"This work serves not only to educate everyone who reads it, but also to help LGBT youth feel seen, to know people like them exist in the world, and to have role models that are among the most revered of leaders. Do I wish I'd had this in junior high school? You bet!"

—Dr. Judy Grahn, author of *Another Mother Tongue*

"Lee Wind has done a fabulous job pulling back the curtain to reveal some long suppressed history. Not only is *No Way, They Were Gay?* fascinating reading, I firmly believe it is a book that is literally going to be a lifesaver for some young readers."

—Bruce Coville, author of the groundbreaking short story "Am I Blue?" as well as *My Teacher Is an Alien* and more

"I think as a teen I might've chosen to major in History if I'd read Lee Wind's fun, fast-paced, and thought-provoking book. I love how it lays out the evidence about some of our past's greatest heroes, invites us to draw our own conclusions, and inspires us, regardless of our sexual orientation or gender identity to be true to who we are."

—Alex Sanchez, author of *Rainbow Boys* and *You Brought Me the Ocean*

"Lee's work reminds readers, especially LGBTQ readers, that we all come from somewhere and that even though the history books may seek to silence or throw a shadow over our truths, our truths are ours to share with the world with pride."

—Matthew C. Winner, host of *The Children's Book Podcast*

"Lee Wind offers LGBTQ youth (and anyone who cares about them) a compelling and often surprising look at a history they may not have been conscious of. A powerful and necessary book."

—Ellen Wittlinger, author of *Hard Love* and *Parrotfish*

THE QUEER HISTORY PROJECT

NO WAY, THEY WERE GAY?

HIDDEN LIVES AND SECRET LOVES

LEE WIND

ZEST BOOKS
MINNEAPOLIS

FOR MY HUSBAND, MARK, WHOSE LOVE GIVES ME WINGS;
FOR OUR DAUGHTER, WHO FILLS OUR DAYS WITH JOY AND GRATITUDE;
AND FOR YOU, READER.
THIS BOOK IS FOR US ALL.

Zest Books™
An imprint of Lerner Publishing Group, Inc.
241 First Avenue North
Minneapolis, MN 55401 USA

For reading levels and more information, look up this title at www.lernerbooks.com. Visit us at zestbooks.net. 🖪 🖻

Design by Lindsey Owens.
Main body text set in Janson Text LT Std. Typeface provided by Linotype AG.

Library of Congress Cataloging-in-Publication Data

Names: Wind, Lee, author.
Title: No way, they were gay? : hidden lives and secret loves / Lee Wind, M.Ed.
Description: Minneapolis : Zest Books, [2021] | Series: The queer history project | Includes bibliographical references. | Summary: "History has often ignored men who loved men, women who loved women, and people who lived outside gender boundaries. Lee Wind examines primary source letters, poems, and more to rethink the lives and loves of historical figures" —Provided by publisher.
Identifiers: LCCN 2020013115 (print) | LCCN 2020013116 (ebook) | ISBN 9781541581586 (library binding) | ISBN 9781541581623 (paperback) | ISBN 9781728419169 (ebook)
Subjects: LCSH: Gays—Biography—Juvenile literature. | Gays—Identity—Juvenile literature.
Classification: LCC HQ75.2 .W56 2021 (print) | LCC HQ75.2 (ebook) | DDC 306.76/60922—dc23

LC record available at https://lccn.loc.gov/2020013115
LC ebook record available at https://lccn.loc.gov/2020013116

Manufactured in the United States of America
1-47342-47968-12/29/2020

In 1961, when I was twenty-one, I went to a library in Washington, D.C., to read about homosexuals and Lesbians, to investigate, explore, compare opinions, learn who I might be, what others thought of me, who my peers were and had been. The books on such a subject, I was told by indignant, terrified librarians unable to say aloud the word *homosexual*, were locked away. They showed me a wire cage where the "special" books were kept in a jail for books. Only professors, doctors, psychiatrists, and lawyers for the criminally insane could see them, check them out, hold them in their hands.

—Judy Grahn, *Another Mother Tongue*

Just think. You're holding *this* book in your hands. We've come a long way.

It's our same world. Only looked at from a different perspective. Just like the history in this book.

CONTENTS

HiDDEN HISTORY

HISTORY SOUNDS REALLY OFFICIAL. Like it's all fact. Like it's what happened.

But that's not necessarily true. History was crafted by the people who recorded it.

Imagine you got into a fight at school. Afterward, there will be different versions of what happened. You'll have your story, the other kid will have their story, and a third person, who maybe saw the fight happen, will have a third story. Whose story will the principal believe? Which version will become the official story, the *history*, of that moment?

What if that third person doesn't like you?

What if that third person is your best friend?

What if your fight was with the principal's kid?

Whose story will become history now?

In the same way, many stories of the past were changed by those in power to support the people they liked, the beliefs they held, and the things that were important to them, such as keeping their power. Some historians may have tried to protect people they cared about from stigma and laws that might have targeted them. Other historians were biased against, didn't see, or couldn't even imagine anyone different from themselves.

The result? History has often left out the stories of women, people of color, disabled people, and LGBTQ people—men who loved men, women who loved women, people who loved without regard to gender, and people who lived outside gender boundaries.

SOMETIMES, PEOPLE TRIED TO DESTROY OUR STORIES.

In Berlin, Germany, in 1919, in an effort to make men loving men, women loving women, and people living outside gender boundaries no longer a crime, Dr. Magnus Hirschfeld founded an institute to research and advocate for them, including himself (Magnus was gay). With a museum, clinic, and offices, the institute also served as a social club and political lobby. Its vast library was world famous. But with the rise of the Nazi Party, anyone different was vilified for being *un-German*, and the institute was raided in 1933. As an eyewitness reported:

On 6 May at 9:30 am, several vans with roughly a hundred students and a brass band appeared before the institute. They took up a military-style position in front of the house and then forced their way into it to musical accompaniment. . . . The students tried to gain

Book burning at the Opernplatz, Berlin, Germany, May 1933

entry to all the rooms; when these were locked . . .
they smashed down the doors. . . . They tore most of
the other pictures, photographs of important persons,
from the walls and played football with them, so
that large piles of ruined pictures and broken glass
were left behind. When one student objected that the
material was of a medical nature, another replied that
the real point, their real concern, was not to seize a
few books and pictures but to destroy the institute . . .
all the writings and pictures were burned three days
later on the Opernplatz, along with many works from
other sources. The number of volumes destroyed
from the institute's special library came to more
than ten thousand. The students carried a dummy of
Dr Magnus Hirschfeld on the torchlight procession,
before throwing it onto the pyre.

The book burning by Nazi students and soldiers in Berlin's
Opernplatz (Opera Square) is infamous. What is less well
known is that so many of the books burned that night were
about men who loved men, women who loved women, and
people who lived outside gender boundaries.

SOMETIMES, WE FELT WE HAD TO HIDE THE TRUE STORIES OF WHO WE LOVED.

Cary Grant played the romantic lead in Hollywood films
for more than thirty-five years. In 1932 he met Randolph
Scott on the set of the movie *Hot Saturday*, and they shared a
home (the press called it Bachelor Hall) until 1939. In 1934,
under pressure from Cary's movie studio (which needed their
movie star to be seen as romantically interested in women),
Cary married the first of his five wives, actor Virginia
Cherrill. Before they could leave for England to get married,

Cary insisted that he and Virginia wait for Randolph to finish the movie he was shooting so the three of them could travel together! Cary and Virginia's marriage lasted less than a year, and then Cary was back at the Santa Monica beach house he owned with Randolph.

Poignantly, even with six marriages to women between them, the maître d' at the Beverly Hillcrest Hotel told Cary's biographers that he often saw the aging actors together:

> **In the 1970s, Cary and Scott** _Randolph_
> **would turn up . . . late at night,**
> **after the other diners had gone, and**
> **in the near darkness of their table at the back of**
> **the restaurant, the maître d' would see the two old**
> **men surreptitiously holding hands.**

A 1935 photo of Cary Grant (*right*) and Randolph Scott

SOMETIMES, THEY HID OUR STORIES.

Michelangelo Buonarroti was the Italian Renaissance artist who painted the Sistine Chapel ceiling and sculpted the famous *David* statue. Besides painting, sculpting, and architectural design, he also wrote over three hundred poems—including several love poems to a man, Roman aristocrat Tommaso de' Cavalieri. But when those sonnets were published in 1623, nearly sixty years after Michelangelo's death, the pronouns were changed to make it look as though he'd written them to a woman.

Michelangelo wrote this poem for Tommaso in 1533:

Michelangelo worked on the *David* statue (his ideal of male beauty) for three years when he was only in his twenties. Check out how Michelangelo fashioned the pupils of David's eyes—they're shaped like hearts.

If, through our eyes, the heart's seen in the face,
more evidence who needs, clearly to show
the fire within? Let that do, my lord, that glow
as warrant to make bold to ask your favor.
Perhaps your soul, loyal, less like to waver
than I imagine, assays my honest flame

and, pitying, finds it true—no cause for blame.
"Ask and it shall be given," in that case.
O day of bliss, if such can be assured!
Let the clock-hands end their circling; in accord
sun cease his ancient roundabout endeavor,
so I might have, certain-sure—though not procured
by my own worth—my long desired sweet lord,
in my unworthy but eager arms, forever.

After 240 years, Michelangelo's love poems were restored to how they were originally written. But even decades after Michelangelo's sonnets were restored in Italian to their original love-poems-to-another-guy truth, some translations continued to change the gender of who Michelangelo longed to hold. In 1900, when this same poem was published in English, the original Italian signor mie caro was translated not as my "lord" (as in the third line above) but as "O dear my mistress"!

SOMETIMES, WHEN OuR STORIES WERE TOLD, WE WEREN'T RESPECTED.

Charley Parkhurst escaped from an orphanage in 1820s Massachusetts and found work with horses. A horse kick to the head cost Charley an eye. By the 1850s, One Eyed Charley was a stagecoach driver in the California gold rush. Charley was good at the job and was said to have killed at least one bandit. Records show that Charley voted in the 1868 US presidential election and lived to be sixty-seven years old.

After Charley died, friends discovered that Charley had a woman's body and had been born Charlotte Parkhurst. They hadn't known. Charley's memorial includes the line "First woman to vote in the U.S. Nov 3, 1868."

CHARLEY DARKEY PARKHURST
1812 — 1879

NOTED WHIP OF THE GOLD RUSH DAYS
DROVE STAGE OVER Mt MADONNA IN
EARLY DAYS OF VALLEY. LAST RUN
SAN JUAN TO SANTA CRUZ. DEATH IN
CABIN NEAR THE 7 MILE HOUSE.
REVEALED ONE EYED CHARLIE
A WOMAN THE FIRST WOMAN TO VOTE
IN THE U.S. NOV 3, 1868

ERECTED 1955

PAJARO VALLEY HISTORICAL ASS'N.

One Eyed Charley's memorial in the
Pioneer Cemetery, Watsonville, California

Was that how Charley, who lived nearly their entire life as a man, would have wanted to be remembered?

To be respectful, when referring to a person whose gender identity was outside the boundaries of he/him/his or she/her/hers, I've chosen to use the singular form of they/them/theirs.
The singular *they* also lets us talk about anyone without assigning them a gender label.

SOMETIMES, WE COULD ONLY TELL OUR STORIES IN SECRET CODE.

Anne Lister was born in 1791 to an upper-class family in England. Anne looked and acted differently from most women of the time, and some people even referred to Anne as Gentleman Jack. For more than thirty-four years, Anne kept a diary—parts of which were written in a code of Latin and Greek letters, numbers, and special characters. For example, the word *love* in Anne's secret "crypthand" was δ5g3. Writing in a way that was unreadable to anyone else

NO WAY, THEY WERE GAY?

allowed Anne to express and explore their romantic feelings for other women. Nearly 150 years after Anne's death, in 1988, researchers published the decoded diaries. Then we were finally able to hear Anne say in their own words, **"I love and only love the fairer sex and thus, beloved by them in turn, my heart revolts from any other love than theirs."**

"The fairer sex" is an old-fashioned term for "women."

A decoded section of Anne Lister's diary entry for Monday, January 29, 1821

—burnt all Caroline Greenwoods foolish

notes and Mr. Montagus farewell verses that no trace of any mans admiration may remain

It is not meet for me I love and only love the fairer sex & thus beloved by them in turn my

heart revolts from any other love than theirs

CAN YOU IMAGINE HAVING TO WRITE THE TRUTH OF YOUR HEART IN A SECRET CODE?

Here's the basic code Anne used in her diaries:

A	2	N	\
B	(	O	5
C	)	P	+
D	o	Q	||
E	3	R	P
F	v	S	=
G	n	T	~
H	θ	U	6
I	4	V	g
J	4	W	8
K	I	X	w
L	δ	Y	7
M	–	Z	9

AND SOMETIMES, OUR STORIES WERE HONORED AND OUR HISTORY DID GET TOLD.

This book is one of those times.

These days, so many gay and bi men who love men, lesbian and bi women who love women, and transgender, gender queer, and gender non-conforming people are out and open about their lives. And it can seem as if this is a new thing. That in our grandparents' time, and in *their* grandparents' time, love between men, love between women, and people living outside gender boundaries didn't happen. Or at least, not as much.

It turns out that's not necessarily true.

There's a proud (yet mostly hidden) history, across the world and throughout time. And that's what we're setting off to explore . . .

MAKING CHOICES

HOW DO YOU CHOOSE WHO TO INCLUDE IN A BOOK LIKE THIS?

When you're picking just a few people from thousands of years of history, from all over the globe, you have to have some criteria, some basis for the choices you're making.

How did I choose to profile these men who loved men, women who loved women, and people who lived outside gender boundaries?

They were the ones whose stories were earth-shaking surprises to me.

Abraham Lincoln was in love with another man. *What?*

William Shakespeare wrote more than 120 love sonnets to another guy. *Wow!*

Mohandas Karamchand Gandhi left his wife to live with a man. *Seriously?*

The guy who taught Martin Luther King Jr. about civil disobedience and who helped organize the March on Washington where King gave the famous "I Have a Dream" speech was openly gay. His name was Bayard Rustin. *Amazing!*

Sappho loving another woman is the reason "the kiss of true love" has its power. *No Way!*

Queen Anne ruled Great Britain and Ireland but couldn't rule her own heart when it came to other women. *Nice!*

First Lady Eleanor Roosevelt loved Lorena Hickok and wore her diamond and sapphire ring. *That's incredible!*

Before Western homophobia took hold in the 1960s and '70s, women in Lesotho, including M'e Mpho Nthunya, had public celebrations of their loving relationships with other women that were like weddings. *So cool!*

The pharaoh Hatshepsut ruled Egypt for twenty-two years, and in that time went from being shown with a female body to being presented entirely in men's clothes, wearing a beard and the royal Atef crown. *Amazing!*

Just before taking vows as a nun, Catalina de Erauso escaped a convent in Spain and traveled to South America as the gambler, lover of women, and soldier Francisco Loyola. *Fascinating!*

We'wha visited Washington, DC, in 1886 and was celebrated as a "Princess of the Zuni Tribe." It was only later that anyone outside the Zuni people realized We'wha was not a woman, or a man, but someone with a third gender identity. *Awesome!*

In the 1950s, Christine Jorgensen became famous—world famous—for changing her body to match her internal sense of gender. *BAM!*

Again and again, my mind was blown. Learning about the people in this book forever changed my view of history, and because of that, my idea of my place in the world as a gay man. If LGBTQ people know our proud and important history, then we can believe in a proud and important today, and we can envision a proud and important future. A future of limitless possibilities! For you. For me. For us all.

GOOD STUFF TO KNOW BEFORE YOU DIVE IN

STAYING SAFE

Harvey was one of the first openly gay people to win an election for a public office in the US.

It's easy to say that everyone should come out right now, be their authentic selves and, oh, how the world would change instantly. Harvey Milk meant this in 1978 when he urged queer people to come out, saying in a speech celebrating the defeat of a ballot proposition in California that would have barred gay people from teaching in public schools:

Every Gay person must come out. [cheers] As difficult as it is, you must tell your immediate family. You must tell your relatives. You must tell your friends, if indeed they are your friends. You must tell your neighbors. You must tell the people you work with. You must tell the people in the stores you shop in. You . . . [cheers] . . . and once they realize that we are indeed their children, that we are indeed everywhere, every myth, every lie, every innuendo, will be destroyed once and for all. And, once you do, you will feel so much better!

That is true and wonderful, but, as Harvey acknowledged, sometimes it isn't safe to come out. Sometimes, it isn't safe to hold the hand of a person you love. Sometimes, you aren't in a place where it is safe to be your authentic self. We can all work together to change that—and we must!—but the prerequisite of being authentic with other people and out in the world is feeling safe. I know this firsthand, as I didn't feel safe coming out fully as a gay man until I was twenty-five!

So know your truth. Be inspired by Harvey, and all the amazing people in the LGBTQ community—past and present—and at the same time keep yourself safe. And I hope you will find the safety and freedom to live your authentic life—and celebrate it!—as soon as possible.

WHAT'S THE "CLOSET"?

People who hide being LGBTQ are commonly referred to as being *in the closet. Coming out* (of that metaphorical closet) and being honest and authentic about one's identity is a powerful rite of passage that people raised in heteronormative and cisnormative cultures face. *Heteronormative* is the assumption that every man will fall in love with a woman, and every woman will fall in love with a man. *Cisnormative* is the assumption that all people born with male bodies will identify and live their lives inside the gender boundaries of "male" and all people born with female bodies will identify and live their lives inside the gender boundaries of "female."

A NOTE ON "LIFESTYLE CHOICE"

Sometimes, well-meaning people outside the queer community will say that they support our "lifestyle choice"— language used by opponents of LGBTQ equality to frame the discussion of our rights in a negative way. *Lifestyle choice* implies that an important part of our very nature (how we understand our gender, who we love, or both) is not an internal and natural state of being but, instead, a casual choice.

Having long hair is a lifestyle choice. **Being authentic about who you feel yourself to be and who you are attracted to is not a lifestyle—it's a life.** If there is a choice, it's to either lie and pretend to be someone else or be honest about who you are and how you feel. So to be respectful, *lifestyle choice* is a term to avoid when speaking about queer lives and loves.

Bi ERASURE/PAN ERASURE

This book is in three sections: Men Who Loved Men, Women Who Loved Women, and People Who Lived outside Gender Boundaries. But descriptions of it always include "People Who Loved without Regard to Gender." Here's why: Bi and pan people sometimes face the challenge that depending on the relationship they are in, they can be perceived as "straight" or gay or lesbian. In either situation, their full, authentic identity can feel erased.

That's called bi erasure or pan erasure, and it's not cool. It's important to acknowledge bi and pan people. No matter who they love or how they identify, they deserve respect in history and today.

MORE ON GENDER: CIS, TRANS, AND A FRIENDLY UNICORN

Gender can be a lot more complex than our culture generally lets on. It's more than newborn babies getting a pink or blue knit cap depending on what's under their diaper. When I close my eyes, I feel like a guy. When I open my eyes and look at my body, it matches how I feel inside. That makes me *cisgender*. *Cis* is Latin for "on this side of." My gender and my body match.

Someone whose internal image does not match their physical body could call themself transgender. *Trans* is Latin for "across." Their gender identity and their body are different.

A really useful way to think and talk about gender is a

The Gender Unicorn

Graphic by:
TSER
Trans Student Educational Resources

Gender Identity
- Female/Woman/Girl
- Male/Man/Boy
- Other Gender(s)

Gender Expression/Presentation
- Feminine
- Masculine
- Other

Sex Assigned at Birth
Female   Male   Other/Intersex

Physically Attracted To
- Women
- Men
- Other Gender(s)

Romantically/Emotionally Attracted To
- Women
- Men
- Other Gender(s)

To learn more go to:
www.transstudent.org/gender

Design by Landyn Pan
Illustration by Anna Moore

graphic created by Trans Student Educational Resources called the gender unicorn, which covers gender identity (how you identify inside your mind), gender expression or presentation (how you present yourself to the world), the sex you're assigned at birth, who you are physically attracted to, and who you are romantically and emotionally attracted to.

UNDERSTANDING THE ACRONYM LGBTQ

L is for *lesbian*—a woman who can fall in love with another woman.

G is for *gay*—a man who can fall in love with another man. *Gay* is also used as an umbrella term to include all LGBTQ people. Often statements about *gay rights* refer to the rights of the entire LGBTQ community. Sometimes people say "gay man" or "gay men" when they don't mean the umbrella term.

B is for *bi*, short for *bisexual*—a person who can fall in love with another person no matter that other person's gender identity. A bisexual person may love a man or a woman or someone who identifies outside that binary. *Pan* (short for *pansexual*) is another term for this identity. Some people define *bisexuality* more narrowly, as just someone who can fall in love with either a man or a woman.

T is for *trans*, short for *transgender*—a person whose internal understanding of their gender differs from the gender they were assigned at birth. In relation to gender, individuals self-define and express who they are in many different ways. Other terms include *queer, gender queer, gender fluid, trans man*, and *trans woman*.

Q is for *questioning* and also for *queer*.

Questioning is used to describe a person who is figuring out who they authentically are in regard to gender, who they might be attracted to, or both.

Queer is used in two ways: as a self-defined identity to describe a person who feels their love or gender is different from what is expected by society, and as an umbrella term for LGBTQ. A generational divide exists with the word *queer*, since it is a slur and the LGBTQ community only began reclaiming it in the 1990s and 2000s. Some people may have a difficult time with the word because they remember or experience it being said in a mean way toward them or people they cared about. For those who have reclaimed it, the use of the word *queer* is mostly empowering and positive, with universities offering queer studies programs, where students get to study queer theory and catch some queer cinema too.

SOMETIMES YOU'LL SEE IA2+ ADDED, AS IN LGBTQIA2+

I is for *intersex*—used to describe a person whose physical body has characteristics or traits outside the false binary that says everyone has either a male body or a female body. Not everyone does, and those people can claim the term *intersex*, if they choose.

A is for *asexual*, or *ace*—used to describe a person who does not feel a romantic or physical attraction to other people. There are different kinds of asexuality, including *demisexual* or *demi* (someone who only feels physical attraction for someone they are romantically close to) and *gray-A* or *gray-ace* (someone who identifies as in-between asexuality and sexuality).

2 stands for Two Spirit, to embrace and include Indigenous queer people of North America.

+ is to cover everyone else who feels that they are part of the queer community.

Because LGBTQIA2+ is such an unpronounceable jumble, the term *QUILTBAG* was created. It has the advantage of being a word you can say and of giving a higher priority to traditionally underrepresented groups. Most of the letters are the same.

The numeral 2 and the + are not included in the term QUILTBAG—a good reminder that terms of identity within the queer community are constantly evolving.

Being intersex is more common than you might think. According to the nonprofit Advocates for Informed Choice, "As many as 1.7% of people are born with intersex traits—about the same number who are born with red hair."

Q—questioning, queer
U—unidentified (someone who chooses to not label themself yet still identifies as part of the queer community)
I—intersex
L—lesbian
T—trans
B—bi
A—asexual
G—gay, gay men

HOW DO YOU SAY GAY?

More than twenty-five hundred years ago in what is now China, the ruler of the state of Wei, Duke Ling, was walking through an orchard with the man he loved, Mi Zi Xia. Mi Zi Xia picked a ripe peach from a tree and started to eat it. It was so delicious that after a few bites, Mi Zi Xia gave the rest of the peach to the duke, so he could share it.

The duke was moved by this and said, **"How sincere is your love for me! You forget your own appetite and think only of giving me good things to eat!"**

Later, as the philosopher Han Fei Tzu tells us in his book of essays written sometime between 260 and 230 BCE, the duke fell out of love with Mi Zi Xia and accused him of committing a crime. **"After all,"** said the ruler, listing reasons not to trust his former love, **"another time he gave me a half-eaten peach to eat!"**

Duke Ling's fickle nature aside, the story of sharing the peach, and the symbolism of the love behind that sharing, became famous. So famous that in Chinese the expression *love of the half-eaten peach* [yutao zhipi, 餘桃之癖] was used for over one thousand years as we use the word *gay* in English, to describe two men in love.

THE IMPORTANCE OF SELF-DEFINING

Labels can be constricting, and it's generally not polite to label someone else. Each person should be free to define (or not define) their own gender and who they are (or are not) emotionally and physically attracted to. And some people have their own definitions for the terms they claim and use.

But it's not useful to pretend that gay men and lesbians and bi and pan and trans and queer and gender non-conforming people didn't exist before these modern terms were invented and used by people to describe the love they felt and the lives they lived. Because men who loved men, women who loved women, people who loved without regard to gender, and people who lived outside gender boundaries have always existed.

We have a proud legacy to discover—and that's what this book is about!

ON HATE AND LOVE AND IDENTITY

Homophobia is the fear and hatred of lesbian, gay, bi, and pan people.

Transphobia is the fear and hatred of trans, queer, intersex, Two Spirit, gender queer, and gender non-conforming people.

But in the face of that fear and negativity, remember these words written by Eleanor Roosevelt in her personal journal in 1925: **"No form of love is to be despised."**

"Define yourself in your own terms. In terms of gender, race, anything. We are not what other people say we are. We are who we know ourselves to be, and we are what we love. That's OK. You're not alone in who you are. There are people out there who will love and support you."

—Laverne Cox, actress, activist, and the first trans woman featured on the cover of *Time* magazine, in a 2014 interview

RESEARCHING AND WRITING THIS BOOK

How can we get the full stories—the history—of lesbian, gay, bi, pan, trans, queer, and gender non-conforming people? We need to go back as far as we can, to the primary source material, if it still exists, to hear from those people themselves.

Primary source materials are shared by someone about what happened to them or what they witnessed. A letter, diary entry, interview, or newspaper article written by a reporter who was there would all be considered primary source materials.

Secondary source materials are what someone shares that they didn't witness themselves. Most history books, including this one, are considered secondary source materials.

What's different here is that we're going to put aside the generations of historians who have in many cases hidden the LGBTQ past, and explore what the primary sources can directly reveal to us about these men who loved men, women who loved women, people who loved without regard to gender, and people who lived outside gender boundaries.

To make them easy to spot, primary sources in this book are all formatted **in bold**.

Every time you hear a story, historical or not, you can decide what you think—you interpret meaning from the story. We all do this.

In the following pages, I'll share how I interpret these primary sources as foundational stories from queer history. And then you can interpret meaning from those same primary sources yourself. Make your own decision about what you think. That's the exciting part of history.

Ready? Let's go!

PART I:
MEN WHO LOVED MEN

TCHAIKOVSKY AND THE MEN OF SWAN LAKE

Swan Lake. Sleeping Beauty. The Nutcracker. Famous ballets, all with music composed by Pyotr Ilyich Tchaikovsky. Born in Russia in 1840, Pyotr is one of the most famous composers of all time. He was also gay, "a historical fact," as historian Konstantin Rotikov put it.

Throughout his life, Pyotr was pretty tortured about his attraction to other men. The penalty for loving another man at that time was losing all your rights and being exiled to Siberia for four years or more. Pyotr worried what people were saying about him and even married a woman to **"shut the mouths of all despicable gossips."** But it was only a few days into his honeymoon when Pyotr realized that, even though he had wanted it to, his marriage to Antonina wasn't going to work out.

In 1995 Pyotr's *Swan Lake* was reimagined by director and

Pyotr Tchaikovsky

choreographer Matthew Bourne, whose swans weren't the classic female ballerinas in white tutus but a powerful, bare-chested male ensemble. In Bourne's version, the tortured prince falls in love with the lead male swan, making it a tragic gay love story that echoed the truth and struggle of Pyotr's life.

The swan and the prince

In 2013 (no, that's not a typo: 2013) Russia passed a gay "propaganda" law, making it illegal to present any positive portrayal of LGBTQ people to kids and teens in Russia. Following that law, officials such as Culture Minister Vladimir Medinsky denied Pyotr was gay, saying, "There is no evidence that Tchaikovsky was a homosexual."

Historian Rotikov countered by pointing out that "in the case of Tchaikovsky his homosexuality is so well documented by his own writings and the writings of others that it is simply ludicrous to suggest otherwise."

So, yes, this book would be illegal in Russia. But perhaps Pyotr would be proud.

Like Pyotr's story, the next four chapters will reclaim the queer history of William Shakespeare, Abraham Lincoln, Mahatma Gandhi, and Bayard Rustin.

CHAPTER 1

WiLLiAM SHAKESPEARE

1564–1616 · ENGLAND

**TWO LOVES I HAVE OF COMFORT AND DESPAIR,
WHICH LIKE TWO SPIRITS DO SUGGEST ME STILL;
THE BETTER ANGEL IS A MAN RIGHT FAIR,
THE WORSER SPIRIT A WOMAN COLOR'D ILL.**
—William Shakespeare, Sonnet 144, opening lines

WHo WAS WILLIAM?

Possibly the most famous playwright in Western culture, William Shakespeare wrote *Romeo and Juliet*, *Hamlet*, *King Lear*, *A Midsummer Night's Dream*, and more than thirty other plays.

It's hard to overstate how much cultural influence William has had. One example: In the first 115 years of feature film production in the United States (1898–2013), 525 films gave William some form of writing credit, more than half of them full adaptations of his plays. That's more than four William Shakespeare–based films a year!

A number of William's plays have fun with gender disguises and mistaken identities, though pretty much everyone ends up in male-female pairings by the final curtain. For example, in *Twelfth Night, or What You Will*, the shipwrecked Viola disguises herself as a man, Cesario,

FIND ME A GUY WHO CAN PLAY JULIET!

It wasn't until 1660 that women were allowed to act on the English stage. Before that, all roles were performed by men. So when Romeo saw Juliet at her window in act 2, scene 2 and said, **"But soft, what light through yonder window breaks? It is the east, and Juliet is the sun,"** it was a guy (playing a guy) speaking about a girl (who was played by another guy).

and gets a job as a page for Duke Orsino. She starts to fall in love with the Duke but can't do anything about it since the Duke thinks she's a man. Meanwhile, the Duke is in love with Olivia, also a hopeless cause, as Olivia is in mourning for her dead brother and won't be courted. When Viola (as Cesario) goes to Olivia's house to deliver the Duke's love messages, Olivia falls in love with Cesario. Viola has a twin brother, Sebastian,

A statue of William in the Theatre Royal Drury Lane, in London

who she thought died in the shipwreck but who shows up to complicate things even more. And of course, Sebastian looks just like Cesario. The plot twists and turns until, in the final moments, Viola is out of her Cesario disguise, and the Duke, realizing Viola is a woman, also realizes he loves her and asks her to marry him. Cue the happy heteronormative ending, with multiple male-female marriages.

WILLIAM WAS ALSO A MAN WHO LOVED ANOTHER MAN

William also wrote 154 sonnets—love poems—126 of them to another man. This was pretty daring because men loving other men was a serious crime in England. In 1533, under King Henry VIII, the English Parliament passed a law making a man's love for another man a crime punishable by death, with the government taking the accused man's land and title, rather than leaving it to his family. Queen Mary repealed the act in 1553. But in 1563, one year before William's birth, Queen Elizabeth I reenacted it.

Historians think some of William's sonnets circulated as manuscripts, since in 1598 the critic and clergyman Francis Meres mentioned in one of his own publications William's **"sugred *Sonnets* among his private friends"**—evidence that William shared his unpublished sonnets with a select group of people. When we consider the antigay laws, it helps us understand why William might not have wanted his sonnets published, since they spoke so openly about his forbidden love.

But in 1609 the sonnets were published. Most historians think this happened without William's permission. The publisher, Thomas Thorpe, dedicated the book of Shakespeare's love poems with these words:

English has changed since Shakespeare's time. *Only* was spelled in the dedication as "onlie."

TO. THE. ONLIE. BEGETTER. OF.
THESE. INSVING. SONNETS.
Mr**. W. H. ALL. HAPPINESSE.**
AND. THAT. ETERNITIE.
PROMISED.
BY.
OVR. EVER-LIVING. POET.
WISHETH.
THE. WELL-WISHING.
ADVENTVRER. IN.
SETTING.
FORTH.
T.T.

NO WAY, THEY WERE GAY?

SPREADING HOMOPHOBIA AROUND THE WORLD FOR CENTURIES

England's antigay law was in effect for more than four hundred years, until 1967 (though the penalty changed in 1861 from execution to life imprisonment). This official antigay stance became the law in most of the British empire's colonies as well, including India, Australia, and the thirteen colonies in North America that would become the United States.

Even in 2020, LGBTQ people in former British colonies such as Jamaica and Singapore are still fighting against colonial antigay laws.

Beget means "to produce," so this was dedicated to the only person who caused the sonnets to be produced (the "begetter"): Mr. W. H., the man who inspired 126 love poems, the until-then "unsung" sonnets. And the publisher wished Mr. W. H. all the happiness and the immortality promised in the poems.

Insving was a spelling of *unsung*, which in this case could mean "up-until-now-unpublished."

Historians don't agree on who Mr. W. H. was. To avoid acknowledging the possibility that the great William Shakespeare might have been in love with another man, some have even suggested that "W. H." was a typesetting error, and it was really supposed to be "W. SH."—making the sonnets dedicated to William Shakespeare himself! But that seems ridiculous since the next lines of the dedication speak of William as **"OVR. EVER-LIVING. POET."**

So who was Mr. W. H.? There are a number of candidates:

Henry Wriothesley—Third Earl of Southampton and Baron of Titchfield, a patron of William Shakespeare and the person to whom William dedicated two of his poems, including "Venus and Adonis." And yes, you'd have to flip his initials to make this one work.

William Herbert—Third Earl of Pembroke, who was also a patron of William Shakespeare. William Shakespeare dedicated the first folio of his plays to William Herbert and his brother, Philip.

Shakespeare scholar Katherine Duncan-Jones makes a convincing argument for Mr. W. H. being William Herbert, who would become Earl of Pembroke.

Willie Hughes—an actor or, possibly, a ship's cook

William Hart—William Shakespeare's infant nephew

William Hathaway—William Shakespeare's presumed brother-in-law

Given how famous Shakespeare was, it's not surprising that there are other theories about the sonnets. One of the most interesting was put forth by Katherine Duncan-Jones, editor of the 1997 Arden Shakespeare edition of *Shakespeare's Sonnets*. As Duncan-Jones put it, "There is every reason to believe that the 1609 Quarto [Thorpe] publication of *Sonnets* was authorized by Shakespeare himself."

Why? Duncan-Jones cites the numerous references to the sonnets making their subject immortal, such as the dedication wished for Mr. W. H., **"THAT. ETERNITIE. PROMISED. BY. OVR. EVER-LIVING. POET."** The reasoning goes, the sonnets couldn't make their subject immortal if they were never published, and the world never heard about how amazing he was.

Also, William may have needed the money from selling the sonnets for publication since his London theater had been closed on and off from July 1606 because of the plague.

Duncan-Jones explains the dedication being written by the publisher Thorpe instead of by William himself by citing the tight timeline. The sonnets' publication was announced at the end of May 1609 by entering them in the Stationers' Register, which recorded publishers' rights, and court records show that William was in his hometown of Stratford on June 7, 1609, recovering a debt owed him. With the plague (and the fear of it) widespread in London during those months, "The hasty departure of the author, rather than any kind of conspiracy, most probably accounts for Thorpe's being the signatory of the dedication."

Another reason to believe the sonnets were published *with* Shakespeare's permission is the play on numbers within them, which suggests the whole work was carefully planned out. Sonnet 20 strongly references the human body, and twenty was a number traditionally associated with the body.

Add up your fingers and toes, and you get twenty!

There are twenty-eight sonnets (127–154) addressed to Shakespeare's "dark lady," and Duncan-Jones pointed out that twenty-eight is the number that corresponds "with the lunar month or menstrual cycle." And Sonnet 144, with its gross character of a "woman color'd ill" may be a play on the word *gross*, as 12 x 12 = 144, the dozen-dozen number commonly referred to as a gross. Even Sonnet 60 references minutes in its second line, and we all know how many minutes there are in an hour: sixty! Could these (and still more instances) *all* be coincidences?

The opening lines of Sonnet 60 read, **"Like as the waves make towards the pebbled shore, So do our minutes hasten to their end . . ."**

Who was Mr. W. H.? Was the publication authorized or not?

While the sonnets are surrounded by mystery, in the sonnets themselves, William spoke clearly of his love for another man and a woman.

Sonnet 144

Two loves I have of comfort and despair,
Which like two spirits do suggest me still;
The better angel is a man right fair,
The worser spirit a woman color'd ill.
To win me soon to hell, my female evil
Tempteth my better angel from my side,
And would corrupt my saint to be a devil,
Wooing his purity with her foul pride.
And whether that my angel be turn'd fiend
Suspect I may, yet not directly tell,
But being both from me, both to each friend,
I guess one angel in another's hell.
    Yet this shall I ne'er know, but live in doubt,
    Till my bad angel fire my good one out.

This is the "gross" sonnet. And maybe the most revealing too.

I have two loves. One's a man, and one's a woman.

Here, William is worried that the woman he loves will seduce the man he loves and take that man away from William. Maybe the drama in his actual life inspired William in creating some of the twists and turns in his plays.

Is this autobiographical? We know William was married to a woman, Anne Hathaway, and records show they had three children: Susanna, Hamnet, and Judith. Interestingly, William didn't live with them. During the twenty years William worked in London, Anne and the children remained in Stratford.

So was William Shakespeare gay? Bi? Was he in love with Mr. W. H.?

Let's look at three other sonnets that William wrote to that other man.

A bust of William in the churchyard of St Mary Aldermanbury, London

Sonnet 18

Shall I compare thee to a summer's day?
Thou art more lovely and more temperate:
Rough winds do shake the darling buds of May,
And summer's lease hath all too short a date;
Sometime too hot the eye of heaven shines,
And often is his gold complexion dimm'd,
And every fair from fair sometimes declines,
By chance or nature's changing course untrimm'd;
But thy eternal summer shall not fade,
Nor lose possession of that fair thou ow'st,
Nor shall Death brag thou wand'rest in his shade,
When in eternal lines to time thou grow'st.
    So long as men can breathe or eyes can see,
    So long lives this, and this gives life to thee.

"So long as men can breathe or eyes can see, so long lives this [this sonnet] and this gives life to thee." That's the immortality William promised, which the publisher referenced in the dedication.

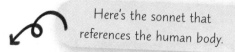
Here's the sonnet that references the human body.

Sonnet 20

A woman's face with Nature's own hand painted
Hast thou, the master mistress of my passion;
A woman's gentle heart but not acquainted
With shifting change as is false women's fashion;
An eye more bright than theirs, less false in rolling,
Gilding the object whereupon it gazeth;
A man in hue all hues in his controlling,
Which steals men's eyes and women's souls amazeth.
And for a woman wert thou first created,
Till Nature as she wrought thee fell a-doting,
And by addition me of thee defeated,
By adding one thing to my purpose nothing.
    But since she prick'd thee out for women's pleasure,
    Mine be thy love, and thy love's use their treasure.

Nature may have created this beautiful man thinking he would be the focus of a woman's interest (what everyone expected in William's heteronormative culture), but here William is saying that the man he's writing this to—this man of gentle heart and bright eye—is the focus of William's passion and love.

Sonnet 36

Let me confess that we two must be twain,
Although our undivided loves are one;
So shall those blots that do with me remain,
Without thy help, by me be borne alone.
In our two loves there is but one respect,
Though in our lives a separable spite,
Which though it alter not love's sole effect,
Yet doth it steal sweet hours from love's delight.
I may not evermore acknowledge thee,

To protect you, I'm going to pretend I don't even know you!

Lest my bewailed guilt should do thee shame,
Nor thou with public kindness honor me,
Unless thou take that honor from thy name.
But do not so, I love thee in such sort,
As thou being mine, mine is thy good report.

> And don't acknowledge me, either. I love you so much that I'll give up being with you to keep you safe.

Here William is saying, *I love you, but we can't be together. People are talking about us . . .*

TRICKY TRICKS

In his introduction to the sonnets in *The Riverside Shakespeare*, that section's editor, Hallett Smith, explained that John Benson republished the sonnets in 1640, "altered so that most of those addressed to the young man were made to seem addressed to a woman." Sonnet 108 originally read, in part:

> A 1,927-page book that boasts it's the "complete collection of Shakespeare's plays and poems."

What's new to speak, what new to register,
That may express my love, or thy dear merit?
Nothing, sweet boy . . .

But in Benson's version, "sweet boy" became "sweet love." For 150 years, the altered versions were the William Shakespeare sonnets the world knew. One publication around the year 1711 presented the 154 Shakespeare love poems as "One Hundred and Fifty Sonnets, all of them in Praise of his Mistress."

In 1974 Smith printed the original versions of the sonnets in *The Riverside Shakespeare*, telling readers it was important to be historically accurate. But even then, he insisted that William's professed love for another man was "the platonic love of a man for a man, more often expressed in the sixteenth century than the twentieth," rather than "any kind of homosexual attachment."

MORE OF THE STORY

The meaning I interpret when I read these sonnets is they are a man writing about his romantic love for another man. Lines where William described the man he was writing to and about as **"a man in hue all hues in his controlling, Which steals men's eyes and women's souls amazeth"** express the passion and wonder William felt about this other man. A few lines later in Sonnet 20, William offered this man William's own love, with **"mine be thy love."**

The sonnets, especially Sonnet 144, also seem very clear about William being in love with both a man and a woman who didn't seem to be his wife. **"Two loves I have of comfort and despair, which like two spirits do suggest me still; The better angel is a man right fair, The worser spirit a woman color'd ill."**

We're not sure what William looked like (even though he's often shown as being bald and having a beard), since most of the paintings, sculptures, and etchings of him were created long after he died. This 1597 illustration from the cover of a book about plants is arguably the only portrait we have of William Shakespeare made while he was alive, when he was thirty-three and already famous. William (*center right*) is holding the ear of corn in his left hand.

NO WAY, THEY WERE GAY?

WHAT IF SHAKESPEARE WASN'T THE TRUE AUTHOR OF SHAKESPEARE'S PLAYS AND SONNETS?

In a June 2019 article in the *Atlantic* magazine, Elizabeth Winkler proposed a twist on the long-standing theory that the person who wrote all of Shakespeare's plays wasn't the guy who took credit for them. While a lot of possibilities have been floated about who the *real* author might have been, Elizabeth thinks that what best explains a brilliant playwright's need to stay anonymous in Elizabethan England is their being a woman!

Elizabeth writes, "Emilia Bassano's life encompassed the breadth of the Shakespeare canon: its low-class references and knowledge of the court; its Italian sources and Jewish allusions; its music and feminism."

If we follow her theory and imagine that the real author of Shakespeare's works (including the sonnets) was the English-Italian poet Emilia Bassano, it's wild to realize that the other twenty-eight sonnets, which speak of Shakespeare's passion for a "dark lady," would still be queer history!

Some historians think the sonnets are fiction, while others, including me, read them as autobiographical—William telling us about his own life and emotions.

Some readers of the sonnets believe that William Shakespeare, in addition to his relationships with women, loved a man . . . maybe the mysterious Mr. W. H. Others don't agree.

What do you think?

CHAPTER 2

PRESIDENT ABRAHAM LINCOLN

1809–1865 • UNITED STATES

I NOW HAVE NO DOUBT THAT IT IS THE PECULIAR
MISFORTUNE OF BOTH YOU AND ME TO DREAM DREAMS
OF ELYSIUM FAR EXCEEDING ALL THAT ANYTHING
EARTHLY CAN REALIZE. FAR SHORT OF YOUR DREAMS
AS YOU MAY BE, NO WOMAN COULD DO MORE TO
REALIZE THEM THAN THAT SAME BLACK-EYED FANNY.

—Abraham Lincoln, in an 1842 letter to Joshua Fry Speed

WE ALL KNOW WHO ABRAHAM WAS

Abraham Lincoln's rise to president is the stuff of legend. Born in a log cabin, he got America through the Civil War, freed the slaves, and preserved the Union.

Or do we?

ABRAHAM WAS ALSO A MAN WHO LOVED ANOTHER MAN

Before that fame, when he was twenty-eight years old, Abraham arrived in Springfield, Illinois, to find work as a lawyer. He was poor and didn't even have a place to sleep. He found a carpenter who could build him a bed, and then went to the A. Y. Ellis & Company general store to buy a mattress, pillow, sheets, and blanket. That's how he met a young store clerk named Joshua Fry Speed.

Abraham couldn't afford the seventeen-dollar bill. Instead of giving Abraham the items on credit, Joshua suggested Abraham move in with him above the store, offering to share the bed he slept in. Abraham agreed. At the time it wasn't unusual for men to share beds. What might be considered unusual is that they continued to share that bed for four years, long past when Abraham succeeded as a lawyer. Long past Abraham's being able to afford his own bed. They lived together, sharing that bed, even while Abraham

Portrait of Joshua Fry Speed from around 1837, when he and Abraham first met

courted a young local woman, Mary Todd.

Around January 1, 1841, Joshua told Abraham he was moving back to his home state of Kentucky. That same week, Abraham broke off his engagement to Mary and entered one of the biggest depressions of his life. A few weeks later, Abraham wrote to his law partner:

A portrait of Abraham used in his 1860 presidential campaign

I am now the most miserable man living. If what I feel were equally distributed to the whole human family, there would not be one cheerful face on the earth. . . . Whether I shall ever be better I can not tell; I awfully forbode I shall not. To remain as I am is impossible; I must die or be better, it appears to me.

In February 1842, Joshua married Fanny Henning.

In November 1842, Abraham married Mary. They would eventually have four sons.

Fast-forward almost twenty years. Abraham was the president, and the American Civil War was raging. Union general William T. Sherman was desperate for supplies, but the government in Washington was ignoring his requests. Sherman went to Joshua to ask for his help, because he'd heard that Joshua knew the president. Joshua told the general to write down everything he needed. Then Joshua went to see Abraham in the White House. Three days later, Sherman got everything he had requested. Astonished, he asked Joshua, **"How is this that more attention is paid to the requests of you, a citizen, than me, a General in the army? . . . You had better take command here."** Joshua told him of his history with the president and said, **"The only mistake you made, General, was not asking for more."**

History has lost most of the letters Joshua wrote Abraham, but we do have a number of the letters Abraham wrote Joshua. Was Abraham Lincoln gay? Bi? Was he in love with Joshua Fry Speed?

Before you form your opinion, read Abraham's own words:

SPRINGFIELD, ILLINOIS, FEBRUARY 13, 1842

Dear Speed: Yours of the 1st instant came to hand three or four days ago. When this shall reach you, you will have been Fanny's husband several days. You know my desire to befriend you is everlasting; that I will never cease while I know how to do anything. But you will always hereafter be on ground that I have never occupied, and consequently, if advice were needed, I might advise wrong. I do fondly hope, however, that you will never again need any comfort from abroad. But should I be mistaken in this, should excessive pleasure still be accompanied with a painful counterpart at times, still let me urge you, as I have ever done, to remember, in the depth and even the agony of despondency, that very shortly you are to feel well again. I am now fully convinced that you love her as ardently as you are capable

This letter was written the day after Abraham's birthday and the day before Valentine's Day, just a few days after Joshua married Fanny.

Their connection is "everlasting."

Abraham hopes that being married to Fanny will meet Joshua's emotional needs.

NO WAY, THEY WERE GAY?

of loving. Your ever being happy in her presence, and your intense anxiety about her health, if there were nothing else, would place this beyond all dispute in my mind. I incline to think it probable that your nerves will fail you occasionally for a while; but once you get them fairly graded now, that trouble is over forever. I think, if I were you, in case my mind were not exactly right, I would avoid being idle. I would immediately engage in some business, or go to making preparations for it, which would be the same thing. If you went through the ceremony calmly, or even with sufficient composure not to excite alarm in any present, you are safe beyond question, and in two or three months, to say the most, will be the happiest of men.

I would desire you to give my particular respects to Fanny; but perhaps you will not wish her to know you have received this, lest she should desire to see it. Make her write me an answer to my last letter to her at any rate. I would set great value upon another letter from her. Write me whenever you have leisure.

Yours forever,
A. LINCOLN.

P.S. I have been quite a man since you left.

> Abraham is trying to convince Joshua that Joshua really does love Fanny.

> Yeah, after that last sentence, Joshua's not going to want to show this letter to Fanny. Or she'll ask him what exactly would have *alarmed* everyone at their wedding . . .

> Is this written in code? Does it mean that just like Joshua (who married Fanny), Abraham is now actively courting women?

Dear Speed: I received yours of the 12th written the day you went down to William's place, some days since, but delayed answering it till I should receive the promised one of the 16th, which came last night. I opened the latter with intense anxiety and trepidation; so much, that although it turned out better than I expected, I have hardly yet, at the distance of ten hours, become calm.

Ten hours later and he's still freaking out. This is really important to Abraham!

I tell you, Speed, our forebodings (for which you and I are rather peculiar) are all the worst sort of nonsense. I fancied, from the time I received your letter of Saturday, that the one of Wednesday was never to come, and yet it did come, and what is more, it is perfectly clear, both from its tone and handwriting, that you were much happier, or, if you think the term preferable, less miserable, when you wrote it than when you wrote the last one before. You had so obviously improved at the very time I so much feared you would have grown worse. You say that something indescribably horrible and alarming still haunts you. You will not say that three months from now, I will venture. When your nerves once get steady now, the whole trouble will be over forever. Nor should you become impatient at their being even very slow in becoming steady. Again you say, you much fear that that Elysium of which you have dreamed so much is never to be realized. Well, if it shall not,

Joshua married Fanny a few weeks earlier and is miserable. Abraham is trying to tell him it will be okay.

Elysium means "heaven."

NO WAY, THEY WERE GAY?

I dare swear it will not be the fault of her who is now your wife. I now have no doubt that it is the peculiar misfortune of both you and me to dream dreams of Elysium far exceeding all that anything earthly can realize. Far short of your dreams as you may be, no woman could do more to realize them than that same black-eyed Fanny. If you could but contemplate her through my imagination, it would appear ridiculous to you that any one should for a moment think of being unhappy with her. My old father used to have a saying that "If you make a bad bargain, hug it all the tighter"; and it occurs to me that if the bargain you have just closed can possibly be called a bad one, it is certainly the most pleasant one for applying that maxim to which my fancy can by any effort picture.

So the dreams of heaven that Joshua and Abraham shared didn't involve women.

The "bad bargain" Joshua needs to hug "all the tighter" was his marrying Fanny.

I write another letter, inclosing this, which you can show her, if she desires it. I do this because she would think strangely, perhaps, should you tell her that you received no letters from me, or, telling her you do, should refuse to let her see them. I close this, entertaining the confident hope that every successive letter I shall have from you (which I here pray may not be few, or far between) may show you possessing a more steady hand and cheerful heart than the last preceding it.

This is a secret letter— sent with a decoy letter that was safe for Joshua to show Fanny!

As ever, your friend,
LINCOLN.

And on October 5, 1842, Abraham wrote Joshua this:

But I began this letter not for what I have been writing, but to say something on that subject which you know to be of such infinite solicitude to me. The immense sufferings you endured from the first days of September till the middle of February, you never tried to conceal from me, and I well understood. You have now been the husband of a lovely woman nearly eight months. That you are happier now than you ever were the day you married her I well know, for without, you could not be living. But I have your word for it, too, and the returning elasticity of spirits which is manifested in your letters. But I want to ask a closer question, "Are you now in feeling as well as in judgment glad that you are married as you are?" From anybody but me this would be an impudent question, not to be tolerated; but I know you will pardon it in me. Please answer it quickly, as I feel impatient to know. I have sent my love to your Fanny so often, I fear she is getting tired of it. However, I venture to tender it again.

Yours Forever,
LINCOLN.

Joshua was so miserable on the day he got married that Abraham is saying if he'd stayed that unhappy, he'd be dead.

Abraham's question reveals that Joshua judged marrying Fanny as the right thing to do, but he didn't feel it. And now Abraham wants to know, Did feelings for his wife come later?

"Please answer it quickly . . ." What was going on in Abraham's life that he needed to know the answer to his question so urgently? We don't have Joshua's reply, but less than a month after he sent this letter, Abraham married Mary.

Did Abraham feel the same way about Mary that Joshua felt about Fanny?

Did Abraham also judge marrying Mary the right thing to do?

Did he hope that feelings for the woman who would become his wife would grow after they were married?

In his early twenties, Abraham wrote this poem to humiliate an adversary. Intent aside, it's fascinating to see that two men marrying each other was even talked about in the 1830s.

Abraham has been on the penny since 1909, the hundredth anniversary of his birth. As of 2020, more than 130 billion pennies were in circulation!

> For Reuben and Charles have married two girls,
> But Billy has married a boy.
> The girls he had tried on every side,
> But none he could get to agree;
> All was in vain, he went home again,
> And since that he's married to Natty.

Natty is a nickname for Nathaniel.

TRICKY TRICKS

Tens of thousands of nonfiction books have been written about Abraham Lincoln, but only a handful have ever directly addressed Abraham's love for another man.

This book is only the second one for young readers to talk about it.

Biographers sometimes spoke about Abraham and Joshua's relationship using coded language, such as Carl Sandburg saying in his 1926 *Abraham Lincoln: The Prairie Years*: "Their births, the loins and tissues of their fathers and mothers, accident, fate, providence, had given these two men streaks of lavender, spots soft as May violets."

Lavender is a shade of purple, "the sacred color associated with Gayness," as gay culture historian Judy Grahn put it. And violets "were worn by both men and women in sixteenth-century England to indicate that they did not intend to marry."

WHO DID JAMES BUCHANAN LOVE?

James Buchanan is often cited as another US president who might have been gay. A lifelong bachelor and the president immediately before Abraham Lincoln, James had a close relationship with William Rufus King. But once again, few of the letters the two men wrote to each other survived.

Here's some of what we do know:

From 1834 to 1844, James and William were both senators (James from Pennsylvania and William from Alabama), and they lived in the same Washington, DC, boardinghouse. They were together so often that other politicians started calling them "Buchanan and his wife," "Mr. and Mrs. Buchanan," and "Aunt Fancy" and "Aunt Nancy" (derogatory terms at the time for gay men).

An 1859 painting of James Buchanan

In the slang of the 1930s, "streak of lavender" meant "an effeminate man," a term often used to describe gay men. Without taking the risk of saying it, was Sandburg trying to tell some readers (gay readers who could decode his language) that Abraham and Joshua were in love?

And in 2012, in a HuffPost article, Sylvia Rhue recalled asking the Reverend Cindi Love why William Herndon

In what some historians see as an effort to stop the gossip, William took a post as a US minister to France. Cue the mean-spirited jokes in Washington about their "divorce."

After William died in 1853 (he was vice president under Franklin Pierce for only forty-five days before his death), James wrote to his friend Cornelia (Mrs. James I.) Roosevelt:

Franklin Pierce was the fourteenth US president, James Buchanan was the fifteenth, and Abraham Lincoln was the sixteenth.

I am now "solitary and alone," having no companion in the house with me. I have gone a wooing to several gentlemen, but have not succeeded with any one of them. I feel that it is not good for man to be alone; and should not be astonished to find myself married to some old maid who can nurse me when I am sick, provide good dinners for me when I am well, and not expect from me any very ardent or romantic affection.

Five years later, James Buchanan became the fifteenth president of the United States. So maybe Abraham wasn't the only male US president to love another man.

(Abraham's law partner, then biographer) never gave any indication in his writings that Abraham had been gay. Love replied, **"William Herndon was my great-great-uncle, and he was gay, and he was Lincoln's lover."** Love told Rhue that the information had been passed down through the years in their family, but had not been made public.

MORE of THE STORY

Perhaps more than for anyone else profiled in this book, the suggestion that Abraham Lincoln was in love with another man seems to upset Americans the most. As if Abraham's place in history would be diminished if it were true. As if his being gay or bi would make him less great. As if just discussing this is an insult to his memory.

The statue of Abraham in the Lincoln Memorial in Washington, DC

But when the truth of people's loves and lives have been purposely hidden, it's time to unlock history's closet door and celebrate that there have been men who loved other men throughout time. Sometimes, they are the historical figures!

We have the surviving letters that Abraham sent Joshua, and transcripts of those letters are reproduced in many different history books as well as online. So the information is available for all of us to read and consider. Each of us gets to decide for ourselves.

Some historians believe that Abraham loved Joshua. Most others don't agree.

What do you think?

CHAPTER 3

MAHATMA GANDHI

A.K.A. MOHANDAS KARAMCHAND GANDHI

1869–1948 • INDIA AND SOUTH AFRICA

WE CAN THEREFORE BUT GO FORWARD AS FAR FORWARD AS OUR LEGS WILL CARRY US AND NO FARTHER AND STILL BE TOGETHER, ONE SOUL AND TWO BODIES.

—Mohandas Gandhi, in a 1914 letter to Hermann Kallenbach

WHO WAS MOHANDAS?

Mahatma means "great soul." Mohandas Gandhi was given the title Mahatma because he was the leader of India's independence movement. India was a colony of Britain, and its people wanted it to be an independent country. Before he helped his homeland become free, Mohandas worked in South Africa, another British colony, protesting the British treatment of Indians there. Starting in 1906, when Mohandas was thirty-seven years old, he used nonviolent methods to protest British rule. For this, Mohandas was jailed a number of times, including for nearly two years during World War II. On August 15, 1947, India finally won its independence.

Mohandas's method of nonviolent protest was also known as civil disobedience, or satyagraha. As Mohandas explained,

Satyagraha is pronounced suht-YAH-grah-ha.

> **Truth (*satya*) implies love, and firmness (*agraha*) engenders and therefore serves as a synonym for force. I thus began to call the Indian movement "satyagraha", that is to say, the Force which is born of Truth and Love or nonviolence, and gave up the use of the phrase "passive resistance" . . . Satyagraha is soul-force pure and simple.**

Satyagraha was so powerful that it freed an entire nation, influencing civil rights movements around the world. The American civil rights leader Bayard Rustin visited India and then returned to teach Mohandas's principles of nonviolent protest to Martin Luther King Jr., who used them to transform the United States. (See chapter 4 for more on Bayard.)

NO WAY, THEY WERE GAY?

BEWARE THE "GREAT MAN" THEORY OF HISTORY

In Gloria Steinem's remarkable autobiography, *My Life on the Road*, the feminist leader recalls visiting India in the late 1970s with the vision of "collecting Gandhian tactics into a pamphlet for women's movements everywhere." In her interview with Kamaladevi Chattopadhyay, a woman leader who had worked with Mohandas in the fight for Indian independence, Steinem learned that the tactics Mahatma Gandhi had become famous for were actually ones he had learned from women—from the Indian women's movement against suttee (the burning of widows on their husband's funeral pyres) and the British women's suffrage movement. As Chattopadhyay put it, women taught Mohandas "everything he knew." This is a powerful example of how, when the history of women isn't told, it can seem as if only men did great things.

History books and websites mention that Mohandas married a girl, Kasturba, when they were both thirteen years old. The couple had four sons, the oldest, Harilal, born when Mohandas and Kasturba were seventeen. Over the next eight years, Manilal, Ramdas, and Devadas were born.

MOHANDAS WAS ALSO A MAN WHO LOVED ANOTHER MAN

History books and websites don't generally include the full scope of Mohandas's relationship with Hermann Kallenbach, a German Jewish architect living in South Africa, who also played a major role in the Indian civil rights movement. Hermann offered his large (1,100 acres, or 445 hectares) farm as a place where the families of imprisoned nonviolent protesters could live. He also helped Mohandas coordinate protests against the British government. And there was a lot to coordinate: What was the plan when and if Mohandas and the other leaders were jailed?

A 1906 photo of Mohandas, when he was a lawyer in South Africa

What about the protesters? What about the funds to keep the fight going?

Besides a political activist connection, there was a personal connection. Mohandas and Hermann lived together, experimenting with their diets and trying to spend the least amount of money possible. Their goal was for Hermann to give up his architectural practice and join Mohandas in living the simplest life that they could. Mohandas said it this way in his autobiography, *The Story of My Experiments with Truth*:

> **In making these experiments I had several companions, the chief of whom was Hermann Kallenbach. . . . Mr. Kallenbach was always with me whether in fasting or in dietetic changes. I lived with him at his own place when the satyagraha struggle was at its height.**

NO WAY, THEY WERE GAY?

Mohandas wrote about meeting Hermann:

We met quite by accident. He was a friend of Mr. Khan's, and as the latter had discovered deep down in him a vein of otherworldliness he introduced him to me.

When I came to know him I was startled at his love of luxury and extravagance. But in our very first meeting, he asked searching questions concerning matters of religion. We incidentally talked of Gautama Buddha's renunciation. Our acquaintance soon ripened into very close friendship, so much so that we thought alike, and he was convinced that he must carry out in his life the changes I was making in mine.

At that time he was single, and was expending Rs. 1,200 monthly on himself, over and above house rent. Now he reduced himself to such simplicity that his expenses came to Rs. 120 per month. After the breaking up of my household and my first release from jail, we began to live together. It was a fairly hard life that we led.

It was during this time that we had the discussion about milk. Mr. Kallenbach said, "We constantly talk about the harmful effects of

At the age of twenty-nine, as a prince of Kapilavastu (in what today is Nepal), Siddhārtha Gautama left his palace, his wife, and newborn baby behind to search for spiritual enlightenment—a renunciation of his previous life. After six years he attained the enlightenment he sought, and became known as Buddha, the Enlightened One. That was the start of Buddhism, one of the world's major religions.

Hermann's drop in spending by a factor of ten is pretty significant!

milk. Why then do not we give it up? It is certainly not necessary." I was agreeably surprised at the suggestion, which I warmly welcomed, and both of us pledged ourselves to abjure milk there and then. This was at Tolstoy Farm in the year 1912.

Mohandas and Hermann named Hermann's South African farm Tolstoy Farm after the famous author Leo Tolstoy, whose writings and ideas about nonviolent resistance they admired.

Some historians use *soul mate* as a way to describe the relationship between Mohandas and Hermann. Most historians, if they mention the relationship between the two men at all, excuse it away as a friendship and nothing more.

TRICKY TRICKS

The information about Mohandas and Hermann's relationship has been publicly available for decades. Yet when it has been spoken or written about, many people don't want to hear it. Some don't even want *other* people to hear it. In 2011 Pulitzer Prize–winning author Joseph Lelyveld's *Great Soul: Mahatma Gandhi and His Struggle with India* included a section on how "it was no secret then, or later, that Gandhi, leaving his wife behind, had gone to live with a man." Because the book discussed Mohandas and Hermann being soul mates, *Great Soul* was banned in parts of India.

How do we know about Mohandas and Hermann's relationship?

Lelyveld explained in his book:

> Gandhi early on made a point of destroying what he called Kallenbach's "logical and charming love notes" to him, in the belief that he was honoring his friend's wish that they be seen by no other eyes. But the architect saved all

of Gandhi's, and his descendants, decades after his death and Gandhi's, put them up for auction. Only then were the letters acquired by the National Archives of India and, finally, published.

Among those published letters are 161 written by Mohandas to Hermann between May 30, 1910, and December 21, 1917—from when Mohandas officially accepted Hermann's offer of his South African farm as a refuge for the families of jailed passive resisters, through to the two men being separated in London during World War I and then losing touch.

What happened? Mohandas, his wife, and Hermann had traveled together from South Africa to London, and the plan was for the three of them to go from there to India together. But while they were on the boat, World War I started. Since Hermann was German (and Britain was at war with Germany), he wasn't allowed to leave London once they arrived. Instead, Hermann was interned by the British as an enemy noncombatant and was eventually sent to Germany. Mohandas kept writing letters to Hermann, even after no more letters came back. Then, for years, Mohandas tried to find him.

Left to right: A 1913 photo of Mohandas Gandhi, his secretary Sonja Schlesin, and Hermann Kallenbach

According to the GandhiServe Foundation, the photo on page 67, of Mohandas with Hermann and Mohandas's secretary, is creased because it was "carried by Kallenbach to England folded and stitched into the collar of his suit, as he was afraid to get it confiscated, due to his German origin." Hermann was arrested in England, but the authorities never discovered the photo.

It's pretty romantic, keeping a photo of the person you love hidden in your collar through years of imprisonment. Is *love* too strong a word? Was Mohandas Gandhi really in love with another man?

Before you form your own opinion, read some of Mohandas's letters to Hermann:

Mohandas and Hermann used nicknames in their correspondence. Mohandas was Upper House and Hermann was Lower House.

7 BUITENSINGLE,
March 15 **[1914]**

MY DEAR LOWER HOUSE,

Mohandas's brother had just died.

. . . I know that I have your sympathy and more in the affliction that has befallen me. But I must not say thanks to you. We are so indivisible one soul in two bodies.

With love,
UPPER HOUSE

Soul mates!

In this next letter, Mohandas started to write *Upper* in addressing Hermann, then crossed out his mistake and wrote *Lower*.

MY DEAR ~~UPP~~ LOWER HOUSE,

I was unconsciously addressing you Upper House.
I note you are angry. . . .

I wish you would forget in our relations that
I am an Indian and you a European. There are
undoubtedly moments when those who are the
nearest to me do not distract my attention at all. You
have given me the privilege of considering you to be
one of the nearest.

I am interrupted. More next time.

With love,
UPPER HOUSE

One of the most amazing documents showing the
relationship between Mohandas and Hermann isn't a letter.
Mohandas was trained as a lawyer, and here he put together
an agreement—a personal contract!—between Hermann
and himself.

[July 29, 1911]

Articles of Agreement between Lower House and
Upper House.

Lower House is to proceed to Europe on a sacred
pilgrimage to the members of his family during the
month of August next. Lower House is not to spend

any money beyond necessaries befitting the position of a simple-living poor farmer.

Lower House is not to contract any marriage tie during his absence. Lower House shall not look lustfully upon any woman.

Lower House is to travel 3rd-class whether by sea or land. Lower House may, if the exigencies of his business in Johannesburg permit it, visit India with Dr. Mehta. In the event of his so doing he will travel the same class as Dr. Mehta.

Lower House will not tarry long in London or any other place, save the homes of the members of the family.

The consideration for all the above tasks imposed by Lower House on himself is more love and yet more love between the two Houses ~ such love as, they hope, the world has not seen. In witness whereof the parties hereto solemnly affix their signatures in the presence of the Maker of all this 29th day of July at Tolstoy Farm.

Mohandas and Hermann are pledging "more love and yet more love between the two Houses"—between each other—"such love as, they hope, the world has not seen." Wow!

UPPER HOUSE

LOWER HOUSE

Written by Mohandas, this document was signed by Hermann.

NO WAY, THEY WERE GAY?

Here are more letters to check out:

ON THE TRAIN,
[Before *June 11, 1911*]

MY DEAR LOWER HOUSE,

Nothing has pained me so much in my leaving Johannesburg, at the present juncture, as your physical and mental condition. If I could have avoided going to Natal, I would certainly have done so, if only so that I could be with you and exercise the privilege and the duty of a friend to nurse you and encourage you. But, I think, to leave for Phoenix was a higher duty. The struggle demands it. . . .

The physical health requires very great attention just now. What I have suggested is, I am sure, the best remedy. The seat of the trouble is undoubtedly the stomach. But it has been accentuated by your mental condition. You are a true man. Any false chord, therefore, shakes your whole system. Your attention is almost divine. You have quite unjustly transferred it all to me. And now you find your idol not satisfying you. This hurts you as if a dagger had gone through you. But why? Who am I? If your affection for me weakens, why suffer agony? It is a passing phase. Let the idol be broken. The residue will be a purer thing. . . .

Whatever Call is, do not worry about him or my affection for him—I cannot do otherwise than love him. He has really some very good points in him. I am sure that you too would like him one day. But what can it matter either way?

MAHATMA GANDHI   71

I shall certainly expect a letter from you every day. You will really do me a favour by writing. I shall be always otherwise.

Yours sincerely
UPPER HOUSE

April 17, 1914

MY DEAR LOWER HOUSE,

How curious! No matter how intimate I may be with Gokhale or Andrews or anyone else, you will always be you and you alone to me. I have told you will have to desert me and not I you. So that I should like you finally to dismiss that fear from your mind. . . . Our joint life does not demand coincidence though that is what you are bringing about. If I can lie on a stone bed and you cannot, you should certainly have a mattress underneath. And though you may lift a ten-stone weight, I shall certainly not attempt to do any such thing myself and still not feel ashamed to be your companion. I shall put up with you and love you just the same notwithstanding what you may call your limitations, even as you have to do likewise to me. We can therefore but go forward as far

A *stone* is another way to measure how much something weighs, a system still used in Britain and some of its former colonies. One stone equals fourteen pounds, so when Mohandas says that Hermann could lift "a ten-stone weight," he's saying that Hermann could lift a 140-pound (64 kg) weight!

NO WAY, THEY WERE GAY?

forward as our legs will carry us and no farther and still be together, one soul and two bodies. Please therefore be at ease so far as my side is concerned. Take care of your own and everything else will follow. . . .

With love,

[PS]
Gokhale has cabled inquiring whether I would visit him in London before going to India. I have answered I might if absolutely necessary, Mrs. Gandhi's health permitting. We shall see.

What a love letter!

We know they did go to London, where Hermann was interned. Later, back in India, Mohandas wrote to him:

AHMEDABAD,
July 22, [1915]

MY DEAR FRIEND,

I have your letter, also the cable sent by Mr. Turner to whom I am writing. . . .
My heart is with you. I have unpacked our goods and as a perpetual reminder I am using your favourite wooden pillow which you will recall you did not want to leave behind. In trying to reduce things to order, I ever think of you, I ever miss you. As it is, I am simply preparing

The nicknames in the letters disappeared when Mohandas was writing to Hermann in the British internment camp during World War I. These letters were addressed and signed differently. This may have been for the censors, whom they both knew were probably reading their mail.

Mohandas misses Hermann so much he's using Hermann's pillow.

the house as if I wanted to receive you. That is, you are positively with me when I am cleaning up the compound and the closets. I ask myself whether you would approve of my work and the method of cleaning. Your suggestions and your nose I miss so much.

But for better or for worse we must live for some time in physical separation. Only we must so act that we should be nearer in spirit if we have to put up with this enforced physical separation. Your internment has brought you nearer to me, if it is possible for you to be nearer than you were.

Your life there must be a model for the others. How I would love to think that you are there vindicating your German birth, your ancestral faith and our joint ideals. You vindicate the first two if you realize the third. And I know you will not fail. . . .

Yours,
OLD FRIEND

In August 1920, after years of separation and unexplained silence from Hermann, Mohandas finally learned that Hermann was alive. He wrote Hermann, telling him, **"Never has a day passed but I have thought of you"** and **"For me you have risen from the dead."** Mohandas signed the letter, **"With love and expectation of seeing your own writing soon. Yours ever, UPPER HOUSE"**

But they didn't see each other right away. Hermann eventually moved back to South Africa and resumed his career as an architect. And though Mohandas asked, again and again, when Hermann would join him in India, it wasn't until 1937 when Hermann finally visited. Lelyveld's biography of Mohandas uses an account from Mahadev Desai to explain what happened:

He [Hermann] arrived before dawn during morning prayers. **"After how many years?"** Gandhi asked when prayers were done. Kallenbach bowed at his feet, **"Twenty-three,"** he said as they embraced. "With childish delight," according to Mahadev, Gandhi lifted up a lantern to examine his long-lost friend's features, then pulled at his hair. **"So the hair has all turned gray,"** he said.

Upper House then asked whether Lower House had sailed in first or second class. It was a test to see how far he had lapsed back into his old materialist ways. **"Tourist class,"** the visitor said. **"I knew that would be the first question you would ask me."**

Kallenbach wore a dhoti, sometimes went bare chested like his host, and slept under the stars near Gandhi. It was almost as if twenty-three years had disappeared, he wrote to his brother. He's **"just like one of us,"** said a gratified Gandhi.

A garment traditionally worn by men, a dhoti is tied around the waist and then folded, tucked, and draped to cover most of the wearer's legs.

After a month with Mohandas in India, Hermann went back to South Africa. World War II was soon to break out (in 1939), and Mohandas would lead the final push for India's independence from Great Britain. The triumph of India's independence in 1947 was followed, tragically, by Mohandas's assassination in January 1948.

MORE OF THE STORY

Since Mohandas and Hermann loving each other isn't exactly common knowledge, it's tempting to assume that it was a secret to everyone while they were alive. But the letters reveal that Mohandas's wife, Kasturba, knew Hermann, and the three of them had their own family dynamics. At one point, Mohandas and Kasturba's son Manilal lived with Hermann, and in April 1914 one of Mohandas's letters to Hermann discussed what the young man was eating and how late Manilal should be allowed to stay up. In a letter to Manilal two days later, Mohandas reminded his son, **"Whatever Mr. Kallenbach's hour for going to bed, you must follow one rule alone. And the same about eating."**

On December 23, 1914, on the boat to India after Mohandas and his wife were forced to leave Hermann behind in London, Mohandas wrote Hermann this:

> **The only thing to complete our happiness would be your presence. We always talk about you at meal times, what you would be doing there at the time, how you would make the stewards work here and how you would have insisted on some cooked things and how you would have wanted more tomatoes and more oil and how I would have protested against both. . . . Mrs. Gandhi, who is sitting by me, wants me especially to send her love to you.**

Not that the relationship between the three of them was always easy. Three days later, on the same journey, Mohandas wrote Hermann, **"Mrs. Gandhi often misses you. It shows how people are sometimes appreciated when they are not available."** Which, of course, meant that when Hermann had been with them, Kasturba hadn't always been that appreciative.

Looking at Mohandas's legacy—knowing about Mohandas's relationship with Hermann—allows us to consider if those feelings for Hermann, who was Jewish, might have helped shape Mohandas's views on religion. Helped shape his philosophy of how we should all be able to live together in

A DUEL?

At one point Hermann was "challenged to a duel by a Volksrust European for his Indian sympathies." Volksrust was a town on the route of the 1913 march (led by Mohandas) of striking miners and their families, who walked 182 miles (293 km) from Newcastle to Hermann's farm. Both Mohandas and Hermann were arrested during the march. As to the duel, Hermann refused, noting that he had **"accepted the religion of peace."**

peace. Here's an excerpt from "Triumph of Satyagraha," which Mohandas published in *Indian Opinion* on October 28, 1911:

> **Let people's religions be different. You worship a Being—a single Entity—as Allah and another adores Him as Khuda. I worship Him as Ishwar. How does anyone stand to lose? You worship facing one way and I worship facing the other. Why should I become your enemy for that reason? We all belong to the human race; we all wear the same skin; we hail from the same land. When the facts are as simple as that, it will be nothing but folly and short-sightedness to bear implacable enmity towards one another.**

Mohandas—Mahatma—Gandhi changed our world. Historians agree about that.

Some, including me, believe Mohandas loved Hermann *while* he changed our world. Others don't agree.

What do you think?

CHAPTER 4

BAYARD RUSTIN

1912–1987 • UNITED STATES

IF WE WANT TO DO AWAY WITH THE INJUSTICE TO
GAYS IT WILL NOT BE DONE BECAUSE WE GET RID OF
THE INJUSTICE TO GAYS. IT WILL BE DONE BECAUSE
WE ARE FORWARDING THE EFFORT FOR THE
ELIMINATION OF INJUSTICE TO ALL.

—Bayard Rustin, in a 1986 interview

BACKGROUND

The term *Jim Crow* was taken from a nineteenth-century song that negatively stereotyped African Americans.

Jim Crow was the name for the system of laws, as well as social codes enforced by mob violence to oppress and segregate Black people in the United States. The Jim Crow era started with the end of slavery (with 1863's Emancipation Proclamation and 1865's Thirteenth Amendment to the Constitution) and lasted nearly one hundred years.

In 1954 the *Brown v. Board of Education* Supreme Court ruling said that separate schools for white and Black students were not equal and so were illegal. Racism wasn't over, and the civil rights movement had many more battles ahead, but Jim Crow was on the way out.

The civil rights movement responded to these oppressive practices, working on many fronts, using nonviolent methods to fight for Black Americans' equality. One of the major fronts in the struggle was the stunningly unfair segregation laws on public buses.

The city code of Montgomery, Alabama, required buses to be segregated into separate sections for white people and for Black people. Bus drivers were given "powers of a police officer of the city" to enforce that law. Most buses posted a sign somewhere toward the middle of the bus, marking the front for white passengers and the back for Black passengers. One sign read:

NOTICE
IT IS REQUIRED BY LAW, UNDER
PENALTY OF FINE OF $500 TO 2500,
THAT <u>WHITE</u> AND <u>NEGRO</u> PASSENGERS MUST
OCCUPY THE RESPECTIVE SPACE OR SEATS
INDICATED BY SIGNS IN THIS VEHICLE

Black passengers got on at the front of the bus to pay their fare, then got off and reboarded the bus at the back. When the front section filled up, the bus driver would move the sign back, expanding the size of the white section and shrinking the Black section, forcing Black passengers who were already sitting to give up their seats so newly arrived white passengers could sit down.

WHO WAS BAYARD?

Pronounced buy-yard

Bayard Rustin was a passionate activist for civil rights.

In 1942, thirteen years before Rosa Parks's famous refusal to get up from her bus seat in Alabama, Bayard Rustin was arrested on a bus trip to Nashville, Tennessee. Why? Because when Bayard got on that bus, he sat in the second seat from the front, a seat reserved for white passengers only. Police officers arrested him, dragging him off the bus and beating him. **"There is no need to beat me. I am not resisting you,"** Bayard told the four police officers. Three white men from the bus tried to stop the attack. In the police car, Bayard caught the eye of the young officer in the front seat. Bayard recalled, **"He looked away quickly, and I took renewed courage from the realization that he could not meet my eyes because he was aware of the injustice being done."** One of the white men from the bus showed up later when Bayard was taken to the Nashville courthouse, calling out to him, **"I'm here to see that you get justice."** Bayard recalled that three of the police officers told their story to the assistant district attorney, **"stretching the truth a good deal in spots and including several lies for seasoning."** When his eyes locked with the young police officer who hadn't been able to meet his gaze earlier, Bayard explained what had occurred to him. **"Did I tell the truth just as it happened?"** Bayard asked the young police officer. The officer couldn't contradict him. An hour later, Bayard was released. He later wrote, **"I left the courthouse, believing all the more strongly in the non-violent approach."**

To learn more about "the non-violent approach," Bayard went to India to study Gandhi's nonviolent protest movement (see chapter 3 for more about Mohandas Gandhi). Bayard taught those principles and techniques to civil rights leader Martin Luther King Jr. Bayard later said:

Mohandas had already been assassinated by the time Bayard visited India to study the strategies of nonviolent protest that had freed the nation.

We need in every community a group of angelic trouble-makers. Our power is in our ability to make things unworkable. . . . The only weapon we have is our bodies. And we need to tuck them in places so wheels don't turn.

Bayard led the team organizing the 1963 March on Washington, which brought more than two hundred thousand people together to demand justice for everyone—of every heritage—under the law. That's when King made his famous "I Have a Dream" speech. Bayard, in glasses, stood to his left.

ROSA PARKS AND THE MONTGOMERY BUS BOYCOTT

On December 1, 1955, Rosa Parks was taking a bus home from work in Montgomery, Alabama. When she refused to get up so a white passenger could sit down, police arrested her. Later, when asked why she didn't get up, Rosa said she was tired. *Tired of giving in.*

Her arrest was the start of the Montgomery bus boycott, when the Black community organized to stop using the city buses, and at the same time took legal action to fight segregation on public transportation. The boycott lasted for more than a year before the US Supreme Court ruled that segregation on public transport was unconstitutional, and the city gave in. On December 20, 1956, Montgomery buses became integrated—a turning point in Black Americans' struggle for civil rights.

In 2013 President Barack Obama called Bayard "a giant in the American Civil Rights Movement" and one of America's "greatest architects for social change and a fearless advocate for its most vulnerable citizens."

If he did so much, how come Bayard is the civil rights leader you may not have heard of? Because he was gay. Unapologetically gay.

BAYARD WAS ALSO A MAN WHO LOVED ANOTHER MAN

In 1962 Bayard had a public debate with civil rights leader Malcolm X about whether Black people should aim to separate completely from white people or to integrate with them. Bayard argued for integration, saying, "The problem can never be stated in terms of black and white."

For Bayard, love could not be stated in terms of black and white, either. Before the United States entered World War II, Bayard spoke at a conference on race held at Bryn Mawr College in Pennsylvania. That's where he met twenty-year-old Davis Platt. Davis recalled:

Bayard when he was thirty years old

> **For some reason, he looked in my direction and I looked in his direction, and something happened. . . . He was an extraordinary person to me. He had such intelligence, such a love of life, such a sense of humor. Really, a lot of wisdom. And he had absolutely no shame about being gay.**

That was the start of their relationship. But because Bayard was a pacifist and wasn't willing to enlist in the military to fight in World War II, he was arrested and then imprisoned in 1944. In prison he led a series of civil disobedience actions to end the segregation there.

While Bayard was in prison, he and Davis wrote each other. Davis explained:

> **We were determined to stay in touch with each other. There's no question that I saw him as my lover, and he saw me as his lover. And it was clear that our letters could not express clearly what we felt. So we developed a code, and I would write about myself as a woman.**

Bayard was in jail for two years, four months. Davis remembered, **"When he got out he called me right away, and we began to really live together for the first time."**

After a year of living together, the two men broke up. But in the documentary *Brother Outsider: The Life of Bayard Rustin*, Davis's memories of Bayard are fond ones.

While Bayard said that **"I never went through any trauma about coming out,"** being gay wasn't always easy for him. The 1950s in the United States was a time of public hysteria about Communists (the "red scare") and gay men and lesbians (the "lavender scare"). Mass firings and public hearings ruined many careers and lives.

In 1953, in California, police arrested Bayard for being intimate with two other men, and a judge sentenced him to sixty days in a county jail. Bayard felt that he had been set up, but the reasons for his being caught didn't matter to the leaders of the civil rights movement. The arrest cost Bayard his leadership position in the Fellowship of Reconciliation, a pacifist and civil rights organization.

In February 1956, during the bus boycott, Bayard arrived in Montgomery to advise King, but was "smuggled out of town in the trunk of a car" when a Black reporter threatened to expose him as a "homosexual and ex-Communist." Instead, Bayard helped the bus boycott effort from New York, organizing a fundraiser where twenty thousand people came to hear celebrities such as the performers Harry Belafonte and Sammy Davis Jr. talk about civil rights. Among the speakers was former first lady Eleanor Roosevelt. (See chapter 7 for more about Eleanor.)

TRICKY TRICKS

Attempted blackmail!

In June 1960, Bayard and King announced a plan for mass rallies outside both the Republican and Democratic National

Conventions to pressure the parties to support civil rights. Not everyone in the civil rights movement thought this would help. Adam Clayton Powell Jr., a Black Democratic congressional representative from Harlem, feared the protests would cost him his influence in Congress. As explained in *Bayard Rustin: The Invisible Activist*, Powell "had an aide phone King with a vicious threat: Unless the marches were called off, Powell would leak a lie to the media that King and Bayard were romantically involved."

What happened next? Devon Carbado and Donald Weise broke it down in their introduction to *Time on Two Crosses: The Collected Writings of Bayard Rustin*: King stalled, maybe hoping Bayard would "make the decision for him." Ultimately, Bayard "stepped down from SCLC and quit his position on the march committee. Much to Rustin's bitter surprise, King quickly accepted his resignation."

As Carbado and Weise explained, "Although Rustin felt utterly betrayed by King, his bitterness toward him eventually softened." As Bayard later said:

The Southern Christian Leadership Conference (SCLC) was formed to coordinate civil rights protest activities across the southern part of the United States. King was its president.

Dr. King came from a very protected background. I don't think he'd ever known a gay person in his life. I think he had no real sympathy or understanding. I think he wanted very much to. But I think he was largely guided by two facts. One was that already people were whispering about him. And I think his attitude was, look, I've got enough of my own problems. . . . Secondly, he was surrounded by people who, for their own reasons, wanted to get rid of me.

Powell never went to the press with his lie about the two having an affair. And on July 10, 1960, King led five thousand civil rights supporters in a march to the Los Angeles Memorial Sports Arena where the convention would begin the next day. In a victory for the movement, a civil rights plank was adopted as part of the Democratic National Convention platform.

Bayard said of the blackmail episode:

> I had come to the SCLC to help. If I was going to be a burden I would leave—and I did. However, Dr. King was never happy about my leaving. He was deeply torn—although I had left the SCLC, he frequently called me in and asked me to help. While in 1960 he felt real pressure to fire me, in 1963 he agreed that I should organize the March on Washington, of which he was one of the leaders.

Two weeks before that famous March on Washington, FBI director J. Edgar Hoover tried to discredit the whole march by releasing wiretapped recordings of King worrying (in a telephone conversation) that their opponents would use Bayard's being gay against the civil rights movement. A senator stood on the floor of Congress and called Bayard some pretty terrible names.

In response to these attacks on Bayard, A. Philip Randolph, a mentor of Bayard's who had hired him to organize the march, said:

> Twenty-two arrests in the fight for civil rights attests, in my mind, to Mr. Rustin's dedication to high human ideals. That Mr. Rustin was on one occasion arrested in another connection has long been a matter of public record. . . . There are those who contend that

this incident . . . voids or overwhelms Mr. Rustin's ongoing contribution to the struggle for human rights. I hold otherwise. . . .

We are not fooled, however, into believing that these [accusers] are interested in Mr. Rustin. They seek only to discredit the movement.

Bayard (along with Tom Kahn) drafted this response for Randolph!

Randolph was a staunch defender and supporter of Bayard. As Bayard told it:

In 1965 Bayard helped found the A. Philip Randolph Institute (APRI), fighting for social, political, and economic justice for all working Americans. Bayard eventually became the APRI's chairperson.

Someone came to Mr. Randolph once and said, "Do you know that Bayard Rustin is a homosexual? Do you know he has been arrested in California? I don't know how you could have anyone who is a homosexual working for you." Mr. Randolph said, "Well, well, if Bayard, a homosexual, is that talented—and I know the work he does for me—maybe I should be looking for somebody else homosexual who could be so useful." Mr. Randolph was such a completely honest person who wanted everyone else also to be honest. Had anyone said to him, "Mr. Randolph, do you think I should openly admit that I am homosexual?" his attitude, I am sure, would have been, "Although such an admission may cause you problems, you will be happier in the long run." Because his idea was that you have to be what you are.

Looking back from 1987, Bayard commented on the Black community's intolerance of gay men and lesbians who "wanted the right to come out of the closet" in the aftermath of World War II:

> Well, I think the community felt that we have, as
> blacks, so many problems to put up with, and we
> have to defend ourselves so vigorously against being
> labeled as ignorant, irresponsible, shufflers, etc.,
> there's so much prejudice against us, why do we
> need the gay thing, too? I remember on one occasion
> somebody said to me, "Goodness gracious! You're a
> socialist, you're a conscientious objector, you're gay,
> you're black, how many jeopardies can you afford?"
> I found that people in the civil rights movement were
> perfectly willing to accept me so long as I didn't
> declare that I was gay.

MORE OF THE STORY

By the mid-1980s, Bayard was speaking out about being gay and Black and what that intersectionality allowed him to understand. In 1987 an interviewer asked, "Looking back over your whole life, in what ways did your being a gay man affect the person that you are, the person you have been?" Bayard answered:

> Oh, I think it has made a great difference. When
> one is attacked for being gay, it sensitizes you to a
> greater understanding and sympathy for others who
> face bigotry, and one realizes the damage that being
> misunderstood can do to people. It's quite all right
> when people blast my politics. That's their obligation.
> But to attack anyone because he's Jewish, black, a
> homosexual, a woman, or any other reason over

which that person has no control is quite terrible. But making my peace and adjusting to being attacked has helped me to grow. It's given me a certain sense of obligation to other people, and it's given me a maturity as well as a sense of humor.

In his 1986 speech, "From Montgomery to Stonewall," presented to a gay student group at the University of Pennsylvania, Bayard said:

... the job of the gay community is not to deal with extremists who would castrate us or put us on an island and drop an H-bomb on us. The fact of the matter is that there is a small percentage of people in America who understand the true nature of the homosexual community. There is another small percentage who will never understand us. Our job is not to get those people who dislike us to love us. Nor was our aim in the civil rights movement to get prejudiced white people to love us. Our aim was to try to create the kind of America, legislatively, morally, and psychologically, such that even though some whites continued to hate us, they could not openly manifest that hate. That's our job today: to control the extent to which people can publicly manifest antigay sentiment.

With the repeated use of the pronoun us in reference to the gay community, Bayard is being very public and "out" about his being gay.

In 1987 Bayard responded to the efforts in New York state to change a new law banning discrimination on the basis of sexual orientation. In an eloquent expression of what he had learned in a lifetime of fighting for civil rights, Bayard wrote:

When laws are amended to provide "legal loopholes" that deny equal protection for any group of citizens, an immediate threat is created for everyone, including those who may think they are forever immune to the consequences of such discrimination. History demonstrates that no group is ultimately safe from prejudice, bigotry, and harassment so long as any group is subject to special negative treatment. The only final security for all is to provide now equal protection for every group under the law.

Ten years earlier, in April 1977, Bayard had met Walter Naegle. As Walter later remembered:

The day that I met Bayard I was actually on my way to Times Square. We were on the same corner waiting for the light to change. He had a wonderful shock of white hair. I guess he was of my parents' generation, but we looked at each other and lightning struck. . . . He was my life partner for 10 years.

Partner, life partner, and longtime companion were all ways of saying gay spouse or lesbian spouse, before marriage between two men, and marriage between two women, became legal.

But in the early 1980s, there was no legal way for a gay couple to define or protect their relationship. As Walter explained:

And he was concerned about protecting my rights, because gay people had no protection. At that time, marriage between a same-sex couple was inconceivable. And so he adopted me, legally adopted me, in 1982. That was the only thing we could do to kind of legalize our relationship. We actually had to go through a process as if Bayard was adopting a small child. . . . But, you know, we did what we did because we loved each other and because we were happy together.

Walter remembered:

Bayard (*left*) and Walter

We were kind of an odd couple. I, of course, was faced with the prospect of going home to my mother and telling her, "I'm gay, he's black, and he's older than you." But I was dealing with a 65-year old [Bayard] at that time, who was a much more youthful 65-year old. Full of energy, full of life. Always wanting to find something new. Not thinking about retiring in any sense of the word. You never knew where Bayard was going to be called off to next, or what issue he would be asked to become involved in or make a statement about. He was working for Soviet Jewry, he would travel to Israel, he was in refugee camps in Thailand. In the last years of his life he was returning to where he had started, the belief that we are all members of one human family.

Five years after making their relationship as legal as it could be then, Bayard died. He was seventy-five years old. In Bayard's *New York Times* obituary, Walter was identified as his "administrative assistant and adopted son"—even though they were a couple and in love.

NO WAY, THEY WERE GAY?

On November 20, 2013, twenty-six years after Bayard's death, President Obama awarded Bayard the Presidential Medal of Freedom. Walter accepted the award on Bayard's behalf. Here are Obama's remarks at that ceremony:

Now, early in the morning the day of the March on Washington, the National Mall was far from full and some in the press were beginning to wonder if the event would be a failure. But the march's chief organizer, Bayard Rustin, didn't panic. As the story goes, he looked down at a piece of paper, looked back up, and reassured reporters that everything was right on schedule. The only thing those reporters didn't know was that the paper he was holding was blank. (Laughter.) He didn't know how it was going to work out, but Bayard had an unshakable optimism, nerves of steel, and, most importantly, a faith that if the cause is just and people are organized, nothing can stand in our way.

So, for decades, this great leader, often at Dr. King's side, was denied his rightful place in history because he was openly gay. No medal can change that, but today, we honor Bayard Rustin's memory by taking our place in his march towards true equality, no matter who we are or who we love. (Applause.)

A year before he died, an interviewer asked Bayard, "What remarks do you have for other Black gay activists who hope to follow in your footsteps?" Here's his answer:

Well, I think the most important thing I have to say is that they should try to build coalitions of people for the elimination of *all* injustice. Because if we want to do away with the injustice to *gays* it will not be done

because we get rid of the injustice to gays. It will be done because we are forwarding the effort for the elimination of injustice to all. And we will win the rights for gays, or blacks, or Hispanics, or women within the context of whether we are fighting for all.

Although being gay cost Bayard in some ways, as his life progressed, he became more outspoken about being gay, and more public in living as his full, authentic self.

How do you think Bayard's role in the civil rights movement might have been different, had discrimination against gay people not existed in the 1950s and '60s?

How can Bayard's legacy—and insights—impact our world's continuing struggles for equality?

SPEAKING OUT AND STANDING UP

In 1959 Bayard was part of an international team protesting France's test of an atomic bomb in Algeria. Bayard and his fellow protesters went to the testing site and were arrested. As Bayard remembered:

"It didn't stop the tests, and I suppose, in our heart of hearts, we thought it very unlikely that it would. But there are times when you can do nothing but you have to cry out against injustice. Even the stones would cry out if you did not cry out."

PART II:

WOMEN WHO LOVED WOMEN

FREDA DU FAUR AND THE MOUNTAIN SHE NAMED FOR THE WOMAN SHE LOVED

Visiting New Zealand's South Island, twenty-six-year-old Freda du Faur set her sights on climbing the mountains she saw. Back in 1908, it wasn't considered proper for women to climb mountains, but Freda was determined. She trained for over a year and made her first significant climb—Mount Sealy—on December 19, 1909. A male chaperone had to join Freda because her mountain guide was a man, and society said an unmarried man and woman couldn't be left alone together. The chaperone slipped while they were climbing—and Freda grabbed his rope and held on, saving him!

The next year, Freda trained for three months with Muriel Cadogan at the Dupain Institute of Physical Education in Sydney, Australia. That's how the two women met and their romance began.

Mountain climber Freda du Faur

On December 3, 1910, Freda was the first woman to climb New Zealand's highest peak, Mount Cook. She was in such good shape and was such a skilled climber that she and her guides made the ascent in the then-record time of six hours. Just over two years later, Freda, along with two guides, completed the first "grand traverse" of Mount Cook's three peaks. That, as the *Australian Dictionary of Biography* put it, was "the feat with which her name will always be associated."

Freda and Muriel lived as a couple in England. The dedication of Freda's 1915 book, *The Conquest of Mount Cook and Other Climbs: An Account of Four Seasons' Mountaineering on the Southern Alps of New Zealand*, reads:

TO
MY FRIEND
MURIEL CADOGAN
WHOSE LOVE AND SYMPATHY HAVE NEVER FAILED ME
I DEDICATE
THIS BOOK

In 1927 Muriel fell ill, and once their relationship was understood to be romantic, Freda and Muriel were separated by doctors and family. Tragically, after they were no longer together, neither woman lived long.

The first person to scale four different mountain peaks, Freda had the honor of naming them. New Zealand's Du Faur Peak and Cadogan Peak remain a lasting tribute to Freda and Muriel's love.

Like Freda's story, the next four chapters will reclaim the queer history of Sappho, Queen Anne, Eleanor Roosevelt, and M'e Mpho Nthunya.

CHAPTER 5
SAPPHO

CIRCA 612 BCE–? • LESBOS (MODERN GREECE)

One source said Sappho lived until she was seventy years old, but most historians acknowledge that we don't know how old she lived to be. We have one poem fragment, though, where Sappho sang about getting older:

"All my flesh is wrinkled with age, my black hair has faded to white,

my legs can no longer carry me, once nimble like a fawn's . . ."

"NOW, FAR AWAY, ANACTORIA
COMES TO MY MIND.
FOR I WOULD RATHER WATCH HER
MOVING IN HER LOVELY WAY,
AND SEE HER FACE, FLASHING RADIANT,
THAN ALL THE FORCE OF LYDIAN CHARIOTS
AND THEIR INFANTRY IN FULL DISPLAY OF ARMS"

—Sappho, poem excerpt

WHo WAS SAPPHO?

Sappho was born on the island of Lesbos in the Aegean Sea over twenty-six hundred years ago. She was a famous poet— *the* famous female poet of antiquity.

The Greek philosopher Plato, who lived two hundred years after Sappho, included her among the goddesses the ancient Greeks believed inspired the different kinds of literature and arts, saying, **"SOME say the Muses are nine, but how carelessly! Look at the tenth, Sappho from Lesbos."**

There's a story that the Athens politician Solon, who lived at the same time as Sappho, was an old man when he heard his nephew singing one of Sappho's songs. Solon asked the boy to teach it to him. When asked why, Solon said, **"So that having learned it, I may die."**

Sappho knew that her poems had made her famous, writing confidently in one of them:

"I have no complaint. Prosperity that the golden Muses gave me was no delusion; dead, I won't be forgotten."

While the fresco image of Sappho at the beginning of this chapter fits our modern idea of what a poet might look

> The island of Lesbos is just off the coast of what today is Turkey.

> Actually pronounced P-saff-oh, according to some historians. Others think that while you should hear the *p*, the final vowel should sound more like *ah*, which would make her name pronounced P-saff-ah. Go with your favorite.

> Quote marks are used around all of Sappho's poetry (even the fragments) in this chapter to remind us that Sappho composed her poems to be sung or spoken aloud.

like, Sappho didn't write her poems for other people to read—she sang or recited them in her native Greek (today we call it ancient Greek), accompanying herself on a stringed instrument called a lyre.

Translator and poet Mary Barnard explained how the poems traveled to us through time. After Sappho performed them, "they were passed on to professional singers who sang them wherever Greek was spoken. Copies were made and these copies were copied. The earliest papyrus text we possess dates from the third century BC, about three hundred years after her death."

Sappho's poems, even the fragments of her poems, give us a glimpse into her world.

Papyrus is a strong kind of paper, made from the stalk of the papyrus water plant. Papyrus books were long rolls, or scrolls. Have more than one? The plural form is *papyri*.

"In the spring twilight

The full moon is shining:
Girls take their places
as though around an altar"

"And their feet move

Rhythmically, as tender
feet of Cretan girls
danced once around an

altar of love, crushing
a circle in the soft
smooth flowering grass"

"Awed by her splendor

**Stars near the lovely
moon cover their own
bright faces
        when she
is roundest and lights
earth with her silver"**

"Now, while we dance

**Come here to us
gentle Gaiety,
Revelry, Radiance**

**and you, Muses
with lovely hair"**

Sappho (*right*) and Alcaeus, another poet who lived at the same time and on the same island as Sappho, are shown on the side of an Attic red-figure kalathos (a type of Greek vase), circa 470 BCE from Akragas (what is now Sicily, Italy). While this was created closer to Sappho's life, it was still made at least a hundred years after Sappho lived. But this time, the artist showed Sappho with a lyre, which is a lot more accurate. Alcaeus sang about Sappho in one of his poems, calling her: **"O weaver of violets, holy, sweet-smiling Sappho."**

SAPPHO WAS ALSO A WOMAN WHO LOVED ANOTHER WOMAN

The famous poet was also famous for openly declaring her love for other women in her poems. The modern word *lesbian*—how we describe a woman who can fall in love with another woman—derives from the name of the island Sappho lived on, Lesbos!

In this poem, Sappho directly addressed the woman she was romancing:

"Be kind to me

**Gongyla; I ask only
that you wear the cream
white dress when you come**

**Desire darts about your
loveliness, drawn down in
circling flight at the sight of it**

**and I am glad, although
once I too quarreled
with Aphrodite**
                     **to whom
I pray that you will
come soon"**

Aphrodite (sometimes called Kypris) was the Greek goddess of love and beauty. The Romans called her Venus.

In this next poem, as historian Christine Downing put it, Sappho expressed "the tenderness of female love":

"The gods bless you

**May you sleep then
on some tender
girl friend's breast"**

As do these lines:

"I do not think there will be at any time
a woman who looks on the light of the sun
with wisdom such as yours."

And there's this longer poem fragment, where Sappho and
a woman she loves (we're not sure who it is) have to part:

"Honestly, I wish I were dead!

She was leaving me, tears in her eyes.

Much she said, this most of all:
'Ah, Sappho, what we've been through;
I swear, I leave not wanting to.'

And I made this reply:
'Be on your way, yet remember me now
and again. You know how

we have cared for you.
If not I'd remind you
of joyous times which we once knew:

Of rosewreaths and crocus,
of violets you donned at my side,
necklace flower-tied

tossed round your gentle neck;
how you anointed yourself
with a queen's costly scent

This marble bust is a Roman copy of a Greek original, with the Greek inscription *Sappho Eresia*, or "Sappho from Eresos." (Eresos was in the southwest part of Lesbos.) The sculpture is from the early fifth century BCE, making its creation (and certainly the original it was based on) the closest in time to when Sappho actually lived.

> A bust is a sculpture of someone from the chest or shoulders up.

and on yielding beds
gentle
desire

and no dance
no shrine   where
we two were not found.'"

Outside of Sappho's poems, we don't know a lot about her life. As Downing explained, "To find Sappho, we have to look at the poems. They are available; she, apart from them, is not."

A daughter, Cleis, is mentioned in some fragments of Sappho's songs, including this one:

"I have a beautiful child
whose body is like golden petals.
She is my darling Cleis
and I would not have for her
all Lydia"

Some historians think (or maybe want to think) that Sappho was married to a man named Kerkylas, but Jane McIntosh Snyder and Camille-Yvette Welsch made a great argument against that theory in their book *Sappho*. "Kerkylas may be a made-up name, for scholars have noticed that it bears a suspicious resemblance to a Greek word for penis, kerkos; in combination with the name of the presumed husband's birthplace, Andros, which suggests the Greek word for man, we may be dealing with a comic allusion to 'Dicky-Boy from the Isle of Man' that somehow worked its way into the biographical tradition."

Sappho used her own relationships, her own experience of love with other women, as inspiration for her poems. And those poems redefined how we think and talk about love.

Have you ever called something *bittersweet*? A piece of chocolate? An experience that was good in some ways and bad in others?

Sappho invented that word.

She wrote about how love could be both bitter and sweet at the same time, and even coined the term glukupikron in Greek, which translates as "sweet-bitter."

Here's the surviving fragment of her "bittersweet" poem:

"With his venom

Irresistible
and bittersweet

that loosener
of limbs, Love

reptile-like
strikes me down"

In English, the order of Sappho's new word was flipped. She had love be sweet and then bitter, and we have it as bitter and then sweet.

NO WAY, THEY WERE GAY?

THE POEM WHERE SAPPHO LOVES A YOUNG MAN

"It's no use

Mother dear, I
can't finish my
weaving
        You may
blame Aphrodite

soft as she is

she has almost
killed me with
love for that boy"

"To love women does not mean *not* loving men,"
Downing said and then clarified what we know
about Sappho: "Her own desire, the poems suggest,
was most often directed to women."

TRICKY TRICKS

If Sappho was so famous, and so highly regarded, why do we only have fragments of her poems, fragments of her life?

In the time (and under the rule) of Alexander the Great. Alexander, it turns out, was queer too. He was in love with another guy: Hephaestion!

About 250 years after Sappho lived, all the known songs by Sappho were compiled into nine volumes, kept at the famous library in Alexandria, Egypt. It's thought that scholars gathered an estimated seven thousand lines of Sappho's poetry. But in the destruction of the Library of Alexandria, fire took them all.

Copies of individual poems by Sappho survived in other places. But then came the religiously driven efforts to erase Sappho's words and memory from history. Since much of Sappho's poetry was about love, specifically her love for other women, Sappho's poems were torn up, burned, and trashed. Systematic destruction of her works happened under, among others, a fourth-century bishop of Constantinople, who, as Downing put it, "ordered the burning of Sappho's poetry wherever it might be found because of its alleged immorality" and, nearly seven hundred years later, Pope Gregory VII, who ordered public burnings of Sappho's poems in both Rome and Constantinople. As further explained in *The Ancient World: Dictionary of World Biography, Volume 1*: "The Venetian knights who pillaged Constantinople in April, 1204, further decimated her [Sappho's] extant poetry. Thus, no single collection of her work survived the Middle Ages."

Today, Constantinople is called Istanbul, and it's the biggest city in Turkey.

Today, we have fewer than eight hundred lines of Sappho's work. And only one of her poems has survived intact.

The little of Sappho's poetry that does still exist comes to us in two ways.

In the first, historians and teachers of speech and rhetoric used Sappho's words as examples in their own work. That's how we have the one complete poem by Sappho—the Greek historian Dionysius of Halicarnassus quoted "The Hymn to Aphrodite" in its entirety. In it, Sappho calls on the Goddess of Love for help, and imagines Aphrodite telling her the following:

Rhetoric is the art of persuasive speaking.

IMAGINING SAPPHO'S LOST POEMS

Pulitzer Prize–winning author Willa Cather wrote this in a Nebraska newspaper in 1895:

> If of all the lost richness we could have one master restored to us, one of all the philosophers and poets, the choice of the world would be for the lost nine books of Sappho. Those broken fragments have burned themselves into the consciousness of the world like fire. . . . Twenty centuries have not cooled the passion in them.

Thirteen years after writing that, Willa moved in with the woman she loved, Edith Lewis. The couple were together for the next thirty-nine years—the rest of Willa's life.

"For if indeed she flees, soon will she pursue,
and though she receives not your gifts, she will give them,
and if she loves not now, soon she will love,
even against her will."

Then Sappho beseeches the Goddess:

"Come to me now also, release me from
harsh cares; accomplish as many things as my heart desires
to accomplish; and you yourself
be my fellow soldier."

Since we only have the one full poem, it feels like even more of a crime that historians and translators hid the truth of Sappho's love during the eighteenth and nineteenth centuries by changing the pronouns. As Snyder and Welsch explained, the "Hymn to Aphrodite" was "widely translated from Greek into English and various modern European languages. The poem presents a prayer to the goddess of love for assistance in winning the heart of a beloved person. In the original Greek, it is clear that both the narrator (the *I*) of the song and the beloved person are female; nevertheless, this detail was obscured by many translators, who rendered the beloved as *him* instead of *her*."

The second way Sappho's words survived is that archaeologists have discovered them. Papyrus fragments with Sappho's poems on them have been found in, among other places, a two-thousand-year-old city dump outside Oxyrhynchus, Egypt, and in the wrappings of Egyptian mummies!

Mary Barnard explained what happened to many of the scrolls that held Sappho's poems, "The papyrus scrolls were eventually torn into strips, crosswise of the roll, lengthwise

Sappho's words on fragments of a third-century BCE papyrus

of the poem, and pasted together to form cartonage coffins. Other papyri have been found, torn into strips, on rubbish heaps, and other strips were wadded and stuffed into the mouths of mummified crocodiles."

Researchers and historians are still discovering Sappho's poems. In 2004 researchers at the University of Cologne found three of Sappho's poems in the cartonnage of an Egyptian mummy. One of the poems matched fragments previously found in that ancient trash dump outside Oxyrhynchus.

Cartonnage (or *cartonage* in the UK) is a hard surface created by gluing together layers of papyrus or linen.

In 2012 a small chunk of cartonnage was dissolved in warm water and revealed, as the news reports put it, "a folded-up, post-card size manuscript with lines of text in ancient Greek." When it was carbon-dated, the papyrus was estimated to be from circa 201 CE. University of Oxford papyrologist Dirk Obbink doesn't think it was from a mummy; maybe this piece of cartonnage was used to create a book cover. He believes that the two poems found on that papyrus, the "Brothers Poem" and the "Kypris Poem," are Sappho's words. The poem addressing Kypris (Aphrodite) actually filled in missing pieces of the same poem that we already had!

A papyrologist is someone who studies ancient papyrus texts.

MORE OF THE STORY

What's the most powerful thing of all? Have you ever wondered why so many fairy tales (and books and movies) have a kiss of *true love* break an evil spell? Even though nearly all of those stories show the kiss as being between a woman and a man, the "power of love" as a culturally accepted belief is actually something that comes to us from Sappho.

Check out this next poem, thought to be nearly complete:

> "There are those who say
> an array of horsemen,
> and others of marching men,
> and others of ships, is
> the most beautiful thing on the dark earth.
> But I say it is whatever one loves.

It is very easy to show this to all;
for Helen,
by far the most beautiful of mortals,
left her husband
and sailed to Troy,
giving no thought at all
to her child nor dear parents
but was led
by love alone.

Now, far away, Anactoria
comes to my mind.
For I would rather watch her
moving in her lovely way,
and see her face, flashing radiant,
than all the force of Lydian chariots
and their infantry in full display of arms."

Downing explained, "Valuing personal love above heroic glory separates Sappho [from all the poets before her]. The first woman poet is the first poet to give love this central place." In this poem, Sappho showed a new way of thinking about what was important. Most ancient poets composed tales of war, stories where power was the most important, the most beautiful thing on Earth. What's beautiful, they said, was an army. A fleet of warships. A mass of cavalry. But in this poem, Sappho said they were wrong. Because she knew she would rather see the face of the woman she loved, flashing radiant, than all the supposed splendor of an army.

This was a radical idea.

Sappho took it further by reframing the story of Helen of Troy. In ancient times, Helen was known for two things: being beautiful and causing the Trojan War. In the traditional story, Helen allowed a handsome Trojan prince named Paris to take her away from her Greek husband, King Menelaus. Pretty much everyone agreed that Helen was to blame. Hers was the infamous "face that launched a thousand ships." They said her betrayal of her husband caused a ten-year war that destroyed Troy.

But Sappho saw the story of Helen differently. In her eyes, Helen wasn't the villain. Helen was the hero. She left her arranged marriage and followed her heart. Helen wasn't stolen away—she had agency. She was guided by love. And Sappho praised her for it!

If you look again at the last lines of Sappho's "Hymn to Aphrodite," you can see this theme there as well:

"Come to me now also, release me from harsh cares; accomplish as many things as my heart desires to accomplish; and you yourself be my fellow soldier."

"Be my fellow soldier"—Sappho wants Aphrodite to join her on the battlefield of love.

Reading her poems reveals to us that Sappho was all about the power of love, not war. And that idea—that love is the most powerful thing in the universe—caught on, resonated with what people felt in their hearts, and changed our world forever.

If we recognize love as the most powerful thing of all, we need to acknowledge that it was Sappho who was brave enough—and wise enough—to say it first. That insight came to Sappho because she was in love—and we should recognize and celebrate that her love was for another woman!

Despite all the efforts to silence her voice, we can see that twenty-six hundred years after Sappho sung them, her words came true:

"Although they are

Only breath, words
which I command
are immortal."

What do you think is the most powerful thing of all?
What do you want to do that people will remember forever?

CHAPTER 6
QUEEN ANNE

A.K.A. ANNE, QUEEN OF GREAT BRITAIN AND IRELAND
A.K.A. ANNE, PRINCESS OF DENMARK

1665–1714 (REIGNED 1702–1714) • ENGLAND

I HAD RATHER LIVE IN A COTTAGE WITH
YOU THEN REIGN EMPRESS OF THE
WORLD WITHOUT YOU.

—Princess Anne, in a 1692 letter to Sarah Churchill

BACKGROUND

In 1669 Anne's uncle was King Charles II of England, and her father (who was next in line for the throne) converted from Protestant to Catholic. This was a big deal, and the king insisted that his nieces, Anne and her older sister Mary, be raised Protestant. In 1685 Charles II died, and Anne's father became King James II.

The Catholic king in a mostly Protestant country wasn't popular, and when James II's second wife gave birth to a son in June 1688, it looked as though a new Roman Catholic dynasty would rule England.

But then the "Glorious Revolution" happened. Leading a Dutch army, Mary's Protestant husband, William of Orange, invaded England in November 1688. King James II's army and navy deserted him and sided with William— as did Mary, and the then princess Anne.

William and Mary were crowned King William and Queen Mary, Anne became next in line for the throne, and James II fled in exile to France. He would never reconcile with his daughters.

Revolutions tend to be "glorious" only to the winning side. This one was also known as the Revolution of 1688 and the Bloodless Revolution.

WHO WAS ANNE?

Niece of a king. Then daughter of a king. Then sister-in-law of a king. Then queen.

Much of what we know about Anne is from other people because, even in "the last hours of her life," as historian Ophelia Field wrote, the queen "ordered a package of private letters to be burned, and George I was also responsible for destroying several of Anne's papers, including her will."

Prince George Louis from Hanover (in what today is Germany) became Great Britain and Ireland's King George I after Queen Anne's death.

NO WAY, THEY WERE GAY?

ANNE WAS ALSO A WOMAN WHO LOVED ANOTHER WOMAN

One of the people who told us the most about Queen Anne was Sarah Churchill. Anne and Sarah were close, and their relationship was documented by letters Anne wrote to Sarah full of the flowery language of love. Sarah had asked Anne to destroy all of Sarah's letters, but Sarah kept Anne's letters all her life. Eventually, when Sarah was no longer Queen Anne's favorite and their relationship was combative, Sarah would threaten to publish those letters—a threat to make public what would have been seen as, and what might have been, a lesbian relationship between them.

Born Sarah Jennings (also spelled *Jenyns*), she married John Churchill. Later in her life, Sarah would become Lady Churchill and then Duchess of Marlborough.

Leaving us with only one side of the story.

Sarah was very conscious of how history would view her, and more than twenty-five years after Anne's death, told the history herself in her autobiography, *An Account of the Conduct of the Dowager Duchess of Marlborough—from her First Coming to Court, to the Year 1710—In a Letter from Herself to My Lord—*.

AN

ACCOUNT

OF THE

CONDUCT

OF THE

Dowager Duchess of MARLBOROUGH,

From her first coming to COURT,

To the Year 1710.

In a LETTER from Herself to MY LORD —

LONDON:

Printed by JAMES BETTENHAM,

For GEORGE HAWKINS, at *Milton's Head*, between the two *Temple-Gates*.

MDCCXLII.

The title page of Sarah's autobiography

THE SPENCER-CHURCHILL DYNASTY

Sarah Churchill was an ancestor of Winston Churchill, the British prime minister from 1940–1945 and again from 1951 to 1955.

Sarah was also an ancestor of Diana, Princess of Wales, who was the mother of Prince William, the Duke of Cambridge, and Prince Harry, the Duke of Sussex.

A 1943 photo of Winston Churchill giving his famous "V for Victory" sign during World War II

In her book, Sarah wrote:

I think it would would be making myself no great compliment, if I should say, her chusing to spend more of her time with me, than with any of her other servants, did no discredit to her taste. Be that as it will, it is certain she at length distinguished me by so high a place in her favour, as perhaps no person ever arrived at a higher with queen or princess.

A stylistic pattern in Sarah's autobiography was the repeating of a word (or part of a word) from the end of one page to the start of the next.

NO WAY, THEY WERE GAY?

In 1683, when Sarah was promoted to Princess Anne's Lady of the Bedchamber, she took over the role from Mary Cornwallis, whom Sarah described as Anne's "first favourite." In one version of her memoirs, Sarah wrote, **"K[ing] Charles [II] used to say, 'No man ever loved his Mistress as his niece Anne did Mrs Cornwallis.'"**

A Lady of the Bedchamber, Field explained, was responsible for assisting the princess "at mealtimes and when dressing, for introducing guests then standing beside the Princess in their presence."

When Sarah gave birth to her second daughter, she named the girl Anne, and Princess Anne became the baby's godmother.

Even though Sarah was a member of Anne's court, working for her, we can see another dynamic of their relationship in this 1683 letter, where the teenage princess wrote to Sarah, **"You see that tis no trouble to me to obey your commands."**

Sarah had been married for seven years and Anne for two when Anne wrote her, **"I hope the little corner of your heart that my Ld Churchill has left empty is mine."**

Ld was an abbreviation for the title Lord.

After the Glorious Revolution, Sarah was the one who negotiated an annual salary of £50,000 for Princess Anne directly from Parliament. This gave the princess more independence than if she'd been paid a salary from her sister and brother-in-law, the ruling Queen Mary and King William. As a thank you, Anne bumped Sarah's salary from £400

Anne's salary would be over £9 million (British pounds) in today's money, or more than $12 million (US dollars) a year!

Sarah's salary of £1,000 would be over £180,000 in today's money, or more than $240,000 a year.

to £1,000, writing her, **"I believe you in all things as the Gospel, & could you see my heart you would find I have not one thought but what I ought of that dear woman who my soul loves."**

Sometime around 1692, Sarah and Anne started writing their letters to each other in code. Sarah explained this in her autobiography:

The **PRINCESS** had a different taste. A friend was what she most coveted: and for the the sake of friendship (a relation which she did not disdain to have with me) she was fond even of that *equality* which she thought belonged to it. She grew uneasy to be treated by me with the form and ceremony due to her rank; nor could she bear from me the sound of words which implied in them distance and superiority. It was this turn of mind, which made her one day propose to me, that whenever I should happen to be absent from her, we might in all our letters write ourselves by feigned names, such as would import nothing of distinction of rank between us. **MORLEY** and **FREEMAN** were the names her fancy hit upon; and she left me to chuse by which of them I would be called. My frank, open temper naturally led me to pitch upon **FREEMAN**, and so the **PRINCESS** took the other; and from this time **MRS. MORLEY** and **MRS. FREEMAN** began to converse as equals, made so by affection and friendship.

Early that same year, King William fired Sarah's husband from his posts, in what Sarah saw as an attempt to separate her from Anne. Many people, including Sarah, thought that she controlled Anne, and Mary and William wanted Sarah out of the way. In her autobiography, Sarah published a letter Anne wrote her, that ended:

> No, my dear MRS. FREEMAN, never believe your faithful MRS. MORLEY will ever submit. She can wait with patience for a sun-shine day, and if she does not live to see it, yet she hopes England will flourish again. Once more give me leave to beg you would be so kind never to speak of parting more, for let what will happen, that
> that is the only thing can make me miserable.
> Tuesday morning.

The day after her husband was dismissed, Sarah showed up at court. Queen Mary wrote her sister Anne, complaining that it was **"very unfit LADY MARLBOROUGH should stay with you, since that gives her husband so just a pretence of being where he ought not."**

After getting that letter, Anne wrote to Sarah, **"I had rather live in a cottage with you then reign empress of the world without you."**

After the deaths of Mary (of smallpox) and then William (from a fall from his horse), Anne was crowned queen on April 23, 1702. Right away, Sarah was promoted to Groom of the Stole, Mistress of the Robes, and Keeper of the Privy Purse. Field pointed out that these were "three of the top posts in the Queen's household, and certainly the most lucrative that could be awarded to a woman." As Field further explained, "The symbol of Sarah's power in the household, representing her unique access to the Queen, was the Gold Key. It opened the doors of the bedchamber, other private rooms and galleries, State and reception rooms, and all the garden gates." Portraits of Sarah created after 1702 show the key hanging from a pocket of her dress. Sarah's husband John was put in charge of the allies fighting France (chosen over Anne's own husband Prince George of Denmark), and Sarah's close friend Sidney Godolphin was appointed treasurer.

Check out the gold key in this portrait of Sarah Churchill by Sir Godfrey Kneller.

Sarah used her influence on the queen, and also on her husband and Sidney, to influence the politics of the day. In 1704, as Field told us, Sarah's "strategy . . . proved successful; she persuaded Marlborough to persuade Godolphin to persuade the Queen to dismiss him [Buckingham] and replace him with the Duke of Newcastle."

But things changed between Anne and Sarah once Anne became queen. Political disagreements rose between them, and Sarah was frustrated that Anne wasn't doing what she wanted her to do. As Sarah wrote in her autobiography:

> The intimate friendship, with which the **QUEEN** was known to honour me, afforded a plausible foundation for this opinion : And I believe therefore, it will be a surprise to many, to be told, that the first important step, which **HER MAJESTY** took, after her accession to the government, was against my wishes and inclinations.

In this letter, Anne told Sarah:

> Banish all your fears for there is, nor never will be, any cause for them. Oh no, your poor unfortunate Morley has a constant heart, loves you tenderly, passionately and sincerely & knows the world too well (if I were of a fickle temper) ever to be charmed with anybody but your Dear Self. . . . I hope I shall get a moment or two to be with my dear Mrs. Freeman that I may have one dear embrace, which I long for more than I can express.

Despite those assurances, things continued to sour between Sarah and Anne. Somewhere around 1707, Abigail, a cousin of Sarah's, became the new focus of Queen Anne's emotional life. Sarah wrote about confronting Abigail once she discovered this, saying to her:

> that it was very plain, the QUEEN was very much changed towards me, and that it was now come out [Abigail] being very much with the Queen in private, that she had used many artifices to hide that intimacy from me . . . she answered that the Queen who had loved me so extremely, she was sure, would always be very kind to me. These were her very words and I am sure if I could live a thousand years I could never forget them.

Next came a power struggle for the primary position of intimacy—and influence—with Queen Anne. Sarah was convinced Abigail was steering the queen to ally with Sarah's political enemies. Field found support for that theory in the diary of Jonathan Swift, who wrote that Abigail and the politician Robert Harley would **"retreat after dinner to talk business like a pair of gentlemen. . . . Tis well she is not very handsome: they sit alone together, settling the nation."**

Sarah's letters threatened, railed, and asked again and again for Anne to dismiss Abigail, as in this one, sent to Queen Anne in the summer of 1708:

> **I remember you said . . . of all the things in this world, you valued most your reputation, which I confess surprised me very much, that your Majesty should so soon mention that word after having discovered so great a passion for such a woman. For sure there can be no great reputation in a thing so strange & unaccountable, to say no more of it, nor can I think the having no inclination for any but of one's own sex is enough to maintain such a character as I wish may still be yours.**

But just as Anne wouldn't dismiss Sarah when Queen Mary had demanded it, Anne wouldn't give in to Sarah's jealousy.

TRICKY TRICKS

Sarah used the threat of publicizing Anne's earlier letters to her to blackmail the queen, telling an intermediary that her daughters had better inherit Sarah's posts as Anne had promised years earlier, or **"such things are in my power that if known by a man that would apprehend and was a right politician, might lose a Crown."**

Sarah sent Anne letters that included some of the nasty songs people were singing about Queen Anne and Abigail. "A New Ballad. To the Tune of 'Fair Rosamond,'" was written in 1708 by Sarah's friend Arthur Maynwaring. It opened with these lines:

**When as Queen Anne of great Renoun
Great Britain's Sceptre sway'd
Beside the Church, she dearly lov'd
A Dirty Chamber-Maid.**

Still in control of the Privy Purse (the queen's private income from the government), Sarah withdrew large sums of money. As Field wrote, "It has been calculated that Sarah withdrew about £21,800 . . . between August 1708 and January 1710 . . . so Sarah appeared to be blackmailing her [Queen Anne] on a private level." And in

Over £3.5 million today, or more than $4.6 million.

Queen Anne on a Jacobite broadside (a political flyer) from the time of her reign

1708 and 1709 Sarah was granted more than 6 acres (2.4 h) of land in central London on which to build Marlborough House.

But Sarah, her husband, and Godolphin would all lose their positions of power. The queen promoted Abigail's husband as part of a move to regain control of the British government, leading to a vote against Sarah's husband on January 24, 1712.

The queen then asked Sarah's husband to get Sarah to return the gold key that her former favorite had held since Anne had taken the throne nearly nine years earlier. One of the last things Sarah did with control of the Privy Purse was give herself a payment of £18,000, saying it was money she was owed.

Over £2.7 million today, or more than $3.6 million.

Sarah was pretty bitter and would write of the early years of her relationship with Queen Anne:

> **Though it was extremely tedious to be so much where there could be no manner of conversation, I knew she loved me, & suffered by fearing I did wrong when I was not with her; for which reason I have gone a thousand times to her, when I had rather have been in a dungeon.**

By the end of 1710, Queen Anne's infatuation with Abigail seemed to be waning. The queen had a new favorite, Elizabeth, Duchess of Somerset. At this time, as Field wrote, "Abigail complained to Robert Harley that the Queen no longer listened to her."

Queen Anne would reign for four more years, until she died in 1714.

This statue of Queen Anne stands outside St Paul's Cathedral in London.

NO WAY, THEY WERE GAY?

MORE OF THE STORY

Sarah's influence in government did not end with her dismissal, or even the death of Queen Anne. As Field tells it, "By 1719, Sarah was worth over £100,000 . . . in her own right." When Sarah's husband the Duke of Marlborough died in 1722 and Sarah was given control of his trust, it made Sarah so wealthy that in the 1720s she controlled "the economic stability of the government."

> Over £16.1 million today, or more than $21.4 million.

When we look back at Anne and Sarah, they were very different and yet very similar women.

Anne, by the age of thirty, was "too lame to climb the Palace stairs," as Field recounted. Anne suffered from gout (a painful form of arthritis) and was "morbidly obese." An interesting footnote from history is that even though Great Britain and France were at war, Louis XIV (king of France) sent Anne "a newfangled invention called a 'wheelchair', which she loved."

Sarah's hair was "strawberry blonde, washed every day in honey-water to maintain its glow." Often called beautiful, Sarah, as Field told us, "did not want to be remembered just for her looks. On the 1715 draft of her memoirs, her pen deleted her co-author's sycophantic reference to her beauty. She also crossed out descriptions of her 'wit', 'vivacity' and 'accomplishments'. The only compliment she let stand was to her 'spirit.'" As Sarah wrote later in her life, **"I am confident I should have been the greatest hero that ever was known in the Parliament House, if I had been so happy as to have been a man."**

> Sycophantic means "kissing up," or telling someone only what you think they want to hear.

A QUEER COURT

Neal Broverman wrote in the *Advocate* magazine about six other historical members of the British royal family who, throughout the empire's history, "had tongues wagging over their rumored gay ways." The list includes:

King William II (1056–1100)

William never married and was said to prefer wearing women's clothing.

King Richard I (1157–1199)

Also known as Richard the Lionheart (yes, the same king who was out of the country during the Robin Hood stories, leaving his brother John in charge and abusing his power), Richard reportedly had a romance with King Philip II of France.

King Edward II (1284–1327)

His romances with other men made it into Christopher Marlowe's 1593 play, *Edward II*, which opened with Piers Gaveston (a man) reading a letter from the king:

> My father is deceast, come Gaveston,
> And share the kingdom with thy deerest friend.
> Ah words that make me surfet with delight:
> What greater blisse can hap to Gaveston,
> Then live and be the favorit of a king?
> Sweete prince I come, these thy amorous lines,
> Might have enforst me to have swum from France.

King James I (1566–1625)

Married to a woman and "often remembered as bisexual."
Some members of his court even called him "Queen James."

In a 1623 letter to George Villiers, who he had promoted to
Duke of Buckingham, James wrote:

**I cannot content myself without sending you this
present, praying God that I may have a joyful and
comfortable meeting with you and that we may
make at this Christmas a new marriage ever to be
kept hereafter. . . . I desire to live only in this world
for your sake, and that I had rather live banished in
any part of the earth with you than live a sorrowful
widow's life without you.**

And if King James sounds familiar, it's because the famous
English-language version of the Bible is named after him!

Prince George, Duke of Kent (1902–1942)

He had four older brothers, so he wasn't about to take the
throne, but letters from Noël Coward lead historians to believe
there was a romance between Prince George and the famous
playwright and poet. Noël was, reportedly, "one of several"
men the prince romanced.

Princess Margaret (1930–2002)

Documentaries and biographies about the "wild younger sister
of Queen Elizabeth II" include her romances with both men
and women.

Each woman would become pregnant multiple times. Anne had eighteen pregnancies, yet all of her children died while very young. Prince William, Duke of Gloucester, who died when he was eleven, lived the longest. Sarah also had multiple pregnancies, with three of her children surviving to adulthood.

Beyond their relationship, what Anne and Sarah shared was ambition, the confidence of knowing their own minds, and trust in their own judgment. At a time when women could not even vote, they were both women who, by their position and wealth, were empowered to influence history.

In 1735, more than twenty years after Anne's death, Sarah had a statue of Queen Anne erected at Blenheim Palace, one of the two grand estates she had built to ensure the Marlborough family's legacy. As Sarah told a granddaughter, **"I have a satisfaction in showing this respect to her, because her kindness to me was real."**

Marlborough House was the other.

Looking back on it, Sarah would write that Anne's **"friendships were flames of extravagant passion, ending in indifference or aversion."**

Scotland joined with England and Wales to form the United Kingdom of Great Britain. This is also when the term British began to refer to all the people of the kingdom.

According to England's National Portrait Gallery, "The most important constitutional landmark of her [Queen Anne's] reign was the Act of Union with Scotland in 1707." But maybe there are other landmarks we should be acknowledging as well. That a woman who loved another woman sat on the throne during a crucial time in British history. And that one of the women she loved, Sarah, became one of the richest—and most powerful—women in the Western world.

More than three hundred years later, the laws have changed, and today an openly queer monarch could rule England. If that had been the case in the time of Queen Anne and Sarah Churchill, would it have changed anything?

What do you think?

CHAPTER 7

ELEANOR ROOSEVELT

1884–1962 • UNITED STATES

**YOUR RING IS A GREAT COMFORT,
I LOOK AT IT & THINK SHE DOES LOVE ME,
OR I WOULDN'T BE WEARING IT!**
—Eleanor Roosevelt, in a 1933 letter to Lorena Hickok

WHO WAS ELEANOR?

Anna Eleanor Roosevelt was born a Roosevelt and married one too. Both her parents died when she was young, and she lived with her grandmother until she was fifteen, when she went to live and study at a school for girls in England. At eighteen, Eleanor came back to the United States and dove into a lifetime of social service and helping others. When she was twenty, she married her distant cousin, Franklin Delano Roosevelt, who would later become president of the United States and serve for twelve years.

During World War II, FDR was elected to his third and then fourth terms in office. After that, the Twenty-Second Amendment to the US Constitution changed the rules, and now "no person shall be elected to the office of the President more than twice."

As First Lady, Eleanor transformed the role of president's wife from mainly a hostess into a very public advocate who influenced people and events. From giving speaking tours across the country and around the world to writing a daily newspaper column that was carried by dozens of papers, Eleanor was the first president's spouse to leverage her position and fame to openly affect societal change.

And Eleanor did change things, such as her 1933 decision to hold her own press conferences as First Lady to force news services to hire women reporters. And standing up for Black singer Marian Anderson in 1939 when the singer was refused access to the Daughters of the American Revolution's Washington, DC, stage that was reserved for white artists only. Eleanor arranged a hugely successful public concert for

Eleanor started writing her My Day columns in 1935. She wrote them, six days a week, for the rest of her life . . . twenty-seven years!

NO WAY, THEY WERE GAY?

Anderson that, as one reporter put it, "struck at the very depths of racism in America." In a powerful symbolic move, Eleanor once carried a folding chair to a segregated public meeting in Alabama (where white people sat on one side and Black people on the other), and she carefully placed her own chair in the center aisle.

This was twenty-five years before Dr. King stood in the very same spot to make his famous "I Have a Dream" speech during the 1963 March on Washington!

In 1941, with the world increasingly engulfed in World War II, the United States was preparing for war. This created lots of new jobs, but there was an official policy of all-white defense plants. Civil rights leader A. Philip Randolph told the president that if he didn't sign an executive order ending that discrimination, civil rights marchers would descend on

The same A. Philip Randolph who became Bayard's mentor, and who hired Bayard to organize the 1963 March on Washington. (See chapter 4 for more about Bayard.)

This news photo of Eleanor taking a flight at the Tuskegee Army Air Field, smiling confidently from the back seat of a two-seater airplane, with Black pilot Charles Alfred Anderson Sr. in the front seat, was a powerful message about racial equality.

Washington, DC, in protest. Ultimately, the president signed the order, which said, "There shall be no discrimination in the employment of workers in defense industries or government because of race, creed, color, or national origin." The march was called off. Some historians think that "First Lady Eleanor Roosevelt may also have influenced her husband's decision when she returned from a trip to New York where she had seen militant preparations for the march."

During the war, Eleanor was seemingly everywhere. She traveled to England and Australia to support Allied efforts, and after the Pearl Harbor attack and the United States entered World War II, she visited US troops to support and encourage them.

The Japanese attack on Pearl Harbor, a US naval base in Hawaii, happened on December 7, 1941. Japan, Germany, and Italy were fighting together (leading the Axis powers), and the United States joined Britain and Russia to lead the Allies.

After her husband's death in office in 1945, Eleanor didn't retire to private life. She continued speaking and writing and was appointed (twice) as a US delegate to the United Nations. As chair of the UN Commission on Human Rights, Eleanor successfully led the efforts to create and then convince the General Assembly to adopt the Universal Declaration of Human Rights. Article 1 of the Declaration reads, **"All human beings are born free and equal in dignity and rights. They are endowed with reason and conscience and should act towards one another in a spirit of brotherhood."**

Eleanor wrote about the Declaration, **"One major point guarantees no discrimination because of race, creed or color. We must work in our communities to break down prejudice and eliminate discrimination if we are to be an example to the rest of the world."**

A proud moment: Eleanor and the Universal Declaration of Human Rights. The poster-size copy she's holding is in Spanish, a reminder of how Eleanor's leadership created a document that empowered people all over the world, no matter what language they spoke.

ELEANoR WAS ALSO A WoMAN WHO LOVED ANoTHER WOMAN

Eleanor and Lorena Hickok, the first woman reporter to have her byline appear on the front page of the *New York Times*, loved each other. We know this from the surviving thirty-five hundred letters they wrote each other over their thirty-year relationship. But not all the letters these two women wrote each other were preserved for history. After Eleanor died, Lorena (along with their friend Esther Lape) burned hundreds of letters Eleanor had written her. As historian Blanche Wiesen Cook told it, they "sat around an open fire at Lape's Connecticut estate and spent hours burning letter after letter." As Lorena explained to Eleanor's daughter, Anna Roosevelt Halsted, "Your Mother wasn't always so very *discreet* in her letters to me."

Despite that effort at self-censorship, the letters we do have are astonishing. Many letters have them counting the days until they would see each other again, and sometimes they just wrote to say, **"I love you."** Beyond that, the letters show us that Lorena helped Eleanor reenvision what the role of First Lady could be, and that both women encouraged each other with caring and advice. They also illustrate the ups and downs of a love that burned hot and cold and yet was significant enough to last the rest of both women's lives.

How could Eleanor and Lorena's relationship happen while Eleanor was married to the president of the United States? Back in 1918, long before Lorena was in Eleanor's life, Eleanor had discovered that her husband, Franklin, was having a love affair with Eleanor's own social secretary, Lucy Page Mercer. Eleanor and Franklin agreed to stay married, but from then on their romantic lives were separate.

It's telling that Lucy was with Franklin on April 12, 1945, when the president died of a cerebral hemorrhage while vacationing in Warm Springs, Georgia.

Eleanor and Lorena met in 1928, but when the Associated Press assigned Lorena to cover Eleanor in 1933, their relationship intensified. Historian Rodger Streitmatter wrote in *Empty without You: The Intimate Letters of Eleanor Roosevelt and Lorena Hickok*, "It was Lorena who persuaded Eleanor to become the only first lady in history to conduct weekly press conferences. . . . It was Lorena who helped Eleanor grow into one of history's most powerful humanitarians by giving this woman born to wealth and privilege a close-up view of the plight of the poor and the powerless. . . . It was Lorena who suggested that Eleanor publish a syndicated newspaper column to communicate her vision for humanity to the entire country on a daily basis." As Streitmatter summed up, "Lorena was, in short, the woman behind the woman."

NO WAY, THEY WERE GAY?

For Christmas 1932, Lorena gave Eleanor "an extravagant sapphire and diamond ring." Streitmatter explained, "The gift was far too expensive for a news reporter to have purchased; Madame Ernestine Schumann-Heink had pressed the magnificent piece of jewelry into Lorena's hand in 1916 after the young reporter had written a flattering story about the grand diva. Eleanor protested that the gift was too precious for Lorena to part with, but eventually she slipped the ring onto her left hand where it would remain for the next four years."

In this letter, written on March 7, 1933, Eleanor told Lorena what the ring meant to her. Hick was Lorena's nickname.

The White House
Washington

Hick darling, All day I've thought of you & another birthday I *will* be with you, and yet to-night you sounded so far away & formal, oh! I want to put my arms around you, I ache to hold you close. Your ring is a great comfort, I look at it & think she does love me, or I wouldn't be wearing it! . . .

By Saturday I hope to begin to read, & write, & think & feel again. What shall we read Hick? You choose first.

Eleanor and Lorena read books at the same time so they could talk about them together.

It is late 1:15 & I am very weary, so goodnight my dearest one. A world of love & how happy I will be to see you Tuesday.

After an incredibly long and busy day of settling into the White House and going to the inauguration concert, Eleanor stayed up until 1:15 the next morning to write to Lorena.

Ever Yours,
E.R.

Eleanor signed her letters and sometimes referred to herself with her initials, E.R.

The day before, on March 6, Eleanor wrote Lorena, explaining how her son James (Jimmy) was standing right next to her when they were on the phone, so she couldn't tell Lorena what she wanted to say:

THE WHITE HOUSE
Washington

Hick darling, Oh! how good it was to hear your voice, it was so inadequate to try & tell you what it meant, Jimmy was near & I couldn't say *"je t'aime and je t'adore"* as I longed to do but always remember I am saying it & that I go to sleep thinking of you & repeating our little saying.

French for "I love you and I adore you."

Well, now for the diary! . . .

At last 12:10, bed & a talk with you—the nicest time of the day. A week from to-morrow I came back from the telephone & began marking my calendar, Tuesday week is so much better than Thursday!

. . . Give Jean my love she is a swell person. No one is like you though. Hick—I love you & good night.

Devotedly,
E.R.

Eleanor wrote Lorena about kissing Lorena's picture, pressed a rose into one letter, penned a Valentine's Day poem, wrote of missing the feel of Lorena's hair, and even imagined the furniture they'd have in a future home together. Here's where she mentions kissing Lorena's picture, in a letter written on March 9, 1933:

Hick dearest, It was good to talk to you & you sounded a bit happier. . . . The one thing which reconciles me to this job is the fact that I think I can give a great many people pleasure & I begin to think there may be ways in which I can be useful. I am getting some ideas which I want to talk over with you—

Life is pretty strenuous—one or two a.m. last night & 12:15 now & people still with F.D.R. but this should settle things more or less.

My pictures are nearly all up & I have you in my sitting room where I can look at you most of my waking hours! I can't kiss you so I kiss your *picture* good night & good morning! This is the first day I've had no letter & I missed it sadly but it is good discipline. . . .

Anna & the children left to-day at 2. So I have asked John to go for a drive with me to-morrow a.m. Remind me to show you a note he wrote me, he is pretty sweet & I am so sorry for them. . . .

One more day marked off my dear. My dear if you meet me may I forget there are other reporters present or must I behave? I shall want to hug you to death. I can hardly wait!

A world of love to you & good night & God bless you "light of my life,"

E.R.

"I am so sorry for them" is a reference to Eleanor's daughter Anna and the man she loved. Anna was married to Curtis Dall at the time, but she was involved romantically with John

Boettiger (who was married to someone else as well). They had to keep their love a secret, but ultimately they each divorced so they could be together. When the news of John's divorce hit the press in November 1933, Eleanor wrote Lorena:

Louis tells me one of the newspaper men casually mentioned the other day to a group of them "now that John Boettiger has his divorce I supposed we'll soon hear of Mrs. Dall's getting hers"! One cannot hide things in this world, can one? How lucky you are not a man!

"How lucky you are not a man!" Eleanor was saying that if Lorena were a man, they would have no chance to keep their own relationship private.

And here's the Valentine's poem Eleanor wrote Lorena, on February 12, 1935, on the back of a card that showed a black-and-white puppy holding a small heart, inscribed **"To My Valentine"**:

May the world be full of sunshine,
And our meetings frequent be
Hours of joy & quiet time,
Take us over life's rough seas.

For her part, Lorena wrote Eleanor of feeling like an outsider when she wanted to feel like family, of how she missed her (**"At times life becomes just one long, dreary ache for you."**), of how wonderful their time together was, of how much she loved her (**"you are still the person I love more than anyone else in the world."**), and about kissing her.

Being a reporter and in a close relationship with the First Lady was a difficult combination, and in 1933 Lorena took a new job for FDR's administration, traveling the country to report back about how the government's relief efforts were going. Those efforts were to help people, and the economy, recover from the Great Depression. It also meant that when Lorena was in Washington, DC, she could stay at the White House, close to Eleanor.

The years 1929–1939, for those of you who like knowing when things happened.

In this letter (the one about kissing) from December 5, 1933, Lorena wrote Eleanor from Minnesota:

Dear:

Tonight it's Bemidji, away up in the timber country, not a bad hotel, and one day nearer you. Only eight more days. Twenty-four hours from now it will be only seven more—just a week! I've been trying today to bring back your face—to remember just *how* you look. Funny how even the dearest face will fade away in time. Most clearly I remember your eyes, with a kind of teasing smile in them, and the feeling of that soft spot just northeast of the corner of your mouth against my lips. I wonder what we'll do when we meet—what we'll say. Well—I'm rather proud of us, aren't you? I think we've done rather well. . . .

Darling, I've been thinking about you so much today. What a swell person you are to back me up the way you

There's a lot of other great political material in this letter. Lorena even gives advice to members of the administration, including this line: **"If I were Harry Hopkins or Henry Morgenthau or any of the rest of the boys down in Washington, I'd never forget it—not for a moment."** Clearly, she hoped (or expected) Eleanor to pass the information along.

do on this job! We *do* do things together, don't we? And it's fun, even though the fact that we both have work to do keeps us apart.

Good night, dear one. I want to put my arms around you and kiss you at the corner of your mouth. And in a little more than a week now—I shall!

H

As hot as the relationship was at times, Streitmatter pointed out the underlying tension in the letters: Eleanor had family responsibilities (as the mother of five grown children), and as First Lady of the United States, she saw all the possibilities of expanding her role in the world and using her influence and position to help others. Lorena wanted Eleanor to herself, and for the two of them to retreat from the world together. The two women even came up with a nickname for Eleanor if she weren't famous and didn't have her position in the world: *Mrs. Doaks*. In a November 18, 1933, letter to Lorena, Eleanor wrote:

> **"Time" has a dreadful cover picture of me & pages on me, not too scathing I'm told.**
>
> **Does it ever occur to you that it would be pleasant if no one ever wrote about me? Mrs. Doaks would like a little privacy now & then!**

Eleanor and Lorena took vacations that were supposed to be just the two of them, but Eleanor was famous, and even their private times were crashed by enthusiastic admirers of the First Lady. Eleanor was always gracious. Lorena was less pleased.

Lorena described the struggle between the private versus the public in this letter to Eleanor on November 11, 1940:

My trouble, I suspect, has always been that I've been so much more interested in the *person* than in the *personage*. I resented the personage and fought for years an anguished and losing fight against the development of the person into the personage. I still prefer the *person*, but I admire and respect the *personage* with all my heart!

Eleanor (*second from the left*) and Lorena (*far right*) were interrupted by fans during their July 1922 holiday. They posed for this photo, but Lorena couldn't even look at the camera.

Eleanor and Lorena never got the shared house they'd dreamed about, and as Lorena aged, she struggled with both physical and financial troubles. As she wrote to Eleanor on August 7, 1935, she couldn't go back to being a reporter:

> If you got a laugh out of my idea of the possibility of a "happy family" at Campobello—I was equally amused at your idea that I could get a newspaper job, telling them I never saw you and didn't know what was going on. They'd NEVER believe it, dear—unless I actually did quit seeing you. And that would be expecting a good deal of me. Gosh I'm not prepared to give you up *entirely!* (And I don't believe you would want that, either.)

TRYING TO LOSE THE PRESS

It reads like a scene from a wacky comedy.

In August 1934, Eleanor and Lorena planned a vacation in California. But the press was there, waiting in the hotel lobby when Lorena showed up the night before at their "secret" meeting spot. As Streitmatter told it, trying to fool the reporters, Lorena left her car at the hotel and took a taxi to meet Eleanor at the airport. Followed by the press, they went back to the hotel. Lorena got out of the taxi and asked the reporters to be patient and let the First Lady wash her face before they spoke to her and took her picture. The group of reporters agreed.

Lorena then led Eleanor into the hotel elevator, but instead of going up to a room, they went down to the garage where Lorena's car was waiting and, with a state trooper driving them, tried to make their getaway. But two reporters, who suspected something was up, hopped in their own car and chased after them, determined to get the story. Lorena later wrote, **"With dismay I watched the speedometer go up and up and up— 50, 55, 60, 75, 77 miles [80, 89, 97, 121, 124 km] an hour."**

The trooper eventually stopped because they couldn't outrun the reporters. Eleanor and Lorena had a meal with the reporters, who, after asking the First Lady all their questions, let the two women drive away. The resulting news articles on the chase included one on the front page of the *Sacramento Union* with the headline:

"President's Wife Tells Union She Plans 'Secret' Auto Tour of California"

With Eleanor's help, Lorena got some writing work. Lorena's first book for young readers, *The Story of Helen Keller*, was made possible by a scoop Eleanor got her—an interview with Helen Keller.

In 1936, at a low point in their relationship, Eleanor offered to return the sapphire and diamond ring Lorena had given her. (Eleanor had heard the news that the diva who had originally given it to Lorena had died.) A week later, Lorena was at the White House, rereading the letters she had sent Eleanor over the past four years, as research for a book she wanted to write about the Great Depression. She wrote Eleanor this:

December 6

Dearest:

A long, dreary, rainy Sunday. I have spent the whole day in Louis Howe's room, while I plodded through those letters. I should say I am now about half way through. Today I stumbled into a lot of the early letters, written when I was still with the AP. Dear, whatever may have happened since—whatever may happen in the future—I was certainly happy those days, much happier, I believe, than most people ever are in all their lives. You gave me that, and I'm deeply grateful. There were other times, too—many, many of them.

What do you want me to do with these letters when I have finished? Throw them away? In a way, I'd like to keep them, or have them kept somewhere. They constitute a sort of diary, as yours to me probably do, too. They might be of some use when I get around to that biography.

When it was published in 1962, Lorena's biography of Eleanor was called *Reluctant First Lady.*

What do you think? In a way, I haven't minded reading them so much today, although some of them make me feel a little wistful. I don't suppose anyone can ever stay so happy as I was that first year or so, though. Do you?

Good night, dear. You have been swell to me these last four years, and I love you—now and always.

H

TRICKY TRICKS

Even though these letters have been public since 1978, Eleanor and Lorena's relationship continues to be ignored and misrepresented. As of this writing, the *Encyclopædia Britannica* entry on Eleanor doesn't mention Lorena. Neither does Eleanor's History.com First Ladies Biography. And the one mention of Lorena on the "Eleanor Roosevelt: Facts and Figures" page at the Franklin D. Roosevelt Presidential Library and Museum website doesn't say anything about their relationship beyond, "She [Lorena] developed a deep attachment to Eleanor which compromised her objectivity and she resigned from the AP." That's it. That last one is particularly ironic, since the FDR Presidential Library and Museum holds the correspondence between Eleanor and Lorena, including "approximately 2,300 of Mrs. Roosevelt's letters and 1,000 of Miss Hickok's."

As recently as November 22, 2020, the Getty Images listing of a photo of Eleanor and Lorena from August 1, 1934, was

You know it's a lot of letters when they can't even get the numbers right. The FDR Presidential Library and Museum puts it at thirty-three hundred. Streitmatter's figure is thirty-five hundred. But as Streitmatter explains, "Their total correspondence . . . runs in its entirety to some 16,000 pages."

titled "Eleanor Roosevelt Dining with Her Secretary Lorena Hickok."

Lorena was never Eleanor's secretary.

One of the seventeen tags on the photo is "Lesbian photos," so at least there's a hint about the queer history it represents . . .

MORE OF THE STORY

Some publications have acknowledged Eleanor and Lorena's relationship, such as Streitmatter's *Empty without You*. Their relationship is also mentioned in Linas Alsenas's *Gay America*. Alsenas quoted Wiesen Cook's response to historians who dismiss the relationship as a simple friendship: Eleanor "was very aware of lesbian life—in fact, her closest friends during the 1920s were two lesbian couples." Paul Russell's chapter on Eleanor in his *The Gay 100* also talks about Eleanor and Lorena's relationship, with the reminder that "the correspondence was initially suppressed by those who felt it would be 'misunderstood.'" And the LGBT History Month biography of Eleanor includes these lines: "While First Lady, Roosevelt developed an intimate relationship with Lorena Hickok, a journalist who covered the White House. The relationship lasted for the rest of Roosevelt's life."

Despite the thousands of letters, some historians don't think that Eleanor and Lorena loved each other romantically. Others, including me, do believe their relationship was Love with a capital *L*. And does having loved another woman, making Eleanor a lesbian or bisexual, take away from her position in history as an icon and role model? Or does it maybe inform our understanding of why Eleanor had such compassion for those marginalized by society?

Perhaps it's not a coincidence that Eleanor championed the Universal Declaration of Human Rights. Perhaps Eleanor's loving Lorena shaped who she was and, so, shaped history.

What do you think?

CHAPTER 8

M'E MPHO NTHUNYA

1930–2013 • LESOTHO

**WHEN A WOMAN LOVES ANOTHER WOMAN, YOU
SEE, SHE CAN LOVE HER WITH A WHOLE HEART.**
—M'e Mpho Nthunya, from her 1996 autobiography

WHo WAS M'e MPHO?

Pronounced Mem-Po.

M'e Mpho Nthunya was an elder and storyteller who cleaned and did laundry at the university guesthouse where oral and written history researcher, university teacher, performance artist, and author K. Limakatso Kendall stayed upon arriving in Lesotho in 1992. The women became friends and then fell in love, and over the next two years, M'e Mpho dictated her autobiography to Kendall. It was first published in South Africa, and then in 1997 it was published in the United States as *Singing away the Hunger: The Autobiography of an African Woman*.

At the time, M'e Mpho supported eleven people with her salary.

As M'e Mpho put it in the opening chapter:

I'm telling stories for children and grown people in other places, because I want people who know how to read and have time to read, to know something about the Basotho—how we used to live and how we

WHAT'S IN A NAME?

The country is *Lesotho*.

The people of Lesotho are *Basotho*.

A single Basotho is a *Mosotho*.

The language and culture are known as *Sesotho*.

SHOWING RESPECT

While it literally means "mother," *M'e* is the polite honorific (like our culture's *Miss* or *Ms.* or *Mrs.*) added to the first name of a mature Basotho woman. In Sesotho culture, it's actually an insult to speak of a woman without using the honorific. As one Mosotho woman told Kendall, **"To speak of a grown woman without using M'e is the same as stripping off all her clothes."**

live now, how poor we are, and how we are living together in this place called Lesotho. I'm also telling stories for Basotho like my grandchildren, who read books but don't know the old ways of their own people. If they can read these stories, maybe it will teach them where they come from.

M'e Mpho's autobiography was nominated for South Africa's Alan Paton Award, and was one of five books honored at that award's ceremony in Johannesburg. Kendall and M'e Mpho attended together. As Kendall recalled:

There were some television interviews with her [M'e Mpho] at that time, and there was a photograph of her with Ellen Kuzwayo and one of the members of Mandela's cabinet in *Ebony South Africa* (July 1997).

I told her about Andy Warhol's "fifteen minutes of fame," and she laughed that yes, this was her fifteen minutes. There was a big spread about her, with three portraits of her and a photo of the cover of the book, in a magazine called *True Love* (February 1998). She was very proud of that because many domestic workers read that magazine.

The American pop artist Andy Warhol created paintings of everyday objects such as Campbell's soup cans, which challenged people to think about the question, *What is art?* He was also very intentional about being a celebrity, and became most famous for the concept that in the future, everyone will be famous for fifteen minutes (and then it will be someone else's turn). He even hosted a television show on MTV, *Andy Warhol's Fifteen Minutes*. In a bit of irony that Warhol clearly loved, it turns out the quote he was most famous for saying was one he never actually said! Oh, and Warhol was gay.

M'E MPHO WAS ALSO A WOMAN WHO LOVED ANOTHER WOMAN

In her autobiography, M'e Mpho shared that, in addition to her marriage to a man (something all women in her culture were expected to do), she was also ritually married to a woman.

That woman was M'e M'alineo, who chose M'e Mpho as her special friend, or motsoalle, and sealed it with a kiss. M'e Mpho told it this way:

Pronounced Mo-tswall-eh.

> When I was living in the mountains I got a special friend. She was living in another village, and I passed her house when I was going to church every month. One day she saw me and said, "What is your name?"

I told her I was 'M'atsepo Nthunya. So she said, "I always see you passing here. Today I want to talk to you. I want you to be my *motsoalle*." This is a name we have in Sesotho for a very special friend. She says, "I love you."

It's like when a man chooses you for a wife, except when a man chooses, it's because he wants to share the blankets with you. The woman chooses you the same way, but she doesn't want to share the blankets. She wants love only. When a woman loves another woman, you see, she can love her with a whole heart.

I saw how she was looking at me, and I said, "*Ke hantle*, it's fine with me." So she kissed me, and from that day she was my *motsoalle*.

Their relationship was a public one, as M'e Mpho wrote:

She [M'e M'alineo] told her husband about it, and he came to my house and told my husband, and these two husbands became friends too. . . .

Most of the time I would only see her once a month, when I went to church. We would meet outside her house and walk to church together. She would sit by me in church, and we would hold hands. There was a café near her village, and when I went to the café, I would meet her, or if she was not around I would see a child and say, "Go tell M'e M'alineo I'm here in the café." Then she would come, and we would talk until it's time for me to go.

The women exchanged gifts, and even held two feasts observed by their husbands and friends to recognize and honor their relationship. M'e Mpho described that first celebration, held around 1958:

> She loved me so much that she bought me a *seshoeshoe* dress and two brooms. One day my *motsoalle* said she wanted me to come [to] her house for a feast to celebrate our friendship. She cooked for days to get ready, and even me, I made much bread and *joala* and two chickens to add to her feast.
>
> I went to her house with five women, my husband, and two other men.
>
> When we arrive at her house we find that she has prepared a sheep. She shows us the sheep and says, "There is your food." It was like a wedding.
>
> So we say our thanks, and they take the sheep and slaughter it. We go into the house and begin singing, everyone feeling happy. We sing while we wait for the meat, and those who drink *joala*, drink all day. Those who don't drink *joala* have *motoho* and Coke. So when the food is ready and the meat is cooked, then we sit down. We eat meat, bread, *samp*, everything we can think of. It was summer, so it was hot. We stayed the whole day. In the afternoon, around six, I kissed my *motsoalle* goodbye and we went back to our village, singing all the way. I remember it was late, about ten, when we got home, walking by foot, and when we got home we kept on singing till two o'clock in the morning.

Joala is a type of homemade beer.

"It was like a wedding"— wow!

Motoho is a nonalcoholic drink made from ground sorghum, a grain.

Samp is a food made from corn.

M'e Mpho remembered the second feast:

M'e Mpho (*seated*) and her motsoalle M'e M'alineo, circa 1959–1962

Another time, a year later, my *motsoalle* comes for a feast at my house. So she comes with many women and many husbands carrying *joala* and *motoho*. They arrive at noon or so, and we took the whole day. When they arrived I showed them the sheep, and after that we slaughtered it and cooked it. There were many people coming for the party. All these people knew that my *motsoalle* was visiting and they came to honour us for loving each other.

The singing and dancing of that second ritual celebration went on into the next day. As Kendall wrote, **"It would appear from Nthunya's story that long-term loving, intimate . . . relationships between women were normative in rural Lesotho at that time and were publicly acknowledged and honored."**

The historian Judith Gay, writing in the *Journal of Homosexuality* in 1985, reinforced this conclusion when she described a discussion that she had in Lesotho:

A conversation on female friendships with three older women was interrupted by the arrival of a 24-year-old daughter-in-law, who gasped and clapped her hands in amazement when she heard the topic of our discussion. "Why are you clapping so?" asked the straightforward 97-year-old woman. "Haven't you ever fallen in love with another girl?"

Poignantly, the relationship between M'e Mpho and M'e M'alineo would end. M'e Mpho told how that happened:

After some years, my *motsoalle* left her husband to find work in Maseru. He was not treating her well, and they had no children, so it was hard for her to stay alone with him in the mountains.

In Maseru she could not find work. She became a drunkard. I was very sad for that. I saw her last year, on the street. She is no longer my *motsoalle* because she's drinking too much.

M'e Mpho did find love again, with Kendall. Though when she and Kendall became each other's motsoalle in the 1990s, things had changed in Sesotho culture for women who loved women. As Kendall explained, **"The practice**

M'e Mpho and her motsoalle Kendall in 1993

of marriages had stopped." Homophobia had spread to the point where **"M'e Mpho became embarrassed about it. She was uncomfortable with that kind of openness."**

The marriage-like ceremonies M'e Mpho and her motsoalle M'e M'alineo had in the 1950s were among the last cultural expressions of the ritualized and honored love between women in Lesotho. Those women-loving-women relationships didn't stop happening. They just went inside another Western import—the closet.

TRICKY TRICKS

We're so used to our culture's way of looking at the world that it can be easy to forget that other cultures structure and see things (like relationships) differently. Kendall realized this too. She wrote:

> **My search for lesbians in Lesotho began in 1992, when I arrived in that small, impoverished southern African country and went looking for my own kind. That was before the president of nearby Zimbabwe, Robert Mugabe, himself mission-educated, declared moral war on homosexuality and insisted that homosexuality was a "Western" phenomenon imported to Africa by the European colonists. When I left Lesotho two and a half years later, I hadn't found a single Mosotho who identified herself as a lesbian.**

But that doesn't mean Kendall didn't find women who loved other women. She explained:

> **I learned not to look for unconventionality or visible performance of sex-role rejection as indicators of "queerness," for most Basotho women grow up in**

environments in which it is impossible for them to learn, purchase, or display symbols of gay visibility, where passionate relationships between women are as conventional as (heterosexual) marriage, and where women who love women usually perform as conventional wives and mothers. . . . I have concluded that love between women is as native to southern Africa as the soil itself, but that homophobia, like Mugabe's Christianity, is a Western import.

It can be hard to see what we're not looking for. And maybe it takes looking at the stories of women who loved women through other cultural lenses to start seeing that larger, mostly untold, history.

Kendall realized the challenge of looking at one culture through the lens of another. As an out lesbian who grew up in the United States, she wrote about trying to figure out:

Why does it feel important to me to know whether there are or were women in Lesotho who might be called lesbian? . . . After all, constructing or recovering lesbian history is, in a way, an act of legitimation that presumes illegitimacy. If, in Lesotho, love between women was (and still is) perfectly legitimate . . . an activity or a feeling as ubiquitous as air, my prying questions become irrelevant, and the laughter that most often greeted those questions when I put them to Basotho women becomes understandable. . . . The need for legitimacy only arises in cultures (like my own) in which love between women has been pathologized or made illegitimate.

Ubiquitous means "it's everywhere."

Pathologize means "to treat something like an illness."

NO WAY, THEY WERE GAY?

MORE OF THE STORY

M'e Mpho and Kendall lived together in South Africa from 1995 to 1998. As Kendall explained, **"For her [M'e Mpho] it was four years of retirement, of not having to work, of not worrying where her next meal would come from. She called our apartment 'a small heaven.' . . . They were marvelous years for us both."**

In August 2000, M'e Mpho joined Kendall, who had moved back to the United States. As Kendall told me in an email, M'e Mpho **"stayed until May 2001, at which time she missed her culture so much that she returned to Lesotho."** Kendall stayed in the United States.

In 2010 Kendall visited M'e Mpho in Lesotho one last time and took M'e Mpho to see the Indian Ocean. In 2013 M'e Mpho died.

A 1992 photo of M'e Mpho. As Kendall explained, **"This was her favorite of the hundreds of pictures I made of her. The hat is a symbol of the Basotho people, and her father used to weave these from mountain grasses."**

Looking back on the life, and passing, of the woman she loved, Kendall said that at the end of her life, M'e Mpho was **"happy—very satisfied with the work we'd done and the love we'd shared."** After all, **"she'd done what she set out to do—told her story."**

As a woman from Africa whose life included one ritualized—and publicly honored—romantic and loving relationship with a woman, and another unrecognized romantic and loving relationship with a woman, M'e Mpho opens our eyes to her story, and to all the other stories we may not be paying attention to.

As a working Mosotho woman who shared her life story and had it published in English, M'e Mpho helps us see. And as a storyteller brave enough to share her own story, M'e Mpho offers us a window to understanding: even though cultures can seem so different, love is universal. Women loving other women is universal.

M'e Mpho has the final quote of this chapter:

> **In the old days friendship was very beautiful— men friends and women friends. Friendship was as important as marriage. Now this custom is gone; everything is changing. People now don't love like they did long ago.**

How do our cultural blinders prevent us from seeing and acknowledging the history of women who loved women in other cultures?

How much more could we see if we looked closer, listened without bias, and made room for previously unheard voices?

PART III:

PEOPLE
WHO LIVED
OUTSIDE
GENDER
BOUNDARIES

THE CHEVALIER D'ÉON AND MADEMOISELLE DE BEAUMONT WERE THE SAME PERSON

Charles-Geneviève-Louise-Auguste-André-Timothée d'Éon de Beaumont was born in 1728 in France. He was raised as a boy and lived the first half of his adult life as a man.

As the Chevalier d'Éon, Charles served as a cavalry officer during wartime (the French horse-mounted troops were called dragoons.) In 1763 he moved to London as a diplomat to help negotiate the peace treaty between France and Britain. The effort earned him France's highest honor, the Order of Saint Louis. Few people knew that the Chevalier d'Éon was also a spy for the French king Louis XV. As professor of European history Robert Aldrich explained, while the Chevalier d'Éon was in England, he was collecting "intelligence intended for a possible French invasion of the British Isles."

In 1771 rumors that the chevalier was actually a woman created a sensation in both England and France. People placed bets totaling "over £200,000"

A 1777 engraving that aimed to show both identities of the same person: Mademoiselle de Beaumont and the Chevalier d'Éon.

(more than £26.4 million currently or more than $35 million) on the chevalier's "real" gender. There was a lawsuit, a scandal and, finally, an agreement. The Chevalier d'Éon returned to France to live the rest of her life as a woman: Mademoiselle de Beaumont.

In 1785 Mademoiselle de Beaumont moved back to London, where she earned money by entering—and winning—fencing tournaments. She admitted that she had been born female, and that was the history she told in her autobiography (though it wasn't published until nearly two hundred years later).

When she died in 1810, there was one final twist to her story: the revelation that Mademoiselle de Beaumont had a male body.

More than forty-five years as a boy and man. And then, more than thirty-five years as a woman. What a life outside gender boundaries!

Like the Chevalier d'Éon and Mademoiselle de Beaumont's story, the next four chapters will reclaim the queer history of the Pharaoh Hatshepsut, the Lieutenant Nun, We'wha, and Christine Jorgensen.

Mademoiselle de Beaumont wins a fencing match on April 9, 1787, at London's Carlton House.

CHAPTER 9

PHARAOH HATSHEPSUT

1495–1458 BCE (RULED 1479–1458 BCE) • EGYPT

MY FOES SHALL NOT EXIST. LIFE AND POWER ARE UNITED IN ME. I AM CHOSEN FOR HER CROWN OF UPPER EGYPT AND HER CROWN OF LOWER EGYPT; THAT CROWN IS FIRM ON MY HEAD. I AM SUPPORTED BY THE GREAT MAGICIAN, FIRM ON MY THRONE AS THE KING OF THE TWO LANDS.

—Hatshepsut proclaiming herself king—not queen—in the stone carvings called the *Oracle Text*, circa 1474 BCE

BACKGROUND

Ancient Egyptians believed the world started when a god, Atum, created two children, the brother-sister gods Shu and Tefnut. That brother-sister pair had kids together, and then *that* brother-sister pair had kids, two of whom had a child together, the god Horus. And Horus, the people believed, ruled Egypt by taking the form of Egypt's current king, or pharaoh. Because the family in power wanted to keep their royal line "pure," it was common for siblings and cousins to marry each other. In this patriarchal system, boys were the only heirs who could inherit or take on the rule of the nation.

Patriarchy is what we call a society set up so that men have most of the power, and succession (who becomes ruler next) is determined by the male line.

WHO WAS HATSHEPSUT?

Hatshepsut was born into the ruling family of Egypt, the daughter of Thutmose I. At a young age, Hatshepsut married her half brother. When their father died, Hatshepsut's brother-husband became the new pharaoh, Thutmose II. As the wife of the king, Hatshepsut was also a priestess with the title, God's wife of Amen. Then Hatshepsut's nephew was born, the next—and only—male in line for the throne.

Pronounced like it looks: Hat-shep-sut.

Because inscriptions at the time continued to refer to Hatshepsut using female pronouns even after her transition to being hailed as her father's son, we'll honor that by using *she/her/hers* when referring to Hatshepsut.

Barely two years later, Thutmose II died. Hatshepsut was only sixteen years old, and the fate of her family's dynasty hung in the balance. How could the

country crown a two-year-old?
A toddler couldn't rule Egypt!

Regent is a title for the person who rules a country because the actual ruler can't for some reason— such as being too young.

Hatshepsut convinced the priests and ruling class to stay with her family's succession, rather than start a new dynasty. The two-year-old was crowned pharaoh, and Hatshepsut took over as regent for the boy.

In 1479 BCE, in a time of crisis, Hatshepsut, a teenager, stepped in and kept all of Egypt running. As historian and professor of Egyptian art and architecture Kara Cooney explained, Hatshepsut's "ticket to power was that nephew" because it made a woman ruler more acceptable to the patriarchal power structure.

By year five of her regency, Hatshepsut claimed to be **"the one to whom Ra has actually given the Kingship."**

Two years later, in a weeklong ceremony, Hatshepsut was crowned king. Senior co-king, technically. Her nephew, the child king Thutmose III, was nine years old.

Hatshepsut would rule Egypt until she died in the twenty-second year of her reign.

How did a young woman maintain that position of power over everyone else—for twenty-two years!—in vast, wealthy, patriarchal ancient Egypt?

Historians such as Cooney think there were two reasons. The first: Hatshepsut was all about spreading the wealth and creating jobs. She professionalized the army and priesthood, creating new positions of power, title, income, and lands, which built an upper class invested in their own and their ruler's success. The more generous Hatshepsut was to this inner circle of power, the more support Hatshepsut gained for her own rule.

An inscription about Hatshepsut in the tomb of one official reads, **"Her Majesty praised me and she loved me. She knew**

my excellence in the palace. She provided me with things, and she made me great."

Hatshepsut also boosted the economy, ordering the building of monuments, innovative temples, and obelisks all over Egypt.

Hatshepsut also created international campaigns, sending expeditions to lands that were almost mythical to Egyptians in those days: Nubia, Punt, and Yemen. The details of those cultures and the wealth (gold, incense, plants, and animals) that were brought back thrilled the upper class. The result of all this was that Egypt was thriving and prosperous, with an elite class that fully supported Hatshepsut's rule.

Nubia was in today's Sudan. Punt was southeast, along the Red Sea coast in today's Somalia, Djibouti, or Eritrea. Yemen is, all these years later, still Yemen.

The second key to Hatshepsut's power, again according to Cooney, was that Hatshepsut created a divine birth mythology for herself, taking control of the priesthood. If the gods wanted Hatshepsut to be king, how could anyone protest?

Hatshepsut's Temple of Millions of Years in Thebes, built in the most holy spot

NO WAY, THEY WERE GAY?

Carved into one of Hatshepsut's most sacred temples, the *Oracle Text* told the story (in images and symbols) of the gods choosing Hatshepsut to rule over Egypt as king. In the story, the statue of the god Amen has been carried out of his sanctuary to perform a ritual, but nothing goes the way the nobles and officials present expect it to.

An oracle is a person others believe a god speaks through, sharing information and predictions about the future.

His Majesty [the god Amen] proceeded with his Ennead behind him to the oracles. Yet he did not make any pronouncements for the king at the "stations of the Lord." The whole land was silent. Their faces aghast, "we can't," said the royal entourage of the palace. They asked, "what?!" Those whose hearts were full found their minds empty, their hearts trembling with suffering from the event. . . .

Ennead is an old term for a group of nine.

In the David Warburton translation used here the god's name is spelled "Amun," while Cooney spelled it "Amen." I've used "Amen" throughout this chapter.

The Mistress of the Two Lands [Hatshepsut] came out of her palace, and worshipped, praising the procession of the Lord of the Gods and then fell upon her body in the presence of His Majesty, saying, "How much greater is this than the plans of Your Majesty! It is my father who conjured all that is! What is the wish of the Lord that will come to pass?! Indeed, I will do all that complies with your command."

Check out how the drama of a ritual not going the way the people attending expected sets up Hatshepsut's big entrance.

As if it wasn't Hatshepsut who was in charge, but the god telling Hatshepsut what the god wanted.

Later in the text, the god Amen speaks to Hatshepsut, saying:

I place you upon my thrones, you seizing the crook and flail. I form you, who I desired to make, you offering in the presence of I who created you. Found anew the chapels of the gods and protect this land as necessary! May terror of you seize the outlaws planning rebellion, caught by you, the victorious Lord of Power! Then this land will be in your hands, the faithful among the people will praise you. You will maintain law and order, driving out chaos. You will end civil conflict, governing the living with your ordinances."

The royal followers were amazed. . . . Awe seized heaven and earth. . . . He [the god Amen] reached out to his child [Hatshepsut]. He had planned that she should seize the two lands.

Then there's the part where Hatshepsut spoke:

I am beneficent king, a lawgiver who judges deeds. . . . I am the wild horned bull descending from heaven that her shape be seen by him. I am the falcon who glides over the lands, landing to apportion. I am the jackal who circles the land in an instant. I am excellent of heart, glorifying her father, looking for deeds to render justice to him. . . . I am the glorious eye of the head of her father, wreathing his head in victory . . . I came down from heaven, knowing his power. I know the deeds he has commanded for me.

I am KING! Here, Hatshepsut claims her right to rule. Oh, and *beneficent* means doing good, being generous.

NO WAY, THEY WERE GAY?

I take this land, bowing, being exalted while still a child. My power makes the northern land tremble at my step. This is no [minor event, insignificant in all the time] since the earliest ancestors. There was never an event like this coup. I am the king whose going forth through him is ordained . . . My foes shall not exist. Life and power are united in me. I am chosen for her crown of Upper Egypt and her crown of Lower Egypt; that crown is firm on my head. I am supported by the Great Magician, firm on my throne as the king of the Two Lands.

Not only am I king, Hatshepsut is saying, I'm the most special king ever!

Whether you believe Hatshepsut really had this revelation and spoke to her gods or just had the whole thing staged, the story gave Hatshepsut a more direct claim to the throne than being the daughter of a king, the sister of a king, the wife of a king, the widow of a king, and the aunt of a king. Hatshepsut was all of those. But this oracle story was Hatshepsut telling all of Egypt: *I am king because the gods want me to be king!*

HATSHEPSUT ALSO LIVED OUTSIDE GENDER BOUNDARIES

As Hatshepsut's kingship went on, there was a growing problem: her nephew. Cooney explained: "Hatshepsut's young co-king was almost a man. As the king reached fifteen or sixteen years old, we can imagine that his opinions were not only more forcefully expressed but reasoned and educated. His bearing was manly, no longer boyish. He was probably now taller than his female co-king. . . . It was quickly becoming unseemly for her to stand next to

Thutmose III in the senior position during sacred rituals and at court. A woman could outrank a boy but not a man. If she was to continue her dominance in this unequal partnership, something had to change."

What changed was how Hatshepsut presented her own gender.

Cooney described how for the first five years of Hatshepsut's reign, Hatshepsut was shown in images "wearing the long dress of a woman and the crown of a king." By five or six years into her reign, Hatshepsut's image was progressively masculinized—with wider shoulders and no shirt—but still with feminine breasts. Eventually, images of Hatshepsut showed her with a fully masculine body, with broad shoulders and a male chest.

Hatshepsut dressed as a woman and portrayed with a woman's body.

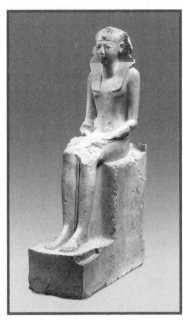

Hatshepsut without a shirt (as a man would be portrayed), with a physique that includes feminine-seeming breasts

This progression from a mostly female, to a blended male-female, to a fully male representation was also seen in the statues of Hatshepsut at her Temple of Millions of Years. The feminine elements in the earliest statues went away in later ones, and even the color of Hatshepsut's skin changed. As Cooney described it, yellow was the color usually used to "depict an elite woman who stayed indoors," while men who were "part of the wider world" were colored with a "deep red ocher." Fascinatingly, Hatshepsut's statues started out yellow and then had an in-between phase, painted with both yellow and red pigment, "resulting in a strange hybrid orange skin color—not at all a part of the established color scheme for Egyptian art"—and ultimately Hatshepsut's statues were colored red.

Hatshepsut wearing a beard and men's clothes, with a fully masculinized body

Cooney explained, "Masculinity was a key component of Egyptian Kingship, and step by step, as her years of royal authority accrued, she [Hatshepsut] concealed her feminine aspects until there was almost no woman left, except in the sacred texts alongside the pictures that continued referring to 'she' and 'her.'"

When Thutmose III was seventeen, in the fourteenth year of Hatshepsut's reign, Hatshepsut staged a Sed festival, "the biggest celebration Egypt had seen in generations." Full of rituals, staged productions that lasted for weeks, and new temples and obelisks, Hatshepsut used the festival to claim, as Cooney put it, that Hatshepsut, "was the rightful successor as the eldest child of Thutmose I, essentially pushing her husband-brother, Thutmose II, out of the picture entirely and giving herself a clean linear succession. While depicting herself as a son, not a daughter, to Thutmose I, and wearing a king's kilt, beard, and wig, she used the jubilee to redefine her person to fit the patriarchal system of succession alongside Thutmose III. Hatshepsut also modified the jubilee to remake her public image as a father figure to Thutmose III. Styled as a man in formal depictions and rituals, she now pivoted 180 degrees from her start as his regent and mother figure when he was a toddler king. The jubilee cemented her role as the senior king in a royal partnership,

HATSHEPSUT DID THE MATH HER OWN WAY

Usually, the Sed festival was celebrated only when a king had reached thirty years of continuous rule, but Hatshepsut added up the thirteen years of her father's reign with the three years of her husband's reign with the seven years of her own regency and the seven years of her own rule as king to get to the number thirty: $13 + 3 + 7 + 7 = 30$ ... and presto! There was a jubilee to celebrate!

thereby creating the foundation for further rule in the next generation, as a father would do for his son, and as she claims Thutmose I did for her."

After that festival, Cooney tells us, "no temple image ever shows her as a woman. She had left that part of herself behind. In her imagery, she had become the son of Thutmose I."

While we don't have diaries or letters from Hatshepsut, historians and archaeologists have reliefs, carvings, statues, inscriptions, and temple writings. Cooney described a number of those carvings: "One image shows the sacred animal licking the hand of the enthroned king; in another, a male Hatshepsut kneels underneath the cow goddess' udders and drinks the divine milk promised only to kings. Hathor was thought to be the mother of the sun god, and to show Hatshepsut suckling from her was to show the king feeding from divinity itself as the predestined son of Re."

Even Hatshepsut's name changed in regards to gender. Originally, *Hatshepsut* meant **"The Foremost of Noble Women."**

But as Cooney explained:

> That's a challenging name to masculinize!

> Just after her accession, she had added the phrase, **"The One United with Amen"** to her birth name. When Hatshepsut said she was "united" with Amen, she meant that she had actually joined her feminine self with his essence, taking on Amen's aspects of divinity, his mind, his intentions, and even, to some extent, his abilities. This particular name modification also suggests that Hatshepsut did not undergo her gender transformation manipulatively or cynically but piously. Possibly, she actually believed Amen had allowed her to transcend her own human body to become an entity greater than herself. Hatshepsut actually feminized the

word *khenem*, "to unite," in her inscriptions by adding a
—*t*, so that her name read **"Hatshepsut the Female One Who Unites with Amen."**

The transition of Hatshepsut's gender expression, or presentation, worked, keeping Hatshepsut the ruling pharaoh of Egypt for the rest of her life.

After twenty-two years of rule, at the age of thirty-eight, Hatshepsut died. Historians believe it was a natural death.

That left Thutmose III as sole king.

TRICKY TRICKS

Twenty-five years after Hatshepsut's death, Thutmose III started a campaign to systematically destroy all of Hatshepsut's statues and reliefs. He tried to erase Hatshepsut from history, changing and sometimes taking the credit for all

Sometimes, Thutmose III's workers were so careful to chisel out *just* Hatshepsut that the silhouette of Hatshepsut's form was still visible!

NO WAY, THEY WERE GAY?

of Hatshepsut's accomplishments. Wherever Hatshepsut's name appeared, he had his workers chisel it out and put in Thutmose I, Thutmose II, or his own name, Thutmose III, instead.

Hatshepsut's most prized sacred temple, the one with the *Oracle Text* carved on its walls, was dismantled block by block and thrown in a pile. Then the images that were still visible (the ones on top) were erased by Thutmose III's workers, who didn't bother with the images underneath. Generations later, when the same black diorite and light red quartzite blocks were used as building materials somewhere else, the carvings that hadn't been chiseled away were exposed. The story was out of order, with parts missing, but the *Oracle Text* was told on Hatshepsut's obelisks and funerary temple as well, and archaeologists pieced it together.

In an ironic twist, some of the erasure was so sloppy that, as Cooney described, in one place "they changed the name of the king from Hatshepsut to Thutmose III but neglected to change 'her' to 'his,' so one inscription about him incongruously reads, **'Amen is satisfied by her monuments.'**"

MORE OF THE STORY

The efforts to erase Hatshepsut from history lasted ten years. Once Thutmose III's own son was crowned co-king with him, the destruction of Hatshepsut's legacy and memorials stopped. But Hatshepsut had been so prolific, with so many projects built, and so many nobles who honored her over twenty-two years of rule, that Thutmose III didn't manage to erase everything. And so we do know about Hatshepsut!

Hatshepsut lived a life outside gender boundaries. With a woman's body, she ruled ancient Egypt first as a woman, and then over the years of their rule transitioned to a publicly male persona.

ONE MORE ROLE FOR THE PHARAOH

Hatshepsut was also a mother, having a daughter with Thutmose II. The girl's name was Nefrure, and we don't know much about her, since she was also erased from monuments. But as Nefrure grew, it's thought that she married Thutmose III, her half brother and Hatshepsut's co-king. As Cooney put it, Nefrure "was a key player for both monarchs: she allowed her mother to have a highborn King's Daughter playing the female role in temple rituals and gave her brother the opportunity to produce offspring of pure royal blood."

By the time Hatshepsut was in their late thirties, she may have been thinking of Nefrure as a possible successor to the throne. Cooney shared the evidence, "Nefrure was labeled on a Sinai inscription as Mistress of the Two Lands and Mistress of Upper and Lower Egypt—titles used by the female king Hatshepsut herself. The stela from the Sinai seems to be dated to Nefrure's own regnal year, an audacity in itself—**'year 11 of the majesty of the God's Wife Nefrure'**—as if she were a king in her own right."

Could Nefrure (and a struggle for who would be pharaoh next) be part of the explanation for Thutmose III's ten-year attempt to erase Hatshepsut from memory? That the campaign of destruction ended once Thutmose III's own son was made co-king with him, thus securing the dynastic line for the men in the family, seems a telling clue.

How much was political necessity versus Hatshepsut's own sense of identity?

We don't know.

But more than thirty-four hundred years later, Hatshepsut's story allows us to reflect on the role gender continues to play in politics and power. And even more, to understand that the public expression of gender is something that can change over time—even for the most famous of people!

Does knowing about Hatshepsut change your view of gender expression being something that cannot—or can—change?

CHAPTER 10

CATALINA DE ERAUSO, THE LIEUTENANT NUN

A.K.A. FRANCISCO LOYOLA • A.K.A. ANTONIO DE ERAUSO

A.K.A. ALONSO DÍAZ RAMÍREZ DE GUZMÁN • A.K.A. LA MONJA ALFÉREZ

1585–1650 • SPAIN, PERÚ, CHILE, PANAMA, AND MEXICO

I KISSED THE FOOT OF HIS HOLINESS URBAN VIII,
AND RELATED TO HIM AS BEST I COULD THE
STORY OF MY LIFE AND TRAVELS, MY SEX, AND
MY VIRGINITY. HIS HOLINESS SHOWED HIMSELF
TO BE ASTONISHED BY SUCH A TALE, AND KINDLY
GRANTED ME PERMISSION TO CONTINUE MY LIFE
DRESSED AS A MAN.

—The Lieutenant Nun, writing in their autobiography

BACKGROUND

Gender was a kind of prison in Spain in the late 1500s and early 1600s. Women were seen by men as lesser-than men physically (not as strong), mentally (not as smart), and morally (more prone to evil). A lot of that stemmed from Christianity's views that blamed Eve in the Garden of Eden story from the Bible. Spain was obsessed with being "purely" Christian, and while Columbus set sail in 1492, it was also the year King Ferdinand II and Queen Isabella ordered the expulsion of Jews from the country. The brutal Spanish Inquisition that tortured and persecuted Jews and Muslims started in the twelfth century and lasted hundreds of years, causing the execution of some thirty-two thousand people.

For centuries, as Benito Jerónimo Feijoo y Montenegro put it in his 1726 *Defense of Women*, the society of men saw a women as **"an imperfect and even monstrous creature, affirming that the design of nature in the work of generation always intends a male, and only by error or defect in either matter or faculty produces a female."**

Even worse, as historian Theresa Ann Smith wrote, "women's enclosure in either convents or marriage was considered essential to uphold their virginity or virtue and thus, by extension, the honor and reputation of their male relatives."

Smith cites a Spanish conduct book written for women by Fray Luis de León in 1583 that explained it this way: **"As men are made for public, women are made for enclosure; and as men are made to speak and go outside, women are made to enclose and cover themselves."**

Born into this gender prison just two years later, Catalina de Erauso was determined to break free.

WHo WAS THE LiEUTENANT NUN?

The Autobiography of doña Catalina de Erauso reads like an action-adventure movie. It opens with their escape, at the age of fifteen, from a Dominican convent in San Sebastián, a village on the northern coast of Spain. From the age of four, Catalina had grown up in the same convent where their aunt was a nun, but just as Catalina was about to enter the Dominican order:

> Since we don't know how Catalina/Francisco would have identified their gender, to be most respectful, I'll use the singular form of the pronoun they/them/their to refer to the Lieutenant Nun.

Near the end of my novitiate year I had a quarrel with a professed nun named doña Catalina de Aliri (a widow who entered and took the vows). She was a strong woman and I but a girl. She beat me and I took it hard. On the night of March 18, 1600, on the eve of St. Joseph, the convent arose at midnight to pray. I entered the choir and found my aunt kneeling there. She summoned me, and giving me the key to her cell, asked me to fetch her breviary. I left to go get it, opened the door and picked it up. Seeing the keys to the convent hanging there on a nail, I left her cell door unlocked and returned the key and prayer book to my aunt. By now all the sisters were in the choir beginning the matins with solemnity.

> A breviary is a religious book of prayers and hymns.

After the first verse, I went to my aunt and asked to be excused because I was ill. Touching my forehead, she said, "Go on, go to bed." I left the choir and, taking a light, went to my aunt's cell. There I grabbed some scissors, a needle and thread, some pieces of eight that were there, and the keys to the convent. Then, I left. I went along, opening doors and shutting them, and in the last one I left my scapular. I went out into the street (which I had never seen before) not knowing which way to turn or where to go.

I don't know where I headed but I ended up in a chestnut grove out behind the rear of the convent. There I hid out for three days tracing and cutting clothing. I made myself a pair of trousers from a skirt of blue cloth that I had, and a shirt and leggings from the green shift that I wore underneath. Not knowing what to make of the rest of my habit, I left it there. I cut off my hair and threw it away.

Pieces of eight were a kind of money used in Spain and in Spanish territories. One gold coin in 1600 would be worth about sixty-three dollars today. Gold doubloons, silver pesos, and silver reales were also used.

A scapular is a piece of fabric worn over a nun's shoulders with an opening for the head.

From the age of four to fifteen, they had been held inside the convent walls and never left—not even to see the street outside!

THE LIEUTENANT NUN ALSO LIVED OUTSIDE GENDER BOUNDARIES

Dressed and groomed as a man, Catalina made their way under the name *Francisco Loyola*, finding work as a page, or servant, for don Juan de Idiáquez, secretary to the king.

Whether Catalina/Francisco knew it or not, that same year Spanish law banned people with female bodies dressing as men. It would be banned again in 1608, and again in 1615, and once more in 1641. As Professor Marjorie Garber put it, "The ban, obviously, proved ineffective, since it needed so frequently to be renewed."

It also means that there were other people with female bodies who tried to escape the gender prison of the time by dressing as men who had been caught. They had *dressed* as men, but didn't successfully *act* as men.

Catalina/Francisco had been gone about ten months when they were almost discovered:

I was standing at the doorway with another page one night when my father arrived asking us if don Juan was at home. My companion replied that he was. My father asked if we would please tell him that he was here. My companion went up leaving us alone. We spoke not a word between us and he didn't recognize me. The page returned saying to go on up and he did, with me following behind.

Did their father not know what Catalina looked like? It was just a haircut and different clothes. Or was it just so unthinkable that a person might present themselves as a different gender that their father didn't even bother to look at the teenage servant boy in front of him?

Don Juan came out onto the stairway and embracing him said, "Captain, what a welcome visit this is!" My father spoke in such a manner that don Juan knew he was upset. Dismissing a visitor whom he was with, he returned and sat down, asking him what was the matter. My father told him about how his daughter had run away from the convent and his search had brought him into this vicinity. Don Juan expressed great sympathy for my father's trouble, as he also was fond of me, and of that convent as

Here it seems don Juan was saying he was fond of Catalina the teenage girl, not Francisco, his teenage page. Neither don Juan (nor Catalina/Francisco's father) knew that Catalina and Francisco were the same person!

well, of which he was a patron (founded as it was by his ancestors, he himself being a native of there).

Hearing this conversation and my father's sentiments, I went back to my room. I gathered up my clothes and left, taking the eight doubloons or so that I had. I went to a tavern to spend the night and met a mule driver there who was leaving in the morning for Bilbao. I made an arrangement with him and we departed the next day. I didn't know what to do or where to go, and so I let myself drift like a feather in the wind.

Catalina/Francisco enlisted as a cabin boy on a ship bound for Panama. The captain was **"my uncle, my mother's cousin."** But he had no idea his cabin boy Francisco was also his niece, Catalina, who had been missing from the convent for three years!

I went through some hard times along the way, being new at my job. Although he didn't know me, my uncle took a liking to me and showed me some favor, having heard where I was from and the supposed name of my family which I had given. In him I had a great protector.

We arrived at Punta Araya and found an enemy force fortified ashore which drove our armada off. Finally we arrived in Cartagena where we remained for eight days. There I was promoted from general cabin boy to the personal service of my uncle, the Captain. . . .

Then, having loaded our cargo of silver ready to return to Spain, I struck my uncle a hard blow, relieving him of five hundred pesos. At ten o'clock at night when he was asleep, I went out and told the guards that the captain was sending me on an errand.

As they knew me, they readily let me go and I jumped ashore. But they never saw me again, for within the hour they weighed anchor and set sail.

Catalina/Francisco seemed to find work, and trouble, everywhere they went in Central and South America. Living as a man, Catalina/Francisco was as aggressive and violent as any man of the time—maybe even *more* aggressive and more violent. Was it an act to keep anyone from suspecting they didn't have a male body, or was it an expression of their true nature? We don't know, but here's one story Catalina/Francisco told from when they were working in a store in Panama:

One holiday I had just taken a seat in the theatre when, without warning, this so-and-so Reyes came in and placed his seat in front of me, so close that it blocked my view. I asked him if he might move aside a little and he responded discourteously. I responded in kind. He told me to get out or he would slash my face. I found myself unarmed except for a dagger, and so I left, very upset, accompanied by some friends who calmed me down.

The next morning—Monday—I was in my store selling when Reyes passed by the doorway twice. I noticed this and closed the store. I grabbed a knife and went to find a barber. I had him sharpen it and file the edge like a saw. I put on my sword, the first I ever wore. I saw Reyes strolling with another fellow in front of the church. I walked up to him from behind saying, "Uh, Señor Reyes!" He turned around and said, "What do you want?" I said, "This is the face that's getting slashed!" and gave him a slice across the face worth ten stitches.

He threw his hands to his wound. Drawing his sword, his friend came at me and I at him. We struck at each other, I ran him through the left side, and he fell.

Immediately I ran into the church which was right there, but right behind me came the sheriff . . . and dragged me back out. He took me to jail (the first I was ever in) and clapped me in stocks and shackles.

Spanish men could do almost anything at that time, and so, as a man, Catalina/Francisco claimed that freedom—to do just what they wanted.

Catalina/Francisco eventually joined the Spanish military, serving as **"a deputy to the sergeant-major,"** in the war against the Ashaninka and other Indigenous peoples of what is now Peru and Colombia.

Catalina/Francisco believed in colonialism: that Spanish men (including themself) and Spanish society were the most advanced expression of humanity, while the Native people they encountered were backward and lesser. Thus, Native lands and wealth and even lives were available for the taking by virtue of the Spanish military's superiority. By virtue of Catalina/Francisco's superiority. And Catalina/Francisco sought to prove their place among men by being a superior soldier. They wrote about the desire shared among the Spanish soldiers **"to conquer and get gold,"** and graphic battles where they slaughtered Indigenous people until **"a gutter of blood like a river flowed down through the place."**

One of many terrible moments where the humanity of people "other" than Catalina/Francisco was completely dismissed. The irony was that their own fellow soldiers would have seen them as "other" if the secret of Catalina/Francisco having female physical characteristics had been known.

NO WAY, THEY WERE GAY?

After deserting with some fellow soldiers because they weren't allowed to conquer another area rich in gold, Catalina/Francisco met one of their brothers in South America, but didn't reveal the connection. Was it thrilling for them to get away with the deception? We don't really know—very little emotion is shared in Catalina/Francisco's autobiography.

But we learn of another quality of Spanish men that Catalina/Francisco embodied: the romancing of women, and the gendered view of women as objects, property, and holding lesser-than status than men. Lesser than Catalina/Francisco, who lived their life as a man:

I remained with my brother as his aide, dining at his table for nearly three years without his ever realizing anything. I went with him sometimes to the house of a girlfriend he had there. Other times I went there without him. He found out about this and took it hard, telling me to keep away from there. He lay in wait for me and caught me at it again. When I came out, he attacked me with his belt and injured my hand. I was forced to defend myself and Captain don Francisco de Aillon, hearing the fracas, came and broke it up.

I ran into the Franciscan church, as I feared the governor who was a hard man, and proved so in this case. Although my brother interceded, he banished me to Paicabí, and with no other recourse I had to go.

Catalina/Francisco visiting the house of their brother's girlfriend, even after being told to **"keep away from there,"** presents themself as a romantic rival for the girlfriend's affections. It's certainly the cause of their brother's jealousy. It's not a flowery love letter, but it reveals to us that Catalina/Francisco had a romantic relationship with a woman.

This led to one of the most dramatic moments of Catalina/Francisco's military career:

After having lived so pleasantly, I had to go off to Paicabí and undergo some hard times for three years. We were always with our weapons in hand owing to the great invasion of Indians there. Finally the governor (Alonso de Sarabia) arrived with all the forces in Chile. We linked up with him and bivouaced in open country on the plains of Valdivia, five thousand men in bitter discomfort.

Bivouac means "to camp somewhere temporarily."

The Indians attacked and took the town of Valdivia. We counter attacked and did battle with them three or four times, beating them back and punishing them always. The last time however, their re-inforcements arrived and it went badly for us. They killed many of our troops and officers, including my lieutenant, and made off with our flag. Seeing it borne away, myself and two other mounted soldiers ran after it, right into the middle of the mob, trampling, killing, and receiving some damage. Soon, one of our three fell dead. The two of us pressed on and reached the flag, but my comrade was felled by a spear. Now badly wounded in the leg, I killed the chief who carried the flag, took it from him, and spurred my horse on, trampling wounding, and killing to infinity. But I was badly hurt, pierced by three arrows and a spear in my left shoulder, which I sorely felt. Finally I made it back to my own people and fell right off my horse. Some people came to my aid, and

This is horrible. And it's a glimpse into what colonization looked like.

among them was my brother whom I had not seen and was a great comfort to me.

They healed me and we remained encamped there nine months. At the end of that period, my brother got me back that flag I won from the governor, and I was commissioned a lieutenant in the company of Alonso Moreno. This company was soon given to Gonzalo Rodríguez, the first captain I had served under, and I was very pleased.

Amazingly, with all those injuries Catalina/ Francisco was able to keep their secret as they were treated and healed.

In Spanish, the word is *alférez*, as in La Monja Alférez. (And, yes, *monja* means "nun.")

There were many more sword fights, battles at sea where their ship was sunk and they had to swim to safety, gambling disputes, and even a duel at night in which Catalina/ Francisco unknowingly killed their own brother. It's one of the few moments where any emotion comes through in Catalina/Francisco's life story—being **"stunned"** at the discovery that the man they'd killed was their brother, Captain Miguel de Erauso. And then watching the burial of their brother's body **"with God only knows what grief."**

Besides Catalina/Francisco's brother's girlfriend, there were more romances—and even a few engagements—and they were all with women. They were engaged to the daughter of a half-Spanish and half-Indigenous widow who had rescued them from the wilderness between the Kingdom of Chile and Tucumán (in today's Argentina). As Catalina/Francisco put it, **"The daughter was very dark, and ugly as the devil, very contrary to my taste, which was always the pretty faces."**

But the mother had saved them, dressed Catalina/Francisco **"gallantly,"** and **"virtually handed over her house and property to me."**

Catalina/Francisco kept stalling the wedding **"on various pretexts"** for two months. Meanwhile, they befriended a canon of the church who arranged for Catalina/Francisco to marry the canon's niece! Catalina/Francisco wrote,

"Then came the part when I mounted the horse and disappeared, and I never learned what became of the [daughter] and the canon's niece afterwards."

> A church official.

> The original Spanish word used by Catalina/Francisco in the 1620s was "negra." It was translated in 1999 as "negress," which feels both dated and disrespectful.

NO! I DON'T WANT THE LIEUTENANT NUN TO BE A RACIST!

But clearly, they were. We want the queer people we look at in history to be perfect. We want to hold up this person who, with a woman's body, lived their life as a man and be like, *There's a role model!* But Catalina/Francisco was also racist, misogynistic, violent, and careless with the emotions of others.

Just like everyone today, people in the past—LGBTQ people too—were three-dimensional and flawed. But even when it is terrible, their stories are still part of our history.

> Misogyny means "to hate, have contempt for, or be prejudiced against women."

After killing another man, el Cid, who stole money from them while they were gambling, Catalina/Francisco was captured in Guamanga, Chile. There, Catalina/Francisco confessed:

The next morning at around ten his Lordship had me brought into his presence and asked me who I was, whose child, and the whole course of my life, and the ways and means wherefore I came to end up there as I did. As he was minutely examining my story, he was throwing in good advice about the risks of life, the terror of death were it to take me unprepared, and he urged me to settle down and kneel before God, which made me feel very small.

He was such a holy man, I seemed in that moment to be in the very presence of God, and I revealed myself to him saying, "Sir, all this I have told your Lordship is not so. The truth is this: that I am a woman; that I was born in such-and-such a place, daughter of such-and-such man and woman; that I was placed at a certain age in such-and-such a convent with my aunt so-and-so; that I grew up there, took the habit and became a novice; that, about to take the vows, I ran off; that I went to such-and-such a place, stripped, dressed myself as a man, cut off my hair, travelled here and there, went to sea, roamed, hustled, corrupted, maimed, and murdered, until coming to end up here at his Lordship's feet."

During this tale, which lasted until one o'clock, the holy lord was spellbound, listening to me without speaking or blinking, and remained so after I had finished, although shedding tears profusely. . . .

Finally after six days, his Lordship decided to place me in the convent of the sisters of Santa Clara— there being no other there—and I was put in a habit. His Lordship came out of his house, taking me by his side. There was such a huge throng that there must not have been a person in the city who did not come, and we were therefore late in arriving. We finally arrived at the gatehouse, for at the church, where the Bishop was thinking of going first, it was not possible, the crowd having filled it in anticipation of his plan. . . . The news of this happening spread everywhere, and those who saw me before and afterwards and knew of my deeds throughout the Indies, were amazed. Within five months, in the year 1620, my Holy Bishop died suddenly and I missed him very much.

After fifteen years living as a man, being a soldier, and romancing women, now they were back to being trapped in a convent, dressed as a nun!

It's possible that revealing their secret was a cynical way to get out of being held responsible for murder. It's also possible this was a spiritual turn in their life. Either way, after the reveal of their having a female body, Catalina/Francisco became famous. As they recalled, **"We entered Lima after nightfall but nevertheless could not avoid the many curious people who came to see the 'Nun Lieutenant.'"**

Once word came back from Spain that Catalina had never actually taken their vows as a nun, they were allowed to leave the gender prison of the convent. In 1624 Catalina/Francisco set sail for Spain with the fleet of General Tomás Larraspuru. On the way to Europe, a fight during a game **"in which I gave somebody a nick in the face with a little**

knife I had" meant that Catalina/Francisco had to change ships. Was this to prove they were more aggressive (and thus masculine) than other men, or was it just a true part of their character? Again, we don't know.

Back in Spain, we do know that Catalina/Francisco wore men's clothes again, as they wrote, **"From Cadiz I went to Seville and stayed there fifteen days, hiding myself as much as I could and fleeing from the crowds who gathered to see me dressed in male attire."**

Amid many more adventures and sword fights, being arrested as a suspected spy in France, and meeting the king of Spain, Catalina/Francisco was awarded a lifetime pension for their military service by the Council of the Indies. And then they made their way to Rome, where they met the pope:

I kissed the foot of His Holiness Urban VIII, and related to him as best I could the story of my life and travels, my sex, and my virginity. His Holiness showed himself to be astonished by such a tale, and kindly granted me permission to continue my life dressed as a man, charging me to live honestly henceforth and to abstain from offending my neighbor, attaching the threat of the wrath of God to his order, "Non Occides."

Non Occides is Latin for "Thou shall not kill." The Jewish, Christian, and Muslim faiths teach that this was one of God's Ten Commandments given to Moses.

The matter became quite notorious there, and it was a noteworthy group I began to see around me: well known personalities, princes, bishops, cardinals. Wherever I found myself it was open house, and such was my luck that during the month and a half that I

remained in Rome, there was seldom a day that I was not regaled by princes.

One Friday in particular I was invited and entertained by some gentlemen by the express order and at the expense of the Roman Senate, and they placed my name in a book as an honorary Roman Citizen.

Hundreds of years before TV, radio, or social media, Catalina/Francisco was a celebrity!

On the day of St. Peter, June 29, 1626, I was taken into the chapel of St. Peter where I saw the cardinals and witnessed the ceremonies they celebrate on that day. All, or almost all of them, showed me great kindness and affection, and many conversed with me. In the afternoon, I found myself in a circle of three cardinals. One of them, who was Cardinal Magalon, told me that the only fault with me was being a Spaniard, to which I replied, "It seems to me, sir, under the correction of your most illustrious Lordship, that that is the only good thing about me."

The narrative of their autobiography ends soon after that visit to Rome. But we know from other historians that Catalina/Francisco later went to Mexico. Here's one account:

The Nun Lieutenant arrived in Mexico when the Marquis of Cerralvo was governing New Spain and on the trip from Veracruz to Mexico fell in love with a woman whose parents had charged her to deliver to Mexico, aware that doña Catalina was a woman, although dressing as a man. That affair produced great displeasure and she [Catalina/Francisco] was at the point of fighting the man whom the lady had

NO WAY, THEY WERE GAY?

married. Doña Catalina challenged him in a letter but some influential people managed to prevent the duel.

With the she/her prounouns and references to "doña" Catalina, this historian uses the binary lens of the time to refer to Catalina/Francisco as a woman, even though they lived their life as a man.

And Mexico is where Catalina/Francisco lived their final days.

They had broken out of the gender prison to live much of their life as a man but kept the gender roles of that time intact. In living as a man, Catalina/Francisco embodied the most stereotypically masculine elements of being a Spanish man: being aggressive and violent, believing in their own superiority to women and certainly to anyone of a different cultural background, and romancing women and being a subject of desire for them too.

A monument in Orizaba, Veracruz, Mexico, honoring the Lieutenant Nun

In looking at why Catalina/Francisco received such attention and even approval from the public and the highest authorities of the day (including the king of Spain and the pope), the historian Smith explains, "Erauso's behavior could be forgiven, even celebrated, because it proved male superiority in the very lengths a woman would go to in order to become a man."

Catalina/Francisco didn't challenge men's superiority—they just claimed it for themself.

ANOTHER PERSPECTIVE
FROM THAT TIME

Looking at anyone from history, it's helpful to have another lens. We know how Catalina/Francisco described themselves, but here's how they were described by the writer Pietro Della Valle, who hosted the Lieutenant Nun in his home:

> **Tall and sturdy of stature, masculine in appearance, she has no more bosom than a little girl. She told me she had applied I don't know what method to make it disappear. I believe it was a plaster administered by an Italian; the effect was painful but much to her liking. She is not bad looking, but well worn by the years. . . . She has the look of a Spanish gentleman and wears her sword as big as life, tightly belted. . . . Only by her hands can one tell that she is a woman as they are full and fleshy, although large and strong, and occasionally gesture effeminately.**

A writer, someone who maybe prided himself on being observant, seized upon a single "tell"—Catalina/Francisco's hands and gestures—that revealed to him (and maybe him alone) that this "masculine" and "Spanish gentleman" had a woman's body. But for fifteen years, from their escape from the convent at the age of fifteen to their confession in Chile at the age of thirty, no one had known.

TRICKY TRICKS

Even though the Lieutenant Nun was famous in their own time, their story didn't exactly survive intact over the centuries.

Sherry Velasco, professor of Spanish, Portuguese, and gender studies, wrote of the different authors who, in telling the story of the Lieutenant Nun, changed the history to be less queer. In the late nineteenth century, Velasco explained, often Spanish writers made Catalina/Fransico either straight or asexual. Velasco called out one version, which "neutralizes the lesbian episodes from her memoirs" and "depicts Catalina as the beautiful but unwilling victim of the passion of other women duped by her disguise."

The reaction to the Lieutenant Nun's story also changed over time, going from fascination in the seventeenth century to Catalina/Francisco being called out as evil in the nineteenth century.

As José Gómez de Arteche put it in the 1866 play he wrote about Catalina/Francisco: "A woman? We are mistaken: she seems like a demon." Velasco described some of the changes made to the Lieutenant Nun's story in that play as "heterosexual plot adjustment," writing how de Arteche created a fictional "heterosexual love" for Catalina/Francisco, rather than sharing the "'verdad histórica' (historical truth)."

MORE of THE STORY

The story of the Lieutenant Nun caught the public imagination enough to survive for four hundred years. Going back to the primary sources lets us see the history without the edits and embellishments of people with other (often anti-LGBTQ) agendas.

An English translation of Catalina/Francisco's autobiography, *Lieutenant Nun: Memoir of a Basque Transvestite in the New World*, was published in 1996 and was named a *New York Times Book Review* Notable Book.

While some parts of Catalina/Francisco's autobiography can seem hard to believe (even for some of the people who translated it), evidence corroborates much of their story, including three petitions the Lieutenant Nun made to King Philip IV of Spain.

This label seems to get a lot wrong. While we don't know how Catalina/Francisco might have identified using the language of LGBTQ communities, *transvestite* is no longer used. The clinical and derogatory term described people who sometimes dressed in clothes associated with a different sex. Today, *cross-dresser* might match that definition, but Catalina/Francisco did much more than just occasionally dress as a man.

Writing your autobiography means you get to shape how you present your story. Catalina/Francisco wanted to make sure readers would know they didn't end their days living a typical woman's life of that time. Here are the final lines of the Lieutenant Nun's autobiography:

> **While strolling along the wharf in Naples one day, I perceived the loud laughter of two girls who were chatting with a couple of boys. We stared at each other and one said to me, "Where to, Lady Catalina?"**
>
> **I answered, "To give you a hundred whacks on the head, my lady whores, and a hundred slashes to whomever may wish to defend you!" They shut up and slipped away.**

What a life! The history of Catalina de Erauso, a.k.a. Francisco Loyola, a.k.a. the Lieutenant Nun, shows us that there is a rich past of people who lived boldly outside the boundaries set for their gender by claiming the rights and freedom of another gender.

What limits do you see society putting on you, based on the gender you present or don't present?

Without the killing-and-deceiving-other-people part, can you see ways to live your life being boldly *you?*

CHAPTER 11

WE'WHA

1849–1896 • HALONA: IDIWAN'A (THE MIDDLE PLACE)i

ZUNI, THE UNITED STATES

THE MEDICINE WHEEL REPRESENTS MEN ON ONE
SIDE AND WOMEN ON THE OTHER, BUT THERE'S A
SPACE IN BETWEEN THAT IS FOR THE TWO SPIRITS.
WE JOIN THE MEN AND WOMEN AND COMPLETE THE
CIRCLE. THAT IS OUR PLACE IN LIFE. THAT IS THE
CREATOR'S PURPOSE FOR US.

—Native American elder, speaking at the Montana Two Spirit
Society's annual gathering in 2015

BACKGROUND

People with male bodies who dress as women and perform many of the tasks generally done by women and people with female bodies who dress as men and perform many of the tasks generally done by men have been documented in North American Native nations "in every region of the continent, among every type of native culture, from the small bands of hunters in Alaska to the populous, hierarchical city-states of Florida." That's a quote from historian Will Roscoe, who explained that these vital and often honored members of their societies are "both and neither men and women" and represent a third and a fourth gender.

Outside of their own languages, people of these other genders were known by many names, including *berdache* (now considered offensive), *hermaphrodites* (an old term to describe someone with both male and female anatomy, which has been replaced by the term *intersex*), *two spirit* (a term with multiple meanings, sometimes including third gender and fourth gender identity), and *lesbian*, *gay*, *bisexual*, and *transgender* Native Americans.

From an estimated total of 400 distinct tribes in North America, Roscoe lists 157 in his "Index of Tribes with Alternative Gender Roles and Sexuality," for which we have documentary evidence of those third and fourth gender roles and identities. That isn't to say the tribes not listed didn't or don't have those roles and identities, only that we don't have documentary evidence of it.

"Are" not "were"— third gender and fourth gender people and traditions are part of Native communities today as well.

Two Spirit Native people are sometimes represented with the numeral 2 in the queer community's acronym LGBTQIA2+.

NO WAY, THEY WERE GAY?

COUNTING GENDERS

- **A third gender.** Some nations have a special title for people with male bodies who live a female gender role. Examples in their languages include: *boté* in Crow, *winkte* in Lakota, and *lhamana* in Shiwi'ma (Zuni)
- **A fourth gender.** Some nations have a special title for people with female bodies who live a male gender role. Examples in their languages include: *hwame* in Mohave, *hetaneman* in Cheyenne, and *tayagigux'* in Aleut
- **Also a third gender.** Some nations have a special title for all people who take on the roles of a gender different from that of their physical body. Examples in their languages include: *tw!inna'ek* in Klamath, *t'übás* in Northern Paiute, and *tangowaip* in Western Shoshone.

The exclamation point inside the word *tw!inna'ek* is not a typo. The *!* represents a brief absence of sound, or "glottal stop." As Paul Kroskrity (a linguistic anthropologist) explained, "It is the sound between syllables of the expression 'oh-oh.'"

The Lakota (a Native people of the Great Plains region of the United States) call third gender individuals winkte. As one Lakota winkte put it, "Winkte is gay with ceremonial powers."

The Navajo call third gender people of their nation nadleeh, "from a word that refers to a constant state of change."

And among the A:shiwi (Zuni people), whose nation is within the borders of New Mexico, third gender people are known as lhamana.

In A:shiwi (Zuni) myth and religion, the mysterious and powerful being Kolhamana represents these people of

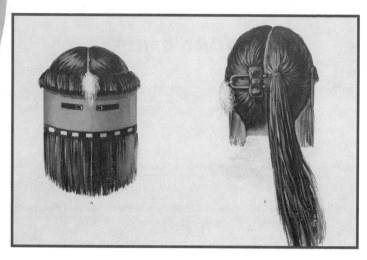

The Mask of Kolhamana (*front view left, back view right*)

the third gender. Kolhamana has a very specific hairstyle. Here's how it was described by Roscoe: "One side wound around a board in a whorl, a female style, while the other side was allowed to hang straight in the male style."

The same male and female and neither male nor female hairstyle appears on a painted figure in a mural found 100 miles (161 kg) northeast of the Zuni Halona: Idiwan'a. Dated between 1300 and 1425 CE, the figure carries both a bow and arrows (a male symbol) and a basketry plaque (a flat basket used in ceremonies and a female symbol).

WE'WHA LIVED INSIDE THE GENDER BOUNDARIES OF A:SHIWI (ZUNI) CULTURE, BUT OUTSIDE THE GENDER BOUNDARIES OF WESTERN CULTURE

In 1879 a small group of anthropologists, including Matilda Coxe Stevenson and her husband, arrived in Halona: Idiwan'a (what they called Zuñi) to study the Native culture and customs.

Stevenson would write it with a ~ over the n, Zuñi. In English, the A:shiwi write it as Zuni.

NO WAY, THEY WERE GAY?

CENTERING AND RESPECTING NATIVE LANGUAGES

The nation uses the term Zuni on their English-language website, but they have their own language.

Halona: Idiwan'a is Zuni land.

A:shiwi are the Zuni people.

Shiwi'ma is the Zunian language.

Language experts say Shiwi'ma "emerged around 7,000 years ago," about 5000 BCE, while English emerged two thousand years after that, around 3000 BCE! Meaning Shiwi'ma is two thousand years older than English!

Among the community were five lhamanas. Twenty-six years later, here's how Matilda described one of them:

We'wha, undoubtedly the most remarkable member of the tribe. This person was a man wearing woman's dress, and so carefully was his sex concealed that for years the writer ← "The writer" is Stevenson.

gave no credence to the story, and continued to regard We'wha as a woman; and as he was always referred to by the tribe as "she"—it being their custom to speak of men who don woman's dress as if they were women—and as the writer could never think of her faithful and devoted friend in any other light, she will continue to use the feminine

By "the story," Stevenson is referring to either rumors or questions she had encountered over the years about We'wha's gender.

gender when referring to We'wha. She was perhaps the tallest person in Zuñi: certainly the strongest, both mentally and physically. . . . She possessed an indomitable will and an insatiable thirst for knowledge. Her likes and dislikes were intense. She would risk anything to serve those she loved, but toward those who crossed her path she was vindictive. Though severe she was considered just. At an early age she lost her parents and was adopted by a sister of her father. She belonged to the Badger clan, her foster mother belonging to the Dogwood clan. Owing to her bright mind and excellent memory, she was called upon by her own clan and also by the clans of her foster mother and father when a long prayer had to be repeated or a grace was to be offered over a feast. In fact she was the chief personage on many occasions. On account of her physical strength all the household work requiring great exertion was left for her, and while she most willingly took the harder work from others of the family, she would not permit idleness; all had to labor or receive an upbraiding from We'wha, and nothing was more dreaded than a scolding from her.

Shiwi'ma does not have gendered pronouns. But Stevenson reported that when speaking English, We'wha's community used "she" when referring to We'wha. I have honored that in this chapter.

We'wha was also a skilled artist, creating pottery as well as woven blankets and sashes. We'wha was one of the first A:shiwi to sell her creations, helping start the shift that would eventually lead to outsiders seeing traditional Native arts as "fine art." Roscoe said, We'wha "discovered a way to build a bridge to the white world through the universal appreciation of the arts. . . . It would be in the realm of the arts

NO WAY, THEY WERE GAY?

that non-Indian Americans would first be able to perceive American Indians as intellectual and social equals."

What was We'wha's life like before Western outsiders came? How did lhamanas live and work? While it was written by one of those outsiders, Stevenson described witnessing part of We'wha's pottery-creating process:

> On one occasion Mr. Stevenson and the writer accompanied We'wha to Corn Mountain to obtain clay. On passing a stone heap she picked up a small stone in her left hand, and spitting upon it, carried the hand around her head and threw the stone over one

AMERICAN INDIAN VS. NATIVE AMERICAN

The labels Indian and Native are debated inside and outside Indigenous communities. An editorial by the *Native Sun News* Editorial Board in 2015 argued that **"political correctness dishonors traditional chiefs of old,"** and that

> As an Indian newspaper we must be very careful that what we call ourselves is not dictated to us by the white media. We have been Indians for a few hundred years and the name carries our history. Crazy Horse, Sitting Bull and Little Wound (Read their quotes) all called themselves "Indian" and they said it with pride. Should we dishonor them by saying they were wrong? Political correctness be damned: We will use "Indian" if and when we choose. We will not be intimidated by the politically correct bunch or the white media.

shoulder upon the stone heap in order that her strength might not go from her when carrying the heavy load down the mesa. She then visited the shrine at the base of the mother rock and tearing off a bit of her blanket deposited it in one of the tiny pits in the rock as an offering to the mother rock. . . . When she drew near to the clay bed she indicated to Mr Stevenson that he must remain behind, as men never approached the spot. Proceeding a short distance the party reached a point where We'wha requested the writer to remain perfectly quiet and not talk, saying: "Should we talk, my pottery would crack in the baking, and unless I pray constantly the clay will not appear to me." She applied the hoe vigorously to the hard soil, all the while murmuring prayers to Mother Earth. Nine-tenths of the clay was rejected, every lump being tested between the fingers as to its texture. After gathering about 150 pounds [68 kg] in a blanket, which she carried on her back, with the ends of the blanket tied around her forehead, We'wha descended the steep mesa, apparently unconscious of the weight.

Making it clear that We'wha did not see herself as a man.

Crossing that bridge between cultures, in 1886 We'wha traveled with Stevenson to Washington, DC. Stevenson wrote of We'wha's experience there:

She had a good memory, not only for the lore of her people, but for all that she heard of the outside world. She spoke only a few words of English before coming to Washington, but acquired the language with remarkable rapidity, and was soon able to join in conversation.

MORE ON THE ANTHROPOLOGIST

Among the first women anthropologists, Stevenson studied the A:shiwi and wrote about their culture for the Smithsonian Institution. After her husband's death in 1888, the Bureau of Ethnology (which he had been working for) hired her in his place, making her one of the first American women to be employed in the sciences.

The A:shiwi also acknowledged her for living outside gender boundaries. In her more than six-hundred-page report on the Zuni culture published in 1904, she wrote about taking part in a ritual of planting prayer plumes, where men offered plumes to the Sun Father and women to the Moon Mother. The A:shiwi

gave her male prayer plumes, telling her, **"Though you are a woman you have a head and a heart like a man, and you work like a man, and you must therefore make offerings such as men make."**

Matilda Coxe Stevenson

We'wha weaves a belt during that 1886 trip to Washington, DC.

For six months, Stevenson introduced We'wha to Washington society, who welcomed We'wha as "an Indian Princess of the Zuni tribe." Photographers documented We'wha demonstrating A:shiwi weaving techniques, and newspapers wrote about the distinguished visitor.

Here's what the *Washington Chronicle* wrote about We'wha on April 18, 1886:

The princess is an eccentric child of nature. Although she is moving at present in the highest circles of Washington and is the pet guest of Mrs. Stevenson, she yet has lapses from the

Calling a human being a "pet guest" is incredibly offensive, and along with calling We'wha a "child of nature" reveals the harsh foundational belief of colonialism: that the A:shiwi and other Native people were lesser-than white American settler society. If white society said that Indigenous people (even the adults) were like children, it functioned as an excuse to deny those people agency, respect, and control over their own lives and lands.

conventionalities of life and goes back to the freer notion of life on the plains. During the late heavy snow fall the princess heard the Stevensons talking about the heavy load of snow on the roof. It was just beginning to thaw and they were fearful that the water would get through the roof. Some way or other through their signs she seemed to understand. A few moments afterwards she disappeared and could not be found. A little later a heavy rush on the roof and then a fall of snow in front of the house indicated where the princess was. She was found on the ridge pole hard at work clearing off the roof. The work was full of peril but the princess would not come down until she had completed it.

During her stay in Washington, DC, We'wha also starred in a charity performance and met President Grover Cleveland. The visit gave We'wha, and the A:shiwi, a high profile when they were, as Roscoe explained, "especially anxious to obtain the government's assistance in protecting their shrinking land base from squatters and encroachment." As a cultural ambassador for the A:shiwi, We'wha wowed Washington—but no one knew of We'wha's third gender status.

Although We'wha acted with great dignity and distinguished the A:shiwi, once word got out about her nontraditional-to-the-West gender identity, some viewed the visit to Washington as a scandal—and a joke. As Stevenson's onetime friend Clara True wrote in a letter to Stevenson's lawyer:

I can't think of any thing so funny as the story of "We-wha." We-wha was a Zuni maiden of wonderful

beauty of character who was taken to Washington on account of her extraordinary qualities. She was a brilliant social success, had an interview with President Cleveland, was entertained at Secretary Carlisle's, etc. Her crowning act in society was leading a "kirmess" charity ball in which wealth and fashion participated. She was given a beautiful bouquet and responded to an encore. She was "studied" by many scientific persons whose names are famous.

The joke of the story is that the beautiful "We-wha" was a "bold bad man," father of a family in Zuni. The fun he had after he got back home you can imagine. . . . It really is one of the best things on Washington which ever occurred, especially scientific Washington.

Although Stevenson reported that We'wha was "beloved by all the children, to whom he was ever kind," there's no evidence that We'wha had children of her own. And Clara calling someone she didn't understand "bad" was an easy way for her to avoid learning what it meant that We'wha wasn't who Clara expected. (It's inconsistent, but Stevenson did use "he" to refer to We'wha in this part of her report.)

We'wha returned to her life in Halona: Idiwan'a as the forces for assimilation (those who wanted to make Native people convert to Christian religions and abandon their traditional ways) gained ground.

Eight years later (December 1893), in a dispute over a witchcraft trial, soldiers arrested tribal leaders, including We'wha's brother. Here's a white eyewitness account of what happened:

An officer who with the sheriff went to the Governor's house to arrest him [We'wha's brother], was bodily

NO WAY, THEY WERE GAY?

We'wha!

thrown out of doors by a woman,—or what at the time was supposed to be a woman, which amounted to the same thing. In making his exit, his coat tails caught in the door which being immediately closed held him in this position, until, thinking of the saber which until now had remained in the scabbard, he valiantly drew it, and extricated himself from his unpleasant predicament, by severing his coat tails from their attachment, becoming again, a free man.

For resisting the soldiers and for her role as a religious leader, We'wha was arrested and spent a month in jail. Four years later, suffering from heart disease, We'wha prepared for an enormous religious festival, Sha'läko. But as Stevenson wrote:

When a week or more had passed after the close of the great autumn ceremonial of the Sha'läko, and the many guests had departed, the writer dropped in at sunset to the spacious home in the house of We'wha's foster father, the late José Palle. We'wha was found crouching on the ledge by the fireplace. That a great change had come over her was at once apparent. Death evidently was rapidly approaching. She had done her last work. Only a few days before this strong-minded, generous-hearted creature had labored to make ready for the reception of her gods; now she was preparing to go to her beloved Ko'thluwala'wa [Sacred Lake].

A few days later, We'wha died. She was forty-nine years old. It was a loss that, as Stevenson would observe, **"caused universal regret and distress in Zuñi."**

TRICKY TRICKS

Just as Stevenson only saw We'wha as a woman, the binary lens of gender sometimes prevented white Americans from even noticing other genders. Tragically, when they did see it, settlers tried to erase the past and destroy the future existence of Native third gender and fourth gender roles. Here are just a few examples:

When artist and anthropologist George Catlin in the 1830s described and drew Native North Americans who were honored in their third gender role, he concluded by writing:

> **This is one of the most unaccountable and disgusting customs, that I have ever met in the Indian country, and so far as I have been able to learn, belongs only to the Sioux and Sacs and Foxes—perhaps it is practiced by other tribes, but I did not meet with it; and for further account of it I am constrained to refer the reader to the country where it is practiced, and where I should wish that it might be extinguished before it be more fully recorded.**

It's interesting to consider how Catlin's negative attitudes toward third gender and fourth gender people affected his ability to see them.

In 1878 Presbyterian minister Taylor Ealy and his family moved into the Halona: Idiwan'a pueblo's mission and ran the day school. Ealy's wife Mary Ealy wrote:

> **All the difficult labor, such as grinding the wheat and corn, carrying the water, etc., is done by the women, while the men do the sewing and knitting. . . . I wish to reverse their labors.**

The hubris of this is shocking, and so revealing of what First Nations people faced from even well-meaning invaders (let's call it what it was). Mary Ealy was so convinced that her Western culture's way was correct that she wanted to completely change how the A:shiwi did things.

Starting in 1879, more than one hundred thousand Native children were sent to government-run boarding schools, whose goal was to **"kill the Indian and save the man,"** and where any crossing of Western-dictated gender lines was suppressed. For punishment at one Hopi school, the white adults in charge shaved boys' heads and forced them to wear dresses, completely reversing the attitude toward third gender people (the Hopi called them ho'va) that those Native children would have learned in their traditional culture.

"Saving the man" inside the Native person was the toxic idea that Native people were uncivilized and backward and needed to deny their own heritage and adopt Western culture and religious beliefs to be saved, both culturally and spiritually.

Another American institution that aimed to erase Native traditions and beliefs was the military. In the 1940s, Native American World War II veterans often returned home with "white GI attitudes" toward any type of gay or transgender people. The anthropologist Nancy Oestreich Lurie reported on her interviews with members of the Ho-Chunk nation just after the war. She wrote about the change in how members of the nation perceived the third gendered people of their community:

White outsiders, including anthropologists like Lurie who published her paper in 1953, called the Ho-Chuck people Winnebago.

It was agreed generally that the berdache was a man who had taken on this role because he had been directed to do so by the moon, a female spirit, at the time of his vision quest. The berdache dressed as a woman, performed women's tasks better than

any normal woman could perform them, and had the ability to foretell future events. However, not all Winnebago prophets were berdaches. One informant mentioned that berdaches sometimes married other men, but no data were obtained concerning the attitude of the society toward the husband of a berdache. Most informants felt that the berdache was at one time a highly honored and respected person, but that the Winnebago had become ashamed of the custom because the white people thought it was amusing or evil. By the time the last known berdache attempted to fulfill the role, his brothers threatened to kill him if he "put on the skirt." This berdache then affected a combination of male and female clothing, fearing that he would die if he did not at least attempt to follow the directions given him in his vision of the moon.

Roscoe reported that in researching his 1991 book he found that

between white intolerance and Indian reticence, memory of berdaches has been almost completely erased from the record on the Pueblo Indians. . . . The otherwise exhaustive Southwest volume of the Smithsonian's 1979 Handbook of North American Indians makes no mention of them at all.

MORE OF THE STORY

Some voices defended third gender and fourth gender Native people. Stevenson's scholarship and friendship with We'wha ensured that history would know We'wha's true qualities of spirit and character.

Others held up the place third gender and fourth gender people occupied in Native American cultures as proof that there were other, successful ways to view gender beyond Western culture's binary options of male or female. It was also held up as proof that there were other ways for Western culture to view gay, lesbian, bi, pan, trans, queer, and gender non-conforming people. As the anthropologist Ruth Benedict wrote in 1934, **"We have only to turn to other cultures . . . to realize that homosexuals have by no means been uniformly inadequate to the social situation. . . . In some societies they have even been especially acclaimed."**

Benedict loved another woman. In her lifetime, she had relationships with both the psychologist Ruth Valentine and fellow anthropologist Margaret Mead.

Two Spirit identity and community still exists and continues to evolve. Whether these are a direct continuation of the traditional roles or a modern Native identity is debated. But being modern doesn't mean not authentic. As a Navajo woman told Roscoe, **"Tradition is reinvented in every generation."**

Reporting on the nineteenth annual gathering of the Montana Two Spirit Society (part of the International Council of Two Spirit Societies), Chadwick Moore wrote in the October 2015 issue of *Out* magazine about Steven Barrios. A Navajo nadleeh, Steven was one of the organizers of the gathering and is also known as Auntie Steven. Moore described Auntie Steven as "perhaps the most respected person here, a statuesque and benevolent figure."

Quoted in that article, a Native American elder attending the Montana Two Spirit Society's annual gathering, described as "a studly woman decked out in beads, with cascading gray hair," explained the role of Two Spirit people:

The Medicine Wheel represents men on one side and women on the other, but there's a space in between that is for the Two Spirits. We join the men and women and complete the circle. That is our place in life. That is the creator's purpose for us.

Steven affirmed that third gender and fourth gender status isn't just history but a living, vibrant, evolving part of Native culture today saying, **"Sometimes young people come to our gathering and they're contemplating suicide. When they realize this was part of our culture, this was part of our tradition, it really instills pride and they feel like they belong."**

As the artist Geo Neptune (Passamaquoddy) put it in a 2018 *InQueery* video on YouTube:

The 1990s.

While the label has only been used since the 90s, the concept of the Two-Spirit is something indigenous groups have identified with for centuries. . . . In recent years, many Native people are returning to the Two-Spirit traditions as a way to heal from the injustices the American colonial project has visited upon their ancestors and traditions. . . .

Two-Spirit identity is resilient and precious. It has survived centuries of colonial violence and prejudice. These sacred ways of knowing live on amongst Native youth seeking to know more about themselves, elders who have kept the traditions alive despite the odds, and anyone in between.

Throughout the 1800s and 1900s, Native Americans were frequently depicted as primitive, savage, or both in entertainment created by white people for white people.

Books, radio plays, TV shows, and films put out the message that Native people were lesser than the white people who settled the North American continent. This colonialist belief was the excuse white people used to steal Native lands and lives from "sea to shining sea." But in many ways, there's a strong argument that Indigenous people were ahead of white people. Especially when it came to how each society treated LGBTQIA2+ people.

Some people who know the traditional and often honored place of third gender and fourth gender people in Native cultures see it as inspiration to rethink the gender binary we cling to in our culture. They believe Native nations can model for us both gender variance and acceptance of that gender diversity. That embracing the gender diverse people among us can be a strength and a light for our culture, as We'wha was a strength and a light for the A:shiwi. Like so many other Two Spirit people, past and present, have been a strength and a light for their nations. That maybe it's time, when it comes to queer people, for white society to embrace this as well.

What do you think?

CHAPTER 12

CHRISTINE JORGENSEN

1926–1989 • UNITED STATES

I THINK WE (THE DOCTORS AND I) ARE FIGHTING THIS THE RIGHT WAY—MAKE THE BODY FIT THE SOUL, RATHER THAN VICE-VERSA.

—Christine Jorgensen, in a 1950 letter to friends who knew about her transitioning from a male body to a female body that matched her gender identity

CHRISTINE JORGENSEN LIVED OUTSIDE GENDER BOUNDARIES

Born George William Jorgensen Jr., Christine wasn't the first person to physically change their body's gender to match how they felt inside. As she would later write in her autobiography, **"There had been perhaps thirty cases of sex conversion on record before mine."** What was different for Christine was that her transition, the press attention she received, the controversy surrounding what people saw as a male soldier becoming a female nightclub singer, and her ultimate openness about her journey combined to make Christine Jorgensen a world-famous celebrity in the 1950s and '60s.

> Since Christine chose the personal pronouns she/her/hers and the name Christine, those are the pronouns and name used when referring to her.

Writing of Christmas when she was five years old, Christine recalled **"asking God for a pretty doll with long, golden hair"** and her **"disappointment when my present turned out to be a bright red railway train."** Christine remembered:

> It must have been about this stage, that I became aware of the differences between my sister, Dolly, and me. Those differences, to me, lay in the order of "masculine" and "feminine" things. Dolly had long blonde hair and wore dresses, both of which I admired but which were not allowed to me, and I was upset and puzzled by this. "Mom," I asked, "why didn't God make us alike?" My Mother gently explained that there was no way of knowing before a baby was born whether it would be a boy or a girl. "You see, Brud," she said, "it's one of God's surprises."

> Brud was Christine's childhood nickname.

"Well," I replied, "I don't like the kind of surprise God made me!"

When Dolly was in college in 1939, she wrote a thesis paper that analyzed her then thirteen-year-old sibling's **"feminine ways,"** which Dolly believed to be partly due, as Christine put it, **"to the fact that I played with girls so much as a child."**

Christine recalled her anger at the time, considering how **"deep within myself, even at that early age, I felt that all these basic feelings were an integral part of me and not highly influenced by outside conditions."**

Before Christine, most psychologists believed that if someone felt their body didn't match the gender they knew themself to be on the inside, something must have gone wrong in their childhood to cause it. Christine helped disprove that.

As Dr. Harry Benjamin put it in his introduction to Christine's autobiography:

> **This was a little girl, not a boy (in spite of the anatomy) who grew up in this remarkably sound and normal family. There was no broken home, no weak or absent father with whom the little boy could not identify. . . . There was a healthy atmosphere and a healthy love relationship which not only is evident from Christine's own description, but also from my personal observation.**

Benjamin described witnessing that love firsthand:

> **A few years ago, Christine drove my wife and me out to her Massapequa home for dinner one day and we spent an afternoon and evening with the family (a visit we could never forget!) where we**

> met her charming, lovable mother, her good-looking
> sister, and a father whose eagerness to understand
> Christine's problem was truly admirable. I heard his
> touching remark which Christine mentions, "She is ours
> and we love her."

When Christine spoke of her transition, she didn't talk about seeking out fame or even of helping medical science. As she said:

> To me, it was a matter of survival. As the object of one
> of Nature's caprices, I was merely searching for my
> own personal expression of human dignity, with no
> thought of what the consequences might turn out to be.

As a fifteen-year-old, Christine realized that what she felt for a male friend wasn't just friendship:

> I remember being overwhelmed by the revelation
> that, despite earlier denials, I was in love with him . . .
> a forbidden emotion—of which I had to feel ashamed,
> and it was abhorrent to me. I couldn't discuss it with
> anyone, not even my beloved Grandma Jorgensen
> and, certainly, I knew I would never mention it to
> Tom. With an accompanying stab of guilt, I added this
> sorrowful secret to the already large burden of my
> inability to cope with life.

Christine didn't know what was wrong. She didn't feel like a young man who loved another young man. It was something else.

On Christine's third attempt, just after World War II ended, she was accepted into the army. Christine recalled a pivotal moment in the enlistment:

When the examining psychiatrist asked me, "Do you like girls?" I knew, as did every other draftee, that the question was designed to weed out the men with homosexual proclivities. Therefore, I answered simply, "Yes."

After leaving the army, Christine went to Hollywood to find photography work in the film industry. Christine remembered stopping at the Grand Canyon:

I looked into the vastness again and watched the colors change with the movement of the sun; red, then coral, and finally, slowly undulating into a thousand variated shades of lavender and purple.

Slowly, one thought separated itself from the others in my mind, at first ephemeral and then a consciously formed idea. "I am looking at the work of God," I thought, "but am I not a work of God, too?"

Hollywood wasn't the job success Christine had hoped for, and instead, she went to photography school. While there, Christine focused on trying to figure out who Christine authentically was. Hormones were a new field of science, and she felt they offered hope—and a possible choice:

If, I wondered, hormones were to be a possible answer, which way should I turn? Should I follow the course already suggested and try to become more masculine by developing the outward physical signs of manhood? However, I reasoned, if that was possible, would I then have a man's desires, attitudes, and emotions? I felt certain, even then, that the answer to that would be "No." Then what of the more drastic measure of trying to become more feminine? Could the

transition to womanhood be accomplished through the magic of chemistry?

Christine felt desperate, but in 1948, after many **"unproductive attempts to find professional medical aid,"** she decided to experiment to see if her body could become "more feminine." Christine managed to buy a bottle of estrogen pills from a pharmacy:

> How strange it seemed to me that the whole answer might lie in the particular combination of atoms contained in those tiny, aspirin-like tablets. As recently as a few years before, science had split some of those atoms and unleashed a giant force. There in my hand lay another series of atoms, which in their way might set off another explosion—one I hoped would not be a destructive force but would help to make me a whole person.

Here, Christine was referring to the invention and use of nuclear weapons.

Two years later, having heard that medical help toward her **"transition to womanhood"** was more available in Europe, Christine headed to Denmark. As Christine recalled:

> All of my planning had to be done in secret, for there were only two people in the world at that time who knew why I was making the trip and it was a lonely thought. I was concealing a terrifying problem that had been insurmountable up to that point, and its solution was an unknown factor. To my friends and family, then, I was merely planning a tourist jaunt, but the Old World was to be the point of no return as George Jorgensen.

NO WAY, THEY WERE GAY?

In Denmark, Christine found Dr. Christian Hamburger, the first medical professional who said that the change she wanted was possible. Christine remembered asking if it would be expensive. Hamburger responded:

> No, I would not charge you anything, but I will tell you quite frankly, that at the same time, you could serve as a guinea pig. There are several questions about the interaction of the hormone which are not quite clear now and I am very much interested in having you help me clear up these complicated matters. They can only be accomplished by observing a person over long periods of time.

That night Christine wrote to the two friends in the know, announcing the decision that would change her life forever. She wrote, **"Just refer to me as guinea pig OOOO!"**

Two months into the tests and treatments, in another letter to those same friends, Christine's hope was palpable:

> Can you realize what success for me will mean to literally thousands of people? For I am not alone in this affliction. It may mean new hope and life to so many people. I think we (the doctors and I) are fighting this the right way—make the body fit the soul, rather than vice-versa. For me, it is the heart, the look in the eyes, tone of the voice, and the way one thinks, that makes the real person.

Two years of daily tests, regular hormone treatments, and a surgery later, Christine named herself to honor the doctor who helped her, using a feminine form of Hamburger's first name, Christian.

Christine's family still didn't know. To tell them, Christine wrote what she called **"the most important letter of my life"**:

June 8, 1952

My Dearest Mom, Dad, Dolly, and Bill:

I am now faced with the problem of writing a letter, one which for two years has been on my mind. The task is a great one and the two years of thought haven't made it any easier. To begin with, I want you to know that I am happier and healthier than ever before in my life. I want you to keep this in mind during the rest of this letter. . . .

Bill was married to Christine's sister, Dolly.

I do not know if you know that both men and women have hormones of both sexes in their bodies. Regardless of many outward appearances, it is the quantity of those hormones which determines a person's sex. All sex characteristics are a result of those hormones. Sometimes, a child is born and, to all outward appearances, seems to be of a certain sex. During childhood, nothing is noticed, but at the time of puberty, when the sex hormones come into action, the chemistry of the body seems to take an opposite turn and, chemically, the child is not of the supposed sex, but the opposite one. . . .

I was one of those people I have just written about. It was not easy to face and had it not been for the happiness it brought me, I should not have had the strength to go through these two years. You see, I was afraid of a much more horrible illness of the mind. One which, although very common, is not

as yet accepted as a true illness, with the necessity for great understanding. Right from the beginning, I realized that I was working toward the release of myself, from a life I knew would always be foreign to me. So, you see, the task was not so difficult at that; not nearly so much so as this letter is for me to write. Just how does a child tell its parents such a story as this? And even as I write these words, I have not yet told you the final outcome of the tests and an operation last September.

I do hope that I have built the letter properly so you already know what I am going to say now. I have changed, changed very much, as my photos will show, but I want you to know that I am an extremely happy person and that the real me, not the physical me, has not changed. I am still the same old "Brud." But nature made a mistake, which I have had corrected, and I am now your daughter.

I do so want you to like me very much and not to be hurt because I did not tell you sooner about why I came over here. . . . ←

Tante means "aunt" in Danish.

Please don't be hurt. Tante Tine can tell you more, for we've had some good talks. She paid me the biggest compliment when she said: "My goodness, you look like both Dolly and Dorothy."

Dorothy was another family member, a second cousin.

I can't write more now. I seem to be all dried up for this time. Waiting at every postal delivery for your letter.

Love,
Chris
('Brud')

Christine wrote of her parents' response in her autobiography:

> They were deeply upset and concerned for me, but in spite of their worry and confusion, they sent me the following cablegram: LETTER AND PICTURES RECEIVED. WE LOVE YOU MORE THAN EVER. MOM AND DAD.

Six months later, Christine had her second transition surgery in Denmark. A reporter showed up while Christine was recovering in the hospital. She handed Christine a telegram, telling her that "tomorrow's newspapers will carry this story in banner headlines." The international press-service wire dispatch read, **"BRONX GI BECOMES A WOMAN. DEAR MOM AND DAD SON WROTE, I HAVE NOW BECOME YOUR DAUGHTER."**

TRICKY TRICKS

Someone in Christine's life had made her story public. (She wouldn't learn it was an acquaintance of her family, someone of her parents' generation, for another fifteen years.) Christine recalled her reaction:

> In the first shock-waves, the world seemed to disintegrate around me with sickening finality. I know at first I felt fear for the safety of my family and horror at the disclosure of an intimate and highly personal event in my life, but the initial shock was replaced by a towering rage. . . . To me, that message was a symbol of a brutal and cruel betrayal. A lifetime of agonizing unhappiness, two years of

THE SCIENCE OF GENDER: "CHRISTINE HAD IT QUITE RIGHT, IN MANY REGARDS"

Dr. Johanna Olson-Kennedy, the medical director of the Center for Transyouth Health and Development at Children's Hospital Los Angeles, weighed in on the modern medical understanding of gender. "I think this letter is probably not too far off from one that might be written by a young adult today," she wrote. "The truth is that we don't know what part of human development is responsible for gender identity. We speculate that gender identity lives in the brain, and that there are a number of developmental factors that are responsible; chromosomes, hormones, hormone receptors, and probably others that we don't have a clue about."

Olson-Kennedy explained that one of the biggest changes since Christine's time is that there are puberty-blocking medications to help young people whose bodies don't match their gender "avoid the development of undesired secondary sex characteristics" and ultimately develop "a body that more closely matches their gender."

medical treatment and two surgical operations had been telescoped into a couple of succinct lines on a telegraphy form, and I knew without being told that it would go far beyond that hospital room.

Christine was right. Her parents wrote her on December 3, 1952, explaining:

The front page of the *New York Daily News* December 1, 1952.

My Dear Chris,

. . . a reporter from the *Daily News* was the first to contact us, asking for information, and he was very threatening. I know you must be very distressed and upset that your letter and pictures have been published, but he told us if we didn't give him further material, he'd print the story anyway. After a long talk, we all decided that it would be the best way of presenting the truth, and I'm sure you must feel as we do, that it's best to have been honest, once they had the story, than to make matters worse by allowing them to slant everything badly. . . .

We are all big enough to face facts with strength and courage, as you have already shown. Do take care. We are okay, so don't worry.

Enclosed, $10.00.

Love,
Mom

**Keep your chin up, everything will be all right. We are with you all the way. Love,
Dad**

What Christine never expected was what happened next. She wrote, **"Like an avalanche, letters and cables poured into my hospital room, and I was inundated with fantastic and extravagant offers."** She ultimately took one of those offers, for an exclusive series of five articles on her in *American Weekly* magazine, for $20,000.

Trying to evade the press, Christine's parents reunited with her in Denmark. Christine wrote of her relief, **"What had been to me the barrier of their possible non-acceptance, was soon dispelled in an atmosphere of love."**

$20,000 would now be worth more than $190,000.

On the eve of the first article's publication, Christine flew back to New York. The plane landed on February 13, 1953. Christine was twenty-six years old and not prepared for what would happen when she exited the airplane. As she later wrote:

I stepped out of the doorway, onto the top step, and met a scene of such chaos and utter madness. . . .

I turned back to see if I had somehow, by mistake, preceded the Danish royal member, but there was no one behind me except the hostess, who seemed less bewildered than I.

I looked into a sea of faces, lined up along the ropes of "quarantine walk" and held back by a squad of determined police, then heard a roar of voices shouting my name. I reeled under the impact.

I thought for a moment that I had entered Dante's Inferno, as flash-bulbs exploded from all directions and newsreel cameras whirred. A crowd of 300 shoving reporters, newsreel and still photographers had converged, all jockeying for position and camera angles. I learned later it was the largest assemblage of press representatives in the history of the airport.

"Hey, Chris, look this way!" "Over here, Miss Jorgensen!" "Come down the steps a little, Miss Jorgensen!" "How about a nice, big smile?" "Just one more, Christine!" "Just one more!"

A famous epic poem by Dante called *The Divine Comedy* includes a section called "Inferno" that describes Dante's vision of Hell.

Suddenly, Christine was a celebrity. Whether she wanted it or not, she was in the public eye and stayed there. The *American Weekly* series was a huge success for the magazine. As Christine noted in her autobiography, the series ended up being **"translated into fourteen languages and distributed throughout seventy countries."**

Fame came with challenges. In a number of months Christine received some twenty thousand letters, some congratulating, some hostile, and some asking for help from people who felt Christine's example offered them hope.

In 1954 a trade magazine for the publishing business wrote that the Christine Jorgensen story had received **"the largest world-wide coverage in the history of newspaper publishing."** Christine admitted that her new fame wasn't what she'd wanted. **"It was frightening to think that after twenty-six years of obscurity, I had emerged in the previous year as the most written about person in the world."**

NO WAY, THEY WERE GAY?

Followed everywhere, with her every movement a headline item (getting her driver's license renewed had been front-page news!), Christine's idea of going back to work in photography was no longer an option. As Charlie Yates, the man who would ultimately become her agent, told her, **"Look, Chris, you're a world-famous personality whether you like it or not. . . . From here on out, there's nothing you can do and no place you can go to lead a normal, quiet life."**

Eventually, Christine took Charlie's advice and created a nightclub act. But in 1954, the Boston Licensing Board pulled the Latin Quarter nightclub's license to keep Christine off the stage—effectively banning her in that city. Eleven years later, she was still controversial, with the US Third Army Division in Frankfurt, Germany, ruling her **"Off Limits!"** and refusing to let her entertain the troops. Detractors accused her of not being a "real" woman, and some even claimed that her whole transition was a hoax. Christine addressed the ongoing controversy in her autobiography, writing:

> **Many times, I've been accused of living a masquerade as a female, but if I have not already made it clear I will state again that, in my view, the real masquerade would have been to continue in my former state. That, to me, would have been living the lie.**

Christine traveled the country and the world as an entertainer. Sometimes, the people she encountered were incredibly rude. Christine recalled one time:

> **In Miami Beach at the Club Morocco, I was sitting with some friends between shows, when someone from behind suddenly grabbed a handful of my hair, and**

gave it a hearty and very painful yank. . . . I whipped around in surprise, to discover a woman who stood open-mouthed, sputtering with chagrin, and what I suspected was a severe case of disappointment when she discovered I wasn't wearing a wig. She hurried away without an apology. As all of my hair was and still is attached to my head in the usual way, I was painfully reminded of her curiosity for days afterward, each time I combed my hair.

A CHRISTINE BY ANY OTHER NAME . . .

Christine wrote of the ways that other people defined her:

At one time or another, I had been called a male homosexual, a female homosexual, a transvestite, an hermaphrodite, a woman since birth who had devised a sensational method of notoriety for financial gain, a true male masquerading as a female, or a totally sexless creature—the last category placing me in the same neutral corner as a table or chair.

The terms used to describe Christine and others who transition their bodies to match their gender have changed over time. These words include *transsexual*, *transgender*, *trans man*, *trans woman*, and *trans*. It's important to let each person define themself and choose their own label—even if their choice is to have no term or label define them at all.

Throughout it all, Christine worked hard to become, as she put it, a **"true performer."** Her determination to **"step over the boundaries of notoriety"** guided the evolution of her cabaret act and led her to take roles in the world of theater.

MORE OF THE STORY

Christine's personal life was news too. Her first engagement, to John Traub, created what she described as another **"storm of publicity and controversy,"** with officials blocking their marriage license and headlines shouting, **"BAR WEDDING FOR CHRISTINE."** The wedding never happened.

In the 1980s, Christine appeared on the television program *Hour Magazine*. When the host, Gary Collins, asked Christine about her romantic life, she responded, **"I've been in love, deeply, twice. And I've been engaged twice. But I was never engaged to the men I was in love with, and I was never in love with the men I was engaged to! [She chuckles.] Which seems to be a pretty female syndrome."**

On another TV program in 1982, Christine performed a song and was interviewed by Tom Snyder. Here's an excerpt from that conversation:

TOM. If George Jorgensen were alive and well today—

CHRISTINE. He is.

TOM. Yes, I know. Yes.

CHRISTINE. I'm part of him!

[*laughter*]

TOM. What would he be doing? What would George be doing?

CHRISTINE. Oh, if I hadn't had the surgery?

TOM. Yeah.

CHRISTINE. I'd probably be behind the cameras in film editing, which I did before. Maybe I wouldn't have lived. I don't know. Maybe life would have been too unnecessary for me. I can't tell. I can only speculate, and it's very foolish to speculate.

TOM. But, George would not be a nightclub entertainer? He wouldn't be singing?

CHRISTINE. Oh no. Heaven, no. Of course not. . . . If the press hadn't made me well-known . . . The *New York Daily News* made me.

What a life. A trailblazer who did it for herself, Christine wasn't allowed to live privately, so she made the best of it—and transformed our world along the way. And she had a sense of humor. As the *New York Times* reported, part of Christine's nightclub act was the song "I Enjoy Being a Girl!"

Christine Jorgensen died in 1989. She was sixty-two years old.

On the final page of her autobiography, Christine wrote:

I suppose the final question to answer is, "Has it been worth it?" I must admit, at certain moments in my life I might have hesitated to answer. I remember times when I lived in a crucible of troubled phantoms, and

THE SURGERY IS NOT THE DIFFICULT PART

In this 1982 interview, Christine helped refocus the discussion about transgender people away from physical changes to their bodies and toward their being their authentic selves:

> People always refer to the surgery. The surgery is sort of an anti-climax. It's done after all the other things. . . . The gender identity clinics insist that the patient live in the role they are going to become assigned to for at least a year . . . and the doctor sees them maybe once every two weeks, even if it's only ten minutes. But in a period of a year the doctor has to have a gut feeling as to who that person is. That's the hard part, is finding out who the person is. The surgery is easy.

faltered in the long, painful struggle for identity. But for me there was always a glimmering promise that lay ahead; with the help of God, a promise that has been fulfilled. I found the oldest gift of heaven—to be myself.

As famous as Christine was in the 1950s and '60s, why is she not widely known today?

And why do you think some people are still prejudiced against transgender people?

IT'S NOT ABOUT THE NUMBERS, IT'S ABOUT A SAFE SPACE

Out of the billions of people who lived and are living, this book has touched on only a few stories of remarkable LGBTQ people from history. But how many queer people were there? And how many queer people are there? Since the late 1940s, different researchers have attempted to figure it out, but there's no definitive answer. Queer people might be 11 percent of the population. Or maybe we're only 3 percent. Some studies say less, others more.

Knowing the *real* numbers of any disenfranchised group is challenging. In a homophobic and transphobic society where people don't always feel safe being or revealing their authentic selves, researchers don't necessarily get honest answers to their questions about LGBTQ lives and loves.

Rumi was a brilliant thirteenth-century Sufi poet who sang of his love for other men. Nearly eight hundred years later, his words sound as though they could have been spoken today:

Sufism is a mystical form of Islam.

I saw you last night in the gathering,
but could not take you openly in my arms,

so I put my lips next to your cheek,
pretending to talk privately

Standing up and finding community starts with having a safe space to be your authentic self, no matter who you are, how you identify, or whom you love. Knowing the LGBTQ history in this book and beyond—that there were men who loved men, women who loved women, people who loved without regard to gender, and people who lived outside gender boundaries in the past and all over the world—helps us build that safe space.

And the numbers shouldn't matter. If we queer people are 50 percent of the population or just one person, every human being should be safe to shine as their most authentic self.

So we need to discover our queer history. Face the terrible parts and celebrate the wonderful. Share it widely. And then, each of us, be safe people and create safe spaces for others.

When we do that, it will make our world a better place for all.

THE HISTORY OF THE RAINBOW FLAG THAT BROUGHT IT ALL TOGETHER

There are many versions of LGBTQIA2+ pride flags, including the light pink, light blue, and white trans pride flag, and the pink, purple, and blue bi pride flag, but the rainbow pride flag is the most universal. With six horizontal stripes (red, orange, yellow, green, blue, and purple), it represents the entire community of men who love men, women who love women, people who love without regard to gender, and people who live outside gender boundaries.

In 1977, after Harvey Milk was elected to the San Francisco Board of Supervisors, he asked Gilbert Baker to come up with a new symbol of pride for the gay community. Gilbert (who was gay as well) created the rainbow pride flag. Gilbert remembered the first time it flew,

Harvey's win was a triumphant moment for the LGBTQ community!

It all goes back to the first moment of the first flag back in 1978 for me. Raising it up and seeing it there blowing in the wind for everyone to see.

NO WAY, THEY WERE GAY?

THERE'S MEANING IN THOSE PRIDE COLORS

Originally eight colors (including hot pink and indigo), each of the six color's of today's pride flag have meaning:

red = life
orange = healing
yellow = sunlight
green = nature
blue = art
purple = human spirit

It completely astounded me that people just got it, in an instant like a bolt of lightning—that this was their flag. It belonged to all of us. It was the most thrilling moment of my life.

In 2017 the marketing and ad agency Tierney worked with Philadelphia's Office of LGBT Affairs to create the diversity pride flag—adding a brown and black stripe on top to pointedly include and honor Black and brown and other people of color within the LGBTQ community. This is the queer pride flag I love the best, and it's represented in the stripes flying proudly on this book's cover.

There's even an ally pride flag for non-LGBTQ people who support those of us who are queer.

So all of us have a history to celebrate, and a flag to fly, as we head proudly into the future.

AUTHOR'S NOTE

My hope is that these true stories of love and gender have started your journey of discovery—they sure started mine! There are so many more amazing historical figures whose loves and lives speak to today's LGBTQ identities.

And know that if you are lesbian, gay, bi, pan, trans, questioning, queer, intersex, asexual, gender queer, or gender non-conforming, you are not alone. We are not alone. These stories, and so many more, are our legacy.

We have a history.

And that's what the Queer History Project and *No Way, They Were Gay?* is all about.

The light in me recognizes and acknowledges the light in you,

Lee

Los Angeles, California

PUTTING IT IN ORDER

Another fun way to read (or reread) this book is chronologically, mixing up the stories across the categories. Using the year of each person's birth as our marker would make the order:

1495 BCE	Pharaoh Hatshepsut	pages 168–183
612 BCE	Sappho	pages 98–115
circa 554 BCE	Yuan, Duke Ling of Wei and Mi Zi Xia	page 26
1207 CE	Rumi	page 246
1475	Michelangelo	pages 12–13
1564	William Shakespeare	pages 32–45
1585	The Lieutenant Nun	pages 184–205
1665	Queen Anne	pages 116–133
1728	Chevalier D'Éon and Mademoiselle de Beaumont	pages 166–167
1791	Anne Lister	pages 14–16
1809	President Abraham Lincoln	pages 46–59
1812	One Eyed Charley	pages 13–14
1840	Tchaikovsky	pages 30–31
1849	We'wha	pages 206–225
1868	Magnus Hirschfeld	pages 9–10
1869	Mahatma Gandhi	pages 60–77
1882	Freda du Faur	pages 96–97
1884	Eleanor Roosevelt	pages 134–151
1898 1904	Randolph Scott and Cary Grant	pages 10–11
1910	Bayard Rustin	pages 78–94
1926	Christine Jorgensen	pages 226–245
1930	M'e Mpho Nthunya	pages 152–164
1930	Harvey Milk	pages 20–21, 248
1951 "born" in 1978	Gilbert Baker and his rainbow pride flag	pages 248–249

SOURCE NOTES

EPIGRAPH

5: "In 1961, when I was twenty-one, . . . hold them in their hands.": Judy Grahn, *Another Mother Tongue: Gay Words, Gay Worlds* (Boston: Beacon, 1984), xi.

INTRODUCTION: HIDDEN HISTORY

9–10: "On 6 May at 9:30 am . . . before throwing it onto the pyre.": Anonymous eyewitness, in Günter Grau, ed., with a contribution by Claudia Schoppmann, *Hidden Holocaust? Gay and Lesbian Persecution in Germany 1933-45,* trans. Patrick Camiller (Chicago: Fitzroy Dearborn, 1995), 31–33.

11: Cary's marriages to women: Marc Eliot, *Cary Grant: A Biography* (New York: Three Rivers, 2004), 77–112.

11: "In the 1970s, Cary and Scott . . . holding hands.": Charles Higham and Roy Moseley, *Gary Grant: The Lonely Heart* (San Diego: Harcourt Brace Jovanovich, 1989), 315–316, 339.

12–13: "If, through our eyes, the heart's seen in the face / . . . / in my unworthy but eager arms, forever.": Michelangelo, *The Complete Poems of Michelangelo,* trans. John Frederick Nims (Chicago: University of Chicago Press, 1998), 37, 58, 171.

13: Original Italian signor mie caro: Michelangelo, *The Poetry of Michelangelo: An Annotated Translation,* trans. James M. Saslow (New Haven, CT: Yale University Press, 1991), 181.

13: "O dear my mistress": Michelangelo, *Sonnets and Madrigals of Michelangelo Buonarroti: Rendered into English Verse by William Wells Newell,* trans. William Wells Newell (Boston: Houghton Mifflin, 1900), 8–9, https://books.google.com/books?id =4_k3AQAAMAAJ&pg=PP7&dq=Se+nel+volto+per+gli+occhi &source=gbs_selected_pages&cad=2#v=onepage&q =Se%20nel%20volto%20per%20gli%20occhi&f=false.

13: "Charley's memorial . . . Nov 3, 1868.": Daniel M. Hall, "The Strange Life and Times of Charley Parkhurst," *Metro Santa Cruz,* March 5–12, 2003, http://www.metroactive.com/papers/cruz /03.05.03/charley-0310.html.

14: The singular *they*: Mary Norris, "Comma Queen: The Singular 'Their,' Part Two—A Gender-Neutral Pronoun," *New Yorker,* March 21, 2016, http://www.newyorker.com/culture/culture-desk/comma -queen-the-singular-their-part-two-a-gender-neutral-pronoun.

15: "I love and only love the fairer sex . . . my heart revolts from any other love than theirs.": Anne Lister, *The Secret Diaries of Miss Anne Lister,* ed. Helena Whitbread (London: Virago, 2010), 161.

16: "A 2 . . . Z 9": "Treasures of the West Yorkshire Archive Service: The Diaries of Anne Lister (SH:7/ML/E) 1806–1840," West Yorkshire Archive Service, accessed March 24, 2020,

http://wyorksarchivestreasures.weebly.com/the-diaries-of
-anne-lister.html.

INTRODUCTION: MAKING CHOICES

19: "Princess of the Zuni Tribe.": Will Roscoe, *The Zuni Man-Woman*
(Albuquerque: University of New Mexico Press, 1991), 56.

INTRODUCTION: GOOD STUFF TO KNOW BEFORE YOU DIVE IN

20: "Every Gay person must come out . . . you will feel so much better!":
"Harvey Implores," YouTube video, 1:30, posted by bstewart23,
November 22, 2008, https://youtu.be/UvZIoZNYTN8,
0:35; Jonathan Capehart, "From Harvey Milk to 58 percent,"
Washington Post, March 18, 2013, https://www.washingtonpost
.com/blogs/post-partisan/wp/2013/03/18/from-harvey-milk-to
-58-percent/. Harvey Milk is a © and ® of the Harvey Milk
Foundation and the Milk Family. Used with permission. Please
visit www.MilkFoundation.org for more information regarding
Harvey and the work of the Foundation.

25: "As many as 1.7% . . . born with red hair.": "Intersex 101: Everything
You Need to Know," 4intersex.org, accessed March 25, 2020,
http://4intersex.org/#yourself, http://4intersex.org/wp-content
/uploads/2018/07/4intersex-101.pdf.

25: Different kinds of asexuality: "Under the Ace Umbrella: Demisexuality
and Gray-Asexuality," AsexualityArchive, June 16, 2012, http://
www.asexualityarchive.com/under-the-ace-umbrella/.

25: 2 stands for Two Spirit: "What Does Two-Spirit Mean? | InQueery |
Them," YouTube video, 6:16, posted by "them," December 11,
2018, https://youtu.be/A4lBibGzUnE.

26: "How sincere is your love . . . giving me good things to eat!": Han Fei
Tzu, *Han Fei Tzu: Basic Writings*, trans. Burton Watson (New
York: Columbia University Press, 1964), 78–79.

26: "After all . . . peach to eat!": Han Fei Tzu.

26: Half-eaten peach symbolism: Pierre Hurteau, *Male Homosexualities and
World Religions* (New York: Palgrave Macmillan, 2013), 49.

26: Symbolism about eating peach: Bret Hinsch, *Passions of the Cut Sleeve*
(Berkeley: University of California Press, 1990), 20–22, 35, 53,
56, 71, 73–75, 83–85, 89, 93, 95, 147, 161, and 181–182.

27: "No form of love is to be despised.": Rodger Streitmatter, ed., *Empty
without You: The Intimate Letters of Eleanor Roosevelt and Lorena
Hickok* (New York: Free Press, 1998), xix.

27: "Define yourself in your own terms . . . who will love and support
you.": Kelly Korducki and Laverne Cox, "We Are What We
Love: An Interview with Laverne Cox," Rookie Mag, July 17,
2014, https://www.rookiemag.com/2014/07/we-are-what-we
-love-an-interview-with-laverne-cox/.

PART I: WHAT'S AHEAD: TCHAIKOVSKY AND THE MEN OF *SWAN LAKE*

30: "a historical fact": Shaun Walker, "Tchaikovsky Was Not Gay, Says Russian Culture Minister," *Guardian* (US edition), September 18, 2013, http://www.theguardian.com/music/2013/sep/18 /tchaikovsky-not-gay-russian-minister.

30: Pytor's struggles: Bonnie Zimmerman, ed., *Lesbian Histories and Cultures: An Encyclopedia* (New York: Garland, 2000), 656.

30: "shut the mouths of all despicable gossips": Pyotr Tchaikovsky, in a letter to his younger brother Modest, quoted in Tom Cowan, *Gay Men and Women Who Enriched the World* (1996; repr., Los Angeles: Alyson, 1988), 93–99, 96, 106.

30: Pyotr realizes marriage won't work: Cowan, 96; David Brown, *Tchaikovsky: The Man and His Music* (New York: Pegasus Books, 2007), 138–139.

31: In Bourne's version of the ballet: Stephen Farber, "Bourne's 'Swan Lake': An Ill-Fated Flight," *Los Angeles Times*, June 1, 1997, http://articles.latimes.com/1997-06-01/entertainment/ca -64399_1_swan-lake. I saw the Matthew Bourne *Swan Lake* production in Los Angeles in the summer of 1997.

31: "There is no evidence that Tchaikovsky was a homosexual.": Walker, "Tchaikovsky Was Not Gay."

31: "in the case of Tchaikovsky . . . it is simply ludicrous to suggest otherwise.": Walker.

CHAPTER 1: WILLIAM SHAKESPEARE

33: Sonnet 144 "Two loves I have of comfort and despair . . . woman color'd ill.": William Shakespeare, *The Riverside Shakespeare*, ed. G. Blakemore Evans (Boston: Houghton Mifflin, 1974), 1775.

34: Number of Shakespeare films: Stephen Follows, "How Many Movies Based on Shakespeare's Plays Are There?," *Stephen Follows Film Data and Education* (blog), April 14, 2014, https:// stephenfollows.com/movies-based-on-shakespeare-plays/.

34: Women on the English Stage: Elizabeth Howe, *The First English Actress: Women and Drama, 1660–1700* (Cambridge: Cambridge University Press, 1992), 23.

34: "But soft, what light . . . Juliet is the sun": Shakespeare, *The Riverside Shakespeare*, 1068.

34–35: The play *Twelfth Night, or What You Will*: Shakespeare, 403–442.

35–36: England's antigay laws: "Why You Have to Know about the 1533 Buggery Act," F Yeah History, August 29, 2019, https:// fyeahhistory.com/2019/08/29/why-you-have-to-know-about -the-1533-buggery-act/.

36: "sugred *Sonnets* among his private friends": Francis Meres, "Palladis Tamia: Wit's Treasury Being the Second Part of Wits

Common Wealth: A Comparative Discourse of our English Poets, with the Greeke, Latine, and Italian Poets (1598)," Center for Applied Technologies in the Humanities, accessed March 27, 2020, http://spenserians.cath.vt.edu/TextRecord .php?textsid=32924.

36: "TO. THE. ONLIE. . . . / FORTH.": Shakespeare, *The Riverside Shakespeare*, 1749.

37: The impact on England's antigay laws around the world: F Yeah History; "India: Supreme Court Strikes Down Sodomy Law," Human Rights Watch, September 6, 2018, https://www.hrw .org/news/2018/09/06/india-supreme-court-strikes-down -sodomy-law#; Ben Winsor, "A Definitive Timeline of LGBT+ Rights in Australia," Special Broadcasting Service, November 15, 2017, https://www.sbs.com.au/topics/pride/agenda/article /2016/08/12/definitive-timeline-lgbt-rights-australia.

37: The fight for LGBTQ rights in former British colonies: Edward Akintola Hubbard, "Britain Can't Just Reverse the Homophobia It Exported during the Empire," *Guardian* (US edition), July 28, 2017, https://www.theguardian.com /commentisfree/2017/jul/28/britain-reverse-homophobia -empire-criminlisation-homosexuality-colonies; "Jamaica," OutRight Action International, accessed March 27, 2020, https://outrightinternational.org/region/jamaica; "High Court in Singapore Dismisses Challenges to Criminalization of Same-Sex Relations," press release, OutRight Action International, March 20, 2020, https://outrightinternational .org/content/high-court-singapore-dismisses-challenges -criminalization-same-sex-relations.

37–38: Who was the mysterious Mr. W.H.?: William Shakespeare, *Shakespeare's Sonnets: The Arden Shakespeare*, ed. Katherine Duncan-Jones (London: Thomson Learning, 1997), 57–64; Dalya Alberge, "Has the Mystery of Shakespeare's Sonnets Finally Been Solved?," *Guardian* (US edition), January 31, 2015, http://www.theguardian.com/culture/2015/jan/31/shakespeare -sonnets-mr-wh-dedication-mystery; Shakespeare, *Shakespeare's Sonnets*, 52–53, 57; Editors of Encyclopaedia Britannica, "Henry Wriothesley, 3rd Earl of Southampton: English Noble," *Encyclopaedia Britannica*, November 6, 2019, https:// www.britannica.com/biography/Henry-Wriothesley-3rd-earl -of-Southampton.

38: Katherine Duncan-Jones argues for Mr. W.H. being William Herbert: Shakespeare, *Shakespeare's Sonnets*, 57–64, 67–69.

38: "There is every reason . . . Shakespeare himself.": Shakespeare, 34.

38: "THAT. ETERNITIE . . . POET.": Shakespeare, 34.

38–39: William needed money.: Shakespeare, 10–12.

39: "The hasty departure . . . signatory of the dedication.": Shakespeare, 10-12.

39: Number play in the sonnets: Shakespeare, 16, 49, 100, 150.

39: Sonnet 60 "Like as the waves . . . hasten to their end . . .": Shakespeare, *The Riverside Shakespeare*, 1760.

40: Sonnet 144 "Two loves I have of comfort and despair . . . Till my bad angel fire my good one out.": Shakespeare, 1775.

40: William's family life: "Shakespeare's Life: Stratford-upon-Avon," British Library, accessed March 27, 2020, http://www.bl.uk /treasures/shakespeare/stratford.html.

41: Sonnet 18 "Shall I compare thee to a summer's day? . . . So long lives this, and this gives life to thee.": Shakespeare, *The Riverside Shakespeare*, 1752.

42: Sonnet 20 "A woman's face with Nature's own hand painted . . . Mine be thy love, and thy love's use their treasure.": Shakespeare, 1753.

42–43: Sonnet 36 "Let me confess that we two must be twain . . . As thou being mine, mine is thy good report.": Shakespeare, 1755–1756.

43: Tricky Tricks with the sonnets: "altered so that . . . to a woman": Shakespeare, 1745–1748.

43: "complete collection of Shakespeare's plays and poems": "The Riverside Shakespeare," Goodreads, accessed September 1, 2020, https://www.goodreads.com/book/show/1414.The_ Riverside_Shakespeare.

43: "What's new to speak . . . / . . . / Nothing, sweet boy . . .": Shakespeare, *Shakespeare's Sonnets*, 42, 327.

43: "sweet boy . . . sweet love": Shakespeare, 42–43.

43: "One Hundred and Fifty Sonnets, all of them in Praise of his Mistress": Shakespeare, *The Riverside Shakespeare*, 1747–1748.

43: "the platonic love of a man for a man . . . any kind of homosexual attachment.": Shakespeare, 1745–1748.

44: What Shakespeare might have really looked like: Agnes Stamp, "How *Country Life* Revealed the True Face of Shakespeare [VIDEO]," *Country Life*, April 19, 2016, http://www.countrylife.co.uk /country-life/world-exclusive-the-true-face-of-shakespeare -revealed-for-the-first-time-video-72243.

45: What if Shakespeare wasn't the true author of Shakespeare's plays and sonnets?: Elizabeth Winkler, "Was Shakespeare a Woman?," *Atlantic*, June 2019, https://www.theatlantic.com/magazine /archive/2019/06/who-is-shakespeare-emilia-bassano/588076/.

45: "Emilia Bassano's life . . . its music and feminism.": Winkler.

CHAPTER 2: ABRAHAM LINCOLN

47: "I now have no doubt . . . that same black-eyed Fanny.": Robert L. Kincaid, *Joshua Fry Speed: Lincoln's Most Intimate Friend*

(Louisville: Filson Club, 1943), 48–49; Abraham Lincoln, *Abraham Lincoln: His Speeches and Writings*, ed. Roy P. Basler (Cleveland: De Capo, 2001), 143–144; William H. Herndon and Jesse W. Weik, *Herndon's Life of Lincoln: The History and Personal Recollections of Abraham Lincoln* (New York: Albert & Charles Boni, 1930), 176.

48–49: Abraham arriving in Springfield and meeting Joshua: Kincaid, *Joshua Fry Speed*, 9–12.

49: The timing of Lincoln's depression: Kincaid, 14–15; *Abraham Lincoln Chronology*, Historical Documents, 1993. I purchased my copy of the *Abraham Lincoln Chronology* at the Lincoln Memorial Shrine in Redlands, CA, in April 2011.

49: "I am now the most miserable man living . . . it appears to me.": Carl Sandburg, *Abraham Lincoln: The Prairie Years – I, Volume One, The Sangamon Edition* (New York: Charles Scribner's Sons, 1945), 261–262.

49: Joshua's marriage timing: Sandburg, 268.

49: Abraham's family: *Abraham Lincoln Chronology*.

50: Joshua helping General Sherman during the Civil War, "How is this that . . . was not asking for more.": Kincaid, *Joshua Fry Speed*, 25–26.

50–51: Abraham's February 13, 1842, letter to Joshua, "Springfield, Illinois, February 13, 1842 . . . P.S. I have been quite a man since you left.": Kincaid, 47–48; Abraham Lincoln, *A. Lincoln, Speeches and Writings: 1832–1858*, compilation and notes, Don E. Fehrenbacher (New York: Literary Classics of the United States, 1989), 79–80; Abraham Lincoln, *Abraham Lincoln, Complete Works: Comprising His Speeches, Letters, State Papers, and Miscellaneous Writings, Volume One*, eds. John G. Nicolay and John Hay (New York: Century, 1894), 56–57; Herndon and Weik, *Herndon's Life of Lincoln*, 175.

52–53: Abraham's February 25, 1842, letter to Joshua, "Springfield, February 25, 1842 . . . As ever, your friend, Lincoln": Kincaid, *Joshua Fry Speed*, 48–49; Lincoln, *Abraham Lincoln Speeches and Writings*, 143–144; Herndon and Weik, *Herndon's Life of Lincoln*, letter, 176.

54: Abraham's October 5, 1842, letter to Joshua, "But I began this letter . . . Yours Forever, Lincoln": Kincaid, *Joshua Fry Speed*, 54–55; Lincoln, *Abraham Lincoln Speeches and Writings*, 161–162.

55: Abraham on the penny: "Penny Facts," Bankrate, June 17, 2003, https://www.bankrate.com/finance/personal-finance/penny-facts.aspx; "Penny Details," Americans for Common Cents, accessed April 1, 2020, https://pennies.org/penny-details/.

55: Abraham's two men marrying each other poem, "For Reuben and Charles have married two girls, / . . . / And since that he's married to Natty.": Herndon and Weik, *Herndon's Life of Lincoln*, 48.

55: Lots of books on Abraham: "Abraham Lincoln" WorldCat, books search results: 42,127 titles, accessed September 4, 2020, https://www.worldcat.org/search?qt=worldcat_org_bks&q =%22Abraham+Lincoln%22&fq=dt%3Abks.

55: Two books (besides this one) that do mention Abraham's love for another man: C. A. Tripp, *The Intimate World of Abraham Lincoln* (New York: Free Press, 2005); Sarah Prager, *Queer, There, and Everywhere* (New York: HarperCollins, 2017), 51–58.

55–56: "Their births, . . . spots soft as May violets.": Sandburg, *Abraham Lincoln*, 264, 266.

56: "the sacred color associated with Gayness . . . they did not intend to marry.": Grahn, *Another Mother Tongue*, 8, 12.

56: Who did James Buchanan love?: Jerome Pohlen, *Gay & Lesbian History for Kids: The Century-Long Struggle for LGBT Rights, with 21 Activities* (Chicago: Chicago Review, 2016), 12; Robert P. Watson, *Affairs of State: The Untold History of Presidential Love, Sex, and Scandal, 1789–1900* (Lanham, MD: Rowman & Littlefield, 2012), 247; Thomas Balcerski, "The 175-Year History of Speculating about President James Buchanan's Bachelorhood," *Smithsonian Magazine*, August 27, 2019, https://www.smithsonianmag.com/history/175-year-history -examining-bachelor-president-james-buchanans-close -friendship-william-rufus-king-180972992/.

56: "Buchanan and his wife": Pohlen, *Gay & Lesbian History for Kids*, 12; Watson, *Affairs of State*, 245–247.

57: "streak of lavender": Tom Dalzell, ed., *The Routledge Dictionary of Modern American Slang* (New York: Routledge, 2008), 607.

57: James and William's "divorce": Martin Greif, *The Gay Book of Days: An Evocatively Illustrated Who's Who of Who Is, Was, May Have Been, Probably Was, and Almost Certainly Seems to Have Been Gay during the Past 5,000 Years* (New York: Main Street, 1989), 65–66, 73.

57: William Rufus King's time as vice president: "William Rufus King, 13th Vice President (1853)," United States Senate, accessed April 3, 2020, https://www.senate.gov/about/officers-staff /vice-president/VP_William_R_King.htm.

57: James's May 13, 1844, letter to Cornelia, "I am now 'solitary and alone' . . . or romantic affection.": James Buchanan, *The Works of James Buchanan*, ed. John Bassett Moore (Philadelphia: J. B. Lippincott, 1909), 6:3.

58: "William Herndon was . . . Lincoln's lover.": Sylvia Rhue, "A Family History Provides More Evidence That Lincoln Was Gay," HuffPost, November 26, 2012, https://www.huffpost.com /entry/a-family-history-provides-more-evidence-that-lincoln -was-gay_b_2169482?.

CHAPTER 3: MAHATMA GANDHI

61: "We can therefore but go forward . . . one soul and two bodies.":
Mohandas Gandhi, *The Collected Works of Mahatma Gandhi
(Electronic Book)* (New Delhi: Publications Divisison Government
of India, 1999, 98 vols., accessed November 7, 2020, http://www
.gandhiashramsevagram.org/gandhi-literature/collected-works
-of-mahatma-gandhi-volume-1-to-98.php, 14:149–150, #129.

62: "How to Pronounce Satyagraha," Forvo, accessed September 5, 2020,
https://forvo.com/word/satyagraha/.

62: "Truth (*satya*) implies love, . . . Satyagraha is soul-force pure and simple.":
Gandhi, *The Collected Works of Mahatma Gandhi*, 34:93, 96,
"Satyagraha in South Africa," chaps. XII, XIII.

63: Beware the "Great Man" theory of history, "everything he knew":
Gloria Steinem, *My Life on the Road* (New York: Random
House, 2015), 37–39.

63: Mohandas's family life: "Gandhi Timeline—Life Chronology,"
Sabarmati Ashram Preservation and Memorial Trust, accessed
April 3, 2020, http://www.gandhiashramsabarmati.org/en/the
-mahatma/life-chronology.html.

64: Mohandas and Hermann discussed protests and strategy in these
letters: Gandhi, *The Collected Works of Mahatma Gandhi*,
13:288–289, 184:291, 186:296, 190:372–373, 237:381, 242:387,
248:390–391, 252:392–393, 253:394–395, 256.

64: Mohandas on meeting Hermann, "In making these experiments . . .
struggle was at its height.": Gandhi, "Chapter XXVII: More
Experiments in Dietetics," 44:330.

65–66: "We met quite by accident . . . in the year 1912.": Gandhi, "Chapter
XXX: Towards Self-Restraint," 44:88, 335–336.

65: The renunciation and start of Buddhism: S. Priyadarshini, "Life of
Gautama Buddha and His Teachings," History Discussion,
accessed April 4, 2020, http://www.historydiscussion.net
/biography/life-of-gautama-buddha-and-his-teachings/2376;
Utpal Kumar, Prabhat Kumar, and Saurabh Kumar,
"Renunciation of Lord Buddha," BrandBharat.com, accessed
April 4, 2020, http://www.brandbharat.com/english
/buddhabihar/renunciation.html.

66: One historian who called them soul mates: Joseph Lelyveld, *Great Soul:
Mahatma Gandhi and His Struggle with India* (New York: Alfred
A. Knopf, 2011), 95–96. All excerpts from *Great Soul* copyright
© 2011 by Joseph Lelyveld used by permission of Alfred A.
Knopf, an imprint of the Knopf Doubleday Publishing Group,
a division of Penguin Random House LLC. All rights reserved.

66: Hermann is Mohandas's "friend and associate" here: Gandhi, *The
Collected Works of Mahatma Gandhi*, 6:508, #409, footnote 1.

66: One of many examples of Hermann not mentioned in histories of
    Mohandas at all: B. R. Nanda, "Mahatma Gandhi," *Encyclopaedia
    Britannica*, January 26, 2020, https://www.britannica.com
    /biography/Mahatma-Gandhi.

66: The book that mentioned Hermann and Mohandas's relationship:
    Lelyveld, *Great Soul*, 88, 95–96; and that book being banned:
    Vikas Bajaj and Julie Bosman, "Book on Gandhi Stirs Passion in
    India," *New York Times*, March 31, 2011, http://www.nytimes
    .com/2011/04/01/books/gandhi-biography-by-joseph-lelyveld
    -roils-india.html.

66–67: "Gandhi early on . . . National Archives of India and, finally,
    published.": Lelyveld, *Great Soul*, 88.

67: Mohandas's letters to Hermann: Gandhi, *The Collected Works of
    Mahatma Gandhi*, vols. 11–15.

68: The photo of Mohandas and Hermann: "carried by Kallenbach . . .
    due to his German origin.": "Item #IMPHPEMG1913505040,"
    GandhiMedia, accessed March 20, 2016, http://www
    .gandhimedia.org/cgi-bin/gm/gm.cgi?action=view&link=
    Images/Photographs/Personalities/Mahatma_Gandhi
    /1893_-_1914&image=IMPHPEMG1913505040.jpg&img
    =60&tt=&search=hermann%20kallenbach%20gandhi&cat
    =&bool=and.

68: Mohandas's March 15, 1914, letter to Hermann: "7
    BUITENSINGLE, . . . UPPER HOUSE": Gandhi, *The
    Collected Works of Mahatma Gandhi*, 14:120, #105.

69: Mohandas's April 3, 1913, letter to Hermann: "[PHOENIX] Thursday
    [April 3, 1913] . . . UPPER HOUSE": Gandhi, 13:39, #26.

69–70: The love contract between Mohandas and Hermann: "[July 29, 1911]
    Articles of Agreement . . . LOWER HOUSE": Gandhi, 12:11, #8.

71–72: Mohandas's before June 11, 1911, letter to Hermann: "ON THE
    TRAIN . . . UPPER HOUSE": Gandhi, 11:441–442, #446.

72–73: Mohandas's April 17, 1914, letter to Hermann: "April 17, 1917 . . .
    We shall see.": Gandhi, 14:149–150, #129.

73–74: Mohandas's July 22, 1915, letter to Hermann: "AHMEDABAD,
    July 22, [1915] . . . OLD FRIEND": Gandhi, 15:32–33, #33.

74: Mohandas's August 10, 1920, letter to Hermann: "Never has a day . . .
    Yours ever, UPPER HOUSE": Gandhi, 21:131–132, #90.

74: Mohandas asked or otherwise expressed his desire for Hermann to visit
    him in India in these letters: Gandhi, 38:375, #376; 57:55, #83;
    63:98, #107; Even in his letters to others, Mohandas tried to
    get Hermann to come to India, like in this September 22, 1917,
    letter to V. S. Srinivasa Sastri: Gandhi, 40:140, #83; and this
    letter to Mohandas's son Manilal: Gandhi, 41:232, #256.

75: "He [Hermann] arrived . . . a gratified Gandhi.": Lelyveld, *Great Soul*,
    278.

76: Mohandas's letters to Hermann about Manilal: Gandhi, *The Collected Works of Mahatma Gandhi*, 14:144–146, #127.

76: "Whatever Mr. Kallenbach's . . . about eating.": Gandhi, 14:146–147, #128.

76: Mohandas's December 23, 1914, letter to Hermann: "The only thing . . . to send her love to you.": Gandhi, 14:325–327, #263.

76: Mohandas's December 26, 1914, letter to Hermann: "Mrs. Gandhi often misses you . . . they are not available.": Gandhi, 14:328–329, #265.

77: "declined, saying that he had 'accepted the religion of peace.'": Gandhi, 8:212, #107, footnote 1.

77: Mohandas's "Triumph of Satyagraha": "Let people's religions be different . . . enmity towards one another.": Gandhi, 12:81–82, #63.

CHAPTER 4: BAYARD RUSTIN

79: "If we want to do away with . . . the elimination of injustice to all.": Bayard Rustin, *Time on Two Crosses: The Collected Writings of Bayard Rustin*, eds. Devon W. Carbado and Donald Weise (New York: Cleis, 2015), 279.

80: The Jim Crow era: "The Rise and Fall of Jim Crow," Thirteen: WNET New York, PBS, accessed April 10, 2020, http://www.pbs.org /wnet/jimcrow/segregation.html.

80: The 13th Amendment: Ken Drexler, "13th Amendment to the U.S. Constitution: Primary Documents in American History," Library of Congress, September 18, 2018, http://www.loc.gov /rr/program/bib/ourdocs/13thamendment.html.

80: An example of a segregation bus sign: "NOTICE . . . SIGNS IN THIS VEHICLE": *Brother Outsider: The Life of Bayard Rustin*, DVD, produced by Sam Pollard and Mridu Chandra, directed by Nancy Kates and Bennett Singer (New York: Question Why Films, 2003), 37:00.

81: Rosa Parks and bus segregation: "Rosa Parks Biography," Biography.com, January 17, 2020, http://www.biography.com/people/rosa-parks -9433715.

81–82: Bayard's story of protesting bus segregation: "There is no need to beat me . . . the non-violent approach.": Rustin, *Time on Two Crosses*, 2–5.

82: "We need in every community . . . wheels don't turn.": *Brother Outsider*, 3:08.

83: Rosa Parks and the Montgomery bus boycott: "Rosa Parks Biography," Biography.com.

83: President Barack Obama on Bayard: "a giant in the American Civil Rights Movement . . . most vulnerable citizens.": Barack Obama, "Remarks by the President at Presidential Medal of Freedom Ceremony," White House: Office of the Press Secretary, November 20, 2013, https://www.whitehouse.gov /the-press-office/2013/11/20/remarks-president-presidential -medal-freedom-ceremony.

83–84: "The problem can never be stated in terms of black and white.":
"Bayard Rustin," YouTube video, 3:25, posted by Shirley
LeClerc, March 12, 2010, https://youtu.be/L1jfwzMdv2E.

84: Davis Platt on Bayard: "For some reason, . . . about being gay.": *Brother
Outsider*, 15:45.

84: Bayard's time in prison during World War II: Rustin, *Time on Two
Crosses*, xvi; Netisha, "Bayard Rustin: The Inmate That the
Prison Could Not Handle," Rediscovering Black History,
August 16, 2016, https://rediscovering-black-history.blogs
.archives.gov/2016/08/16/bayard-rustin-the-inmate-that-the
-prison-could-not-handle/.

84: Davis on writing Bayard in code: "We were determined . . . as a
woman.": *Brother Outsider*, 19:40.

85: How long Bayard was in prison: Calvin Craig Miller, *No Easy Answers:
Bayard Rustin and the Civil Rights Movement* (Greensboro, NC:
Morgan Reynolds, 2005), 70.

85: "When he got out . . . for the first time.": *Brother Outsider*, 19:40.

85: "I never went through any trauma about coming out": Rustin, *Time on
Two Crosses*, 282.

85: Bayard's arrest in California: Rustin, xx, 299–300.

85: Fellowship of Reconciliation: "Fellowship of Reconciliation (FOR),"
Stanford University, Martin Luther King, Jr. Research and
Education Institute, accessed April 15, 2020, https://kinginstitute
.stanford.edu/encyclopedia/fellowship-reconciliation.

85: Bayard during the Montgomery bus boycott: "smuggled out of town . . .
homosexual and ex-Communist": Rustin, *Time on Two Crosses*,
xxiii.

86: Attemped blackmail: "had an aide . . . romantically involved.": Jacqueline
Houtman, Walter Naegle, and Michael G. Long, *Bayard Rustin:
The Invisible Activist* (Philadelphia: Quaker, 2014), 99.

86: Bayard leaving SCLC because of the blackmail threat: "make the
decision for him": Rustin, *Time on Two Crosses*, xxvi.

86: Southern Christian Leadership Conference (SCLC): "Fellowship of
Reconciliation," Stanford University; "Our History," Southern
Christian Leadership Conference, accessed April 15, 2020,
https://nationalsclc.org/about/history/.

86: "Although Rustin felt . . . eventually softened.": Rustin, *Time on Two
Crosses*, xxvii.

86: "Dr. King came from . . . get rid of me.": Rustin, xxvii.

87: The 1960 civil rights march on the Democratic National Convention:
Maurice Isserman, "Commentary: The Protesters of 1960
Helped Change the World," *Los Angeles Times*, August 13, 2000.

87: "I had come to the SCLC to help . . . one of the leaders.": Rustin, *Time
on Two Crosses*, 285.

87: Attempts to discredit Bayard two weeks before the 1963 march on Washington, D.C.: Rustin, xxx.

87–88: A. Philip Randolph's defense of Bayard: "Twenty-two arrests . . . discredit the movement.": Rustin, xxx; Daniel Levine, *Bayard Rustin and the Civil Rights Movement* (New Brunswick, NJ: Rutgers University Press, 2000), 142.

88: Bayard cowriting A. Philip Randolph's defense of Bayard: Levine, *Bayard Rustin*, 141–142.

88: A. Philip Randolph Institute: "Our History," A. Philip Randolph Institute, accessed April 17, 2020, http://www.apri.org/our-history.html.

88: "Someone came to Mr. Randolph . . . be what you are.": Rustin, *Time on Two Crosses*, 286.

89: "wanted the right to come out of the closet": Rustin, 283–284

89: "Well, I think the community . . . I was gay.": Rustin, 283–284.

89: "Looking back over . . . you have been?": Rustin, 287.

89–90: "Oh, I think it has made a great difference. . . . sense of humor.": Rustin, 287.

90: "the job of the gay community . . . antigay sentiment.": Rustin, 273.

91: "When laws are amended . . . under the law.": Rustin, 296.

91: Walter and Bayard meeting: "The day that I met Bayard . . . for 10 years.": Adrian Brooks, "Walter Naegle, Activist Bayard Rustin's Partner, on Rustin's Enduring Legacy," interview with Walter Naegle, Lambda Literary Foundation, February 25, 2015, http://www.lambdaliterary.org/features/02/25/walter-naegle-activist-bayard-rustins-partner-on-rustins-enduring-legacy/; "Long before Same-Sex Marriage, 'Adopted Son' Could Mean 'Life Partner,'" NPR, *Weekend Edition Sunday*, June 28, 2015, http://www.npr.org/2015/06/28/418187875/long-before-same-sex-marriage-adopted-son-could-mean-life-partner.

91–92: "And he was concerned . . . happy together.": "Long before Same-Sex Marriage," NPR.

92: "We were kind of an odd couple. . . . one human family.": *Brother Outsider*, 1:17:40.

92: "administrative assistant and adopted son": Eric Pace, "Bayard Rustin Is Dead at 75; Pacifist and a Rights Activist," *New York Times*, August 25, 1987, http://www.nytimes.com/1987/08/25/obituaries/bayard-rustin-is-dead-at-75-pacifist-and-a-rights-activist.html.

93: "Now, early in the morning . . . who we love. (Applause.)": Obama, "Remarks by the President."

93: "What remarks do you have . . . in your footsteps?": Rustin, *Time on Two Crosses*, 279.

93–94: "Well, I think the most important . . . fighting for all.": Rustin, *Time on Two Crosses*, 279.

94: "It didn't stop the tests . . . you did not cry out.": *Brother Outsider*, 40:00.

PART II: WHAT'S AHEAD: FREDA DU FAUR AND THE MOUNTAIN SHE NAMED FOR THE WOMAN SHE LOVED

96: Freda du Faur: Graham Langton, "Story: Du Faur, Emmeline Freda," *Te Ara: The Encyclopedia of New Zealand*, December 2005, http://www.teara.govt.nz/en/biographies/3d17/du-faur -emmeline-freda.

96: Freda meets Muriel: Langton; Sally Irwin, *Between Heaven and Earth: The Life of Mountaineer, Freda du Faur* (Hawthorn, Australia: White Crane, 2000), 130–135, 153–154, 157, 231; Susan Hawthorn, *The Butterfly Effect* (North Melbourne, Australia: Spinifex, 2005), 12.

97: Freda's fame, "the feat with which her name will always be associated": E. J. O'Donnell, "Du Faur, Emmeline Freda (1882–1935)," *Australian Dictionary of Biography*, vol. 8 (Melbourne: Melbourne University Publishing, 1981), http://adb.anu.edu.au /biography/du-faur-emmeline-freda-6025.

97: Freda's book dedication to Muriel, "TO MY FRIEND . . . I DEDICATE THIS BOOK": Freda du Faur, *The Conquest of Mount Cook and Other Climbs: An Account of Four Seasons' Mountaineering on the Southern Alps of New Zealand* (London: George Allen & Unwin, 1915), dedication page, https://en.wikisource.org/wiki /The_Conquest_of_Mount_Cook; Irwin, *Between Heaven and Earth*, 231, 298.

97: Freda and Muriel separated: Irwin, 287–299, 333.

97: Mountains named for Freda and Muriel: O'Donnell, "Du Faur, Emmeline Freda."

CHAPTER 5: SAPPHO

98: How old did Sappho live to be?: "Sappho 620 BC–550BC: Biography," Poetry Foundation, accessed May 6, 2020, https://www .poetryfoundation.org/poets/sappho.

98: "All my flesh is wrinkled with age, / . . . / once nimble like a fawn's . . .": Christine Downing, *Myths and Mysteries of Same-Sex Love* (New York: Continuum, 1996), 229.

99: "Now, far away, Anactoria / . . . / and their infantry in full display of arms": Downing, 225.

100: How to pronounce "Sappho": Jane McIntosh Snyder, and Camille-Yvette Welsch, *Sappho* (Philadelphia: Chelsea House, 2005), 12; "Sappho 620 BC–550BC: Biography," Poetry Foundation.

100: Who was Plato: Constance C. Meinwald, "Plato: Greek Philosopher," *Encyclopaedia Britannica*, March 31, 2020, http://www .britannica.com/biography/Plato.

100: Plato on Sappho, "SOME say the Muses are nine, . . . Sappho from Lesbos.": *The Greek Anthology, with an English Translation by W. R. Paton, in Five Volumes*, Vol. III (London: William

Heinemann, New York: G.P. Putnam's Sons, 1925), Book IX. EPIGRAMS 506-507, 281, https://archive.org/details /greekanthology03pato/page/280/mode/2up?q=plato.

100: "So that having learned it, I may die.": Snyder and Welsch, *Sappho*, 16–17.

100: "I have no complaint. / . . . / won't be forgotten": Sappho, *Sappho*, trans. Mary Barnard (Berkeley: University of California Press, 1958), 100. All quotes and Barnard translations © 1958 by the Regents of the University of California. Renewed 1986 by Mary Barnard. Used by permission of University of California Press.

101: Sappho sang or recited her poems: Snyder and Welsch, *Sappho*, 16, 37.

101: "they were passed . . . after her death.": Sappho, *Sappho*, 104.

101–102: "In the spring twilight / . . . / with lovely hair": Sappho, 22–25.

102: Alcaeus on Sappho: Snyder and Welsch, *Sappho*, 13.

102: "O weaver of violets, holy, sweet-smiling Sappho.": "Alcaeus: Greek Poet," *Encyclopaedia Britannica*, May 2, 2008, http://www .britannica.com/biography/Alcaeus.

103: "Be kind to me / . . . / come soon": Sappho, *Sappho*, 93.

103: "the tenderness of female love": Downing, *Myths and Mysteries*, 233.

103: "The gods bless you / . . . / girl friend's breast": Downing, 233; Sappho, *Sappho*, 96.

104: "I do not think there will be any at the time / . . . / such as yours": Snyder and Welsch, *Sappho*, 70.

104–105: "Honestly, I wish I were dead! / . . . / we two were not found": Downing, *Myths and Mysteries*, 234. By permission of Jeffrey M. Duban; see www.jeffreyduban.com (Sappho website).

105: "To find Sappho, . . . is not.": Downing, 221.

105: "I have a beautiful child / . . . / all Lydia": Downing, 226.

106: "Kerkylas may be a made-up name . . . the biographical tradition.": Snyder and Welsch, *Sappho*, 13.

106: Glukupikron translates as "sweet-bitter": Nicola Slee et al., *Making Nothing Happen: Five Poets Explore Faith and Spirituality* (Farnham, UK: Ashgate, 2014), 137, https://books.google.com /books?id=VASUBAAAQBAJ&printsec=frontcover#v =onepage&q=glukupikron%20&f=false.

106: "With his venom / . . . / strikes me down": Sappho, *Sappho*, 53.

107: "It's no use / . . . / love for that boy": Sappho, 12.

107: "To love women . . . directed to women.": Downing, *Myths and Mysteries*, 229.

108: Tricky tricks, the destruction of Sappho's poems: Snyder and Welsch, *Sappho*, 61; Downing, *Myths and Mysteries*, 221; Mostafa El-Abbadi, "Library of Alexandria: Ancient Library, Alexandria, Egypt," *Encyclopaedia Britannica*, May 12, 2016, http://www.britannica.com/topic/Library-of-Alexandria.

108: "ordered the burning . . . survived the Middle Ages": Downing, *Myths and Mysteries*, 221; Frank N. Magill, ed., *The Ancient World: Dictionary of World Biography*, vol. 1 (Pasadena, CA: Salem, 1998), 990–991, https://books.google.com/books?id =7NVFUi7G6TEC&printsec=frontcover#v=snippet&q =decimated%20her%20extant%20poetry&f=false.

109: The Sappho poems that survived: Downing, *Myths and Mysteries*, 221; Katy Waldman, "Read Two Newly Discovered Sappho Poems in English for the First Time," *Browbeat: Slate's Culture Blog*, January 31, 2014, http://www.slate.com/blogs/browbeat/2014 /01/31/read_two_newly_discovered_sappho_poems_in_ english_for_the_first_time.html.

109: The one complete Sappho poem: Sappho, *Sappho*, 105.

109: Willa Cather on Sappho's poems, "If all the lost richness . . . passion in them.": Louis Crompton, *Homosexuality and Civilization* (Cambridge, MA: Belknap Press of Harvard University Press, 2003), 20, https://books.google.com/books?id=TfBYd9xVaXcC &pg=PA20&lpg=PA20&dq=willa+cather+on+sappho&source =bl&ots=OqrKTujyiM&sig=VSTekiUFqTn5R30XFKKJOjbz 560&hl=en&sa=X&ved=0ahUKEwjy0LWqt6vMAhVI72MK HcroDCUQ6AEIQTAH#v=onepage&q=willa%20cather%20 on%20sappho&f=false.

109: Willa and Edith: Maria Popova, "Willa Cather's Only Surviving Letter to Her Partner, Edith Lewis," *Brain Pickings*, April 17, 2013, https://www.brainpickings.org/2013/04/17/willa-cather -letters/; "Willa Cather: Biography," Equality Forum, accessed May 4, 2020, http://www.lgbthistorymonth.com/willa -cather?tab=biography.

110: "For if indeed she flees, soon will she pursue, / . . . / even against her will.": Snyder and Welsch, *Sappho*, 37–38.

110: "Come to me now also, release me from / . . . / be my fellow soldier.": Snyder and Welsch, 37–38.

110: Intentionally mistranslated: "widely translated from Greek . . . *him* instead of *her*.": *Snyder* and Welsch, 19.

110: Archaeologists finding Sappho's poems: "Oxyrhynchus: A City and Its Texts, Virtual Exhibition: Excavations and Finds," Imaging Papyri Project, University of Oxford, accessed May 5, 2020, http://www.papyrology.ox.ac.uk/POxy/VExhibition/finds /sappho.html; Judith Weingarten, "A Lyrical Literary Miracle: More Sappho (2 Updates): The Tenth Muse," *Zenobia: Empress of the East* (blog), February 2, 2014, http://judithweingarten .blogspot.com/2014/02/a-lyrical-literary-miracle-more-sappho .html; John Ezard, "After 2,600 Years, the World Gains a Fourth Poem by Sappho," *Guardian* (US edition), June 24, 2005, http:// www.theguardian.com/uk/2005/jun/24/gender.books.

110–111: Mary Barnard explains what happened to many of Sappho's poems: "The papyrus scrolls were . . . mummified crocodiles.": Sappho, *Sappho*, 104–105.

111: We're still discovering Sappho's poems: Ezard, "After 2,600 Years."

112: "a folded-up, post-card size manuscript with lines of text in ancient Greek": Megan Gannon, "Sappho's New Poems: The Tangled Tale of Their Discovery," Live Science, January 23, 2015, http://www.livescience.com/49543-sappho-new-poems -discovery.html.

112: Two new poems attributed to Sappho: Dirk Obbink, "New Poems by Sappho: Why Is the Discovery Important, What Do the Poems Tell Us about Sappho, and How Do We Know They Are Genuine?," *Times Literary Supplement*, February 5, 2014; Dirk Obbink, "Interim Notes on 'Two New Poems of Sappho,'" *Zeitschrift für Papyrologie und Epigraphik* 194 (2015); 1–8, https://www.jstor.org/stable/43909704.

112–113: "There are those who say / . . . / and their infantry in full display of arms.": Downing, *Myths and Mysteries*, 225.

113: "Valuing personal love . . . this central place.": Downing, 225.

114: Blaming Helen, "face that launched a thousand ships": Christopher Marlowe, "The Tragical History of Dr. Faustus, from the Quarto of 1604," Project Gutenberg EBook, November 3, 2009, 162, http://www.gutenberg.org/cache/epub/779/pg779.txt.

114: "Come to me now also, release me from / . . . / be my fellow soldier": Sappho, *Sappho*, 93.

115: "Although they are / . . . / are immortal": Sappho, 9.

CHAPTER 6: QUEEN ANNE

117: "I had rather live in a cottage . . . world without you.": Ophelia Field, *Sarah Churchill, Duchess of Marlborough: The Queen's Favourite* (New York: St. Martin's, 2002), 70.

118: Background on England 1669: "James II (r.1685–1688)," The Royal Household, accessed May 7, 2020, https://www.royal.uk/james -ii-r1685-1688; John P. Kenyon, "James II: King of England, Scotland, and Ireland," *Encyclopaedia Britannica*, October 10, 2019, https://www.britannica.com/biography/James-II-king -of-England-Scotland-and-Ireland.

118: "Glorious Revolution": "Glorious Revolution: English History," *Encyclopaedia Britannica*, November 5, 2019, http://www .britannica.com/event/Glorious-Revolution.

118: "Glorious Revolution: English History," *Encyclopaedia Britannica*.

118: King James II in exile: "James II," The Royal Household.

118: King George I ruling after Anne's death: "Anne: Queen of Great Britain and Ireland," *Encyclopaedia Britannica*, February 2, 2020, https://www.britannica.com/biography/Anne-queen-of-Great-Britain-and-Ireland.

118: Anne's papers destroyed, "the last hours . . . including her will": Field, *Sarah Churchill*, 37, 338.

119: Sarah's life: Field, 107; John S. Morrill, "Sarah Jennings, Duchess of Marlborough: English Duchess," *Encyclopaedia Britannica*, accessed October 14, 2019, https://www.britannica.com/biography/Sarah-Jennings-Duchess-of-Marlborough.

119: Sarah's autobiography: Sarah Churchill, Duchess of Marlborough, and Nathaniel Hooke, *An Account of the Conduct of the Dowager Duchess of Marlborough, from Her First Coming to Court, to the Year 1710—In a Letter from Herself to My Lord—* (London: James Bettenham, for George Hawkins, 1742), https://archive.org/details/conductofdowager00marliala.

120: The Spencer-Churchill dynasty: "The Royal Family," The Royal Household, May 8, 2020, https://www.royal.uk/royal-family; "The Duke of Cambridge," The Royal Household, May 8, 2020, https://www.royal.uk/the-duke-of-cambridge.

120: "I think it would . . . with queen or princess.": Churchill and Hooke, *An Account of the Dowager Duchess*, 9–11.

121: Lady of the Bedchamber description, "at mealtimes and when dressing . . . in their presence.": Field, *Sarah Churchill*, 38.

121: "K[ing] Charles [II] used . . . Mrs Cornwallis.": Field, *Sarah Churchill*, 33–34.

121: "You see that this no trouble to me to obey your commands.": Field, 38.

121: "I hope the little corner . . . empty is mine.": Field, 49.

121–122: Anne and Sarah's salary: Field, 60.

121: Anne's salary, calculating how much today: "Five Ways to Compute the Relative Value of a UK Pound Amount, 1270 to Present," Measuring Worth, accessed September 5, 2020, https://www.measuringworth.com/calculators/ukcompare/.

121: Anne's salary, calculating how much in US dollars: "Convert Pounds to Dollars, GBP to USD Foreign Exchange," Foreign Exchange, May 11, 2020, 20:01, https://www.foreignexchange.org.uk/fx-rates/conversion/1/GBP/USD.

122: "I believe you in all things . . . my soul loves.": Field, *Sarah Churchill*, 60.

122: Anne and Sarah writing to each other in code: Field, 66.

122: "The PRINCESS had a different taste . . . made so by affection and friendship.": Churchill and Hooke, *An Account of the Conduct of the Dowager Duchess*, 13–14.

123: "No, my dear MRS. FREEMAN, . . . Tuesday morning.": Churchill and Hooke, 84–86.

123: Sarah showing up at court the day after her husband was dismissed: Churchill and Hooke, 44.

123: Queen Mary's complaint: "very unfit LADY MARLBOROUGH . . . he ought not.": Churchill and Hooke, 44.

123: Anne's letter to Sarah: "I had rather live in a cottage . . . world without you.": Field, *Sarah Churchill*, 70.

123–124: Queen Anne giving Sarah top positions: "three of the top posts . . . all the garden gates.": Field, 96–103.

124: Sarah influencing Anne: "strategy . . . proved successful . . . Duke of Newcastle.": Field, 143.

124: "The intimate friendship, . . . was against my wishes and inclinations.": Churchill and Hooke, *An Account of the Conduct of the Dowager Duchess*, 122.

125: "Banish all your fears . . . more than I can express.": Field, *Sarah Churchill*, 102.

125: Abigail's ascension in Anne's favor: Field, 177–189.

125: "that it was very plain, . . . I could never forget them.": Field, 189.

126: Jonathan Swift about Abigail and Robert Harley, "retreat after dinner . . . settling the nation.": Field, 277.

126: Sarah threatening Anne, "I remember you said . . . I wish may still be yours.": Field, 208.

126: Tricky tricks and blackmail, "such things are in my power . . . might lose a Crown.": Field, 285.

127: Nasty songs about Anne and Abigail, "When as Queen Anne of great Renoun / . . . / A Dirty Chamber-Maid": Field, 259–260.

127: Sarah benefits financially, "It has been calculated . . . on a private level.": Field, 212–213, 287–293.

127: Calculating how much today: "UK Pound Values," Measuring Worth.

127: Calculating how much in US dollars: "Pounds to Dollars," Foreign Exchange.

127: Sarah and others lose their positions of power: Field, *Sarah Churchill*, 315.

127–128: Sarah returns the gold key and takes more money: Field, 287–293.

128: Calculating how much today: "UK Pound Values," Measuring Worth.

128: Calculating how much in US dollars: "Pounds to Dollars," Foreign Exchange.

128: "Though it was extremely tedious . . . in a dungeon.": Field, *Sarah Churchill*, 37.

128: "Abigail complained to Robert Harley that the Queen no longer listened to her.": Field, 284.

128: Anne's death: "The Stuarts," The Royal Household, May 13, 2020, https://www.royal.uk/stewarts.

129: Sarah's wealth and power, "By 1719, Sarah . . . the economic stability of the government": Field, *Sarah Churchill*, 372–373, 386.

129: Calculating how much today: "UK Pound Values," Measuring Worth.

129: Calculating how much in US dollars: "Pounds to Dollars," Foreign Exchange.

129: Anne's physical condition, "too lame to clime the Palace stairs . . . morbidly obese . . . 'wheelchair,' which she loved.": Field, *Sarah Churchill*, 29, 86.

129: Sarah's physical condition: "strawberry blonde, washed every day . . . to maintain its glow" and Sarah's description of herself: "I am confident . . . so happy as to have been a man.": Field, 56, 150.

130: A queer court "had tongues wagging over their rumored gay ways.": Neal Broverman "A Queer Court: Could an Openly Gay Queen or King Rule the United Kingdom?," *Advocate*, April/May 2014, 13.

130: King William II: Broverman, 13.

130: King Richard I: Broverman, 13.

130: Christopher Marlowe's play *Edward II*, "My father is deceast, come Gaveston, . . . Might have enforst me to have swum from France.": Christopher Marlowe, *Edward II*, Perseus Digital Library, Tufts University, May 14, 2020, https://www.perseus.tufts.edu/hopper/text?doc=Perseus%3Atext%3A1999.03.0007%3Aact%3D1%3Ascene%3D1.

131: "often remembered as bisexual . . . 'Queen James'": Broverman, "A Queer Court," 13.

131: James I writing to George Villiers, "I cannot content myself without . . . life without you.": Kayla Epstein, "'The King and His Husband': The Gay History of British Royals," *Washington Post*, August 18, 2018, https://www.washingtonpost.com/news/retropolis/wp/2018/08/18/the-king-and-his-husband-the-gay-history-of-british-royals/.

131: King James Bible: Broverman, "A Queer Court," 13.

131: "one of several": Broverman, 13.

131: "wild younger sister of Queen Elizabeth II": Broverman, 13.

132: Anne and Sarah's children: Field, *Sarah Churchill*, 49–50, 92–93; "Family Tree," Blenheim Palace, accessed May 13, 2020, https://www.blenheimpalace.com/visitus/family-tree/.

132: "I have a satisfaction . . . kindness to me was real.": Field, *Sarah Churchill*, 2, 431.

132: "friendships were flames . . . indifference or aversion.": Field, 47.

132: "The most important constitutional . . . Scotland in 1707.": "Queen Anne (1665–1714), Reigned 1702–1714," National Portrait Gallery, accessed May 13, 2020, http://www.npg.org.uk/collections/search/person/mp00111/queen-anne.

132: Scotland joining England and Wales: Lacey Baldwin Smith et al., "United Kingdom," *Encyclopaedia Britannica*, May 10, 2020, https://www.britannica.com/place/United-Kingdom.

133: Sarah's position in history: Field, *Sarah Churchill*, 2.

133: Openly queer monarch is now possible: Daily Mail reporter, "How Our Queen Will Never Be a King: Royal Rule Change Brought in after Same-Sex Marriage Laws Meant Britain Could Have Had a Female 'King,'" *DailyMail.com*, February 22, 2014, http://www.dailymail.co.uk/news/article-2565452 /How-husband-future-King-England-never-Queen-Rules-new -royal-titles-changed-ensure-Queen-Princess-female.html; Gareth Johnson, "Could There Be a Gay King of England?," Means Happy, July 20, 2020, https://meanshappy.com/could -there-be-a-gay-king-of-england/.

CHAPTER 7: ELEANOR ROOSEVELT

135: "Your ring is a great comfort . . . wouldn't be wearing it!": Rodger Streitmatter, ed., *Empty without You: The Intimate Letters of Eleanor Roosevelt and Lorena Hickok* (New York: Free Press, 1998), 19–20.

136: Who was Eleanor Roosevelt?: "Eleanor Roosevelt Facts: General Facts and Figures," Franklin D. Roosevelt Presidential Library and Museum National Archives, accessed May 15, 2020, https://www.fdrlibrary.org/er-facts; Streitmatter, xiii.

136: "no person shall be elected . . . more than twice.": US Congress, "Constitution of the United States: Amendments 11–27," National Archives, November 12, 2019, https://www.archives .gov/founding-docs/amendments-11-27.

136: Eleanor as First Lady: "Eleanor Roosevelt," Franklin D. Roosevelt Presidential Library and Museum; Streitmatter, *Empty without You*, xvi, xxiv–xxv.

136: Eleanor holding her own press conferences: "Eleanor Roosevelt," Franklin D. Roosevelt Presidential Library and Museum.

136–137: Eleanor standing up for Marian Anderson, "struck at the very depths of racism in America": Michelle Roehm McCann and Amelie Welden, *Girls Who Rocked the World: Heroines from Joan of Arc to Mother Teresa*, ill. David Hahn (New York: Aladdin; Hillsboro, OR: Beyond Words, 2012), 123–124.

137: Eleanor bringing her own chair to sit in the aisle: Betty Boyd Caroli, "Eleanor Roosevelt: American Diplomat, Humanitarian and First Lady," *Encyclopaedia Britannica*, November 3, 2019, http:// www.britannica.com/biography/Eleanor-Roosevelt.

137: Eleanor photographed with Black pilot Charles Anderson: Calvin Craig Miller, *No Easy Answers: Bayard Rustin and the Civil Rights Movement* (Greensboro, NC: Morgan Reynolds, 2005), 45.

138: Eleanor's possible role in the executive order to end discrimination in hiring for defense industries and government, "There shall be no discrimination . . . preparations for the march.": Miller, 44–45.

138: Eleanor traveled during World War II to support US troops: Christy Regenhardt and Mary Jo Binker, eds., "The Eleanor Roosevelt Papers Project: First Lady of the World," Department of History of George Washington University, accessed May 15, 2020, https://www.gwu.edu/~erpapers/maps/main_map.html.

138: Eleanor as chair of the UN Commission on Human Rights: "Eleanor Roosevelt Biography," Franklin D. Roosevelt Presidential Library and Museum, accessed May 15, 2020, https://www.fdrlibrary.org/er-biography; "Eleanor Roosevelt and the United Nations," US National Archives, accessed May 15, 2020, https://artsandculture.google.com/exhibit/ARaxRSs-; John Sears, "Eleanor Roosevelt and the Universal Declaration of Human Rights," Franklin D. Roosevelt Presidential Library and Museum, accessed May 15, 2020, https://www.fdrlibrary.org/human-rights.

138: "All human beings are born free . . . spirit of brotherhood.": Sears, 6.

138: "One major point guarantees . . . rest of the world.": Sears, 10.

139: Destroying Eleanor's letters to Lorena, "sat around an open fire . . . burning letter after letter.": Linas Alsenas. *Gay America: Struggle for Equality* (New York: Harry N. Abrams, 2008), 44–45.

139: "Your mother wasn't always . . . in her letters to me.": Streitmatter, *Empty without You*, xxii.

140: Eleanor writing Lorena on April 6, 1934, and Lorena writing Eleanor on April 9, 1934, "I love you": Streitmatter, 96–97.

140: Eleanor and Franklin's relationship: Streitmatter, xx, 1, 266.

140: Lucy was with Franklin when he died: Streitmatter, 266.

140: Eleanor and Lorena's relationship intensified in 1933: Streitmatter, xxii.

140: "It was Lorena who persuaded Eleanor . . . the woman behind the woman.": Streitmatter, xxiii, xxiv.

141: The ring Lorena gave Eleanor: "an extravagant sapphire . . . remain for the next four years.": Streitmatter, 10.

141: Eleanor's letter to Lorena March 7, 1933, "The White House . . . Ever Yours, E.R.": Streitmatter, 19–20.

141: Eleanor and Lorena read books at the same time: Streitmatter, 20, footnote 17.

142: Eleanor's letter to Lorena March 6, 1933, "THE WHITE HOUSE . . . Devotedly, E.R.": Streitmatter, 17–18.

142: More romantic Eleanor letters to Lorena: Streitmatter, 111–112, 76–77, 100.

143: Eleanor's letter to Lorena March 9, 1933, "THE WHITE HOUSE . . . God bless you 'light of my life,' E.R.": Streitmatter, 21–23.

143–144: Eleanor's daughter Anna and her relationships: Streitmatter, xx–xxi, 40.

144: "Louis tells me one of . . . How lucky you are not a man!": Streitmatter, 40.

144: Eleanor's 1935 Valentine's Day card to Lorena, "May the world be full of sunshine / . . . / Take us over life's rough seas.": Streitmatter, 147–148.

144: Eleanor's romantic letters to Lorena, including "At times life becomes . . . ache for you" and "you are still . . . else in the world.": Streitmatter, 68–69, 133, 156–157, 240.

144–145: Lorena's new job in 1933: Streitmatter, xxv–xxvi.

145–146: Lorena's letter to Eleanor December 5, 1933, "Dear: Tonight it's Bemidji. . . . And in a little more than a week now—I shall! H": Streitmatter, 52–54.

145: "If I were Harry Hopkins . . . not for a moment.": Streitmatter, 52–54.

146: Eleanor and Lorena's nickname for Eleanor if she weren't famous: Streitmatter, 37.

146: "'Time' has a dreadful cover picture. . . . Mrs. Doaks would like a little privacy now & then!": Streitmatter, 37.

146: Lorena struggling with having to share Eleanor: Streitmatter, 119–222.

147: "My trouble, I suspect, . . . respect the *personage* with all my heart!": Streitmatter, 235.

147: Lorena couldn't go back to being a reporter, "If you got a laugh . . . (And I don't believe you would want that, either.)": Streitmatter, 159–160.

148: Trying to lose the press, "With dismay I watched the speedometer . . . 'President's Wife . . . California'": Streitmatter, 120–122.

149: Lorena writing *The Story of Helen Keller*: Streitmatter, 284–285, 292.

149: Eleanor offering to return Lorena's ring: Streitmatter, 198–199.

149–150: Lorena letter to Eleanor December 6, 1936, "December 6 Dearest: . . . I love you—now and always. H": Streitmatter, 199.

150: Tricky tricks, Eleanor and Lorena's relationship ignored or misrepresented: Caroli, "Eleanor Roosevelt"; "Eleanor Roosevelt," History.com, April 3, 2020, https://www.history .com/topics/first-ladies/eleanor-roosevelt.

150: "She [Lorena] developed a deep attachment . . . 1,000 of Miss Hickok's.": "Eleanor Roosevelt Facts," Franklin D. Roosevelt Presidential Library and Museum.

150: "Their total correspondence . . . runs in its entirety to some 16,000 pages.": Streitmatter, *Empty without You*, xvi.

150–151: Getty Images photo caption: "Eleanor Roosevelt Dining with Her Secretary Lorena Hickok," Getty Images, September 5, 2020, https://www.gettyimages.com/detail/news-photo/san -francisco-ca-8-1-34-mrs-f-d-roosevelt-and-her-secretary -news-photo/514080764.

151: "was very aware of lesbian life . . . two lesbian couples.": Alsenas, *Gay America*, 44.

151: "the correspondence . . . would be 'misunderstood.'": Paul Russell, *The Gay 100: A Ranking of the Most Influential Gay Men and Lesbians, Past and Present* (Secaucus, NJ: Carol, 1995), 174–175.

151: "While First Lady, . . . rest of Roosevelt's life.": "Eleanor Roosevelt: Biography," Equality Forum, May 16, 2020, http://www .lgbthistorymonth.com/eleanor-roosevelt?tab=biography.

CHAPTER 8: M'E MPHO NTHUNYA

153: "When a woman loves . . . with a whole heart.": Mpho M'Atsepo Nthunya, *Singing away the Hunger: The Autobiography of an African Woman*, ed. K. Limakatso Kendall (Bloomington: Indiana University Press, 1996/1997), 69.

154: M'e Mpho Nthunya's salary: Nthunya, 164.

154: M'e Mpho Nthunya's autobiography: Nthunya, 164–171.

154: What's in a name?: Judith Gay, "'Mummies and Babies' and Friends and Lovers in Lesotho," *Journal of Homosexuality* 11, no. 3–4 (1985): 115.

154–155: "I'm telling stories for children. . . . where they come from.": Nthunya, *Singing away the Hunger*, 2.

155: "To speak of a grown woman . . . all her clothes.": Stephen O. Murray and Will Roscoe, eds., *Boy-Wives and Females Husbands: Studies in African Homosexualities* (New York: Palgrave/St. Martin's, 1998), 318, PDF 190, http://www.arcados.ch/wp-content /uploads/2012/06/MURRAY-ROSCOE-BOY-WIVES -FEMALE-HUSBANDS-98.pdf.

155: K. Limakatso Kendall, email message to the author, September 14, 2016.

155–156: "There were some television interviews. . . . read that magazine.": Kendall.

156: Andy Warhol: Rachel Nuwer, "Andy Warhol Probably Never Said His Celebrated 'Fifteen Minutes of Fame' Line," *Smithsonian*, April 8, 2014, http://www.smithsonianmag.com/smart-news /andy-warhol-probably-never-said-his-celebrated-fame-line -180950456/?no-ist; "Andy Warhol Biography," Biography, March 6, 2020, http://www.biography.com/people/andy -warhol-9523875.

156: M'e Mpho was ritually married to a woman: Nthunya, *Singing away the Hunger*, 69–72.

156–157: "When I was living in the mountains I got a special friend. . . . she was my *motsoalle*.": Nthunya, 69.

157: "She [M'e M'alineo] told her husband. . . . it's time for me to go.": Nthunya, 69.

158: "She loved me so much . . . two o'clock in the morning.": Nthunya, 69–70.

158: Joala, Motoho, and Samp are all defined in a glossary in M'e Mpho's autobiography: Nthunya, 172–173.

159: "Another time, a year later, my *motsoalle* comes for a feast. . . . loving each other.": Nthunya, 70.

159: "It would appear . . . publicly acknowledged and honored." Murray and Roscoe, eds., *Boy-Wives and Females Husbands*, 235, PDF 185.

160: "A conversation on female friendships . . . 'Haven't you ever fallen in love with another girl?': Gay, "Mummies and Babies," 102.

160: "After some years, my *motsoalle* left. . . . she's drinking too much.": Nthunya, *Singing away the Hunger*, 71.

160–161: "The practice of marriages had stopped. . . . that kind of openness.": K. Limakatso Kendall, telephone conversation with the author, September 7, 2016.

161: Tricky tricks: "My search for lesbians in Lesotho began in 1992. . . . identified herself as a lesbian.": K. Limakatso Kendall, "When a Woman Loves a Woman," included in "Lesotho: Love, Sex, and the (Western) Construction of Homophobia," in Murray and Roscoe, eds., *Boy-Wives and Females Husbands*," 223, PDF 178.

161–162: "I learned not to look for unconventionality . . . Western import.": Murray and Roscoe, eds. 223–234, PDF 178.

162: "Why does it feel important . . . ? . . . or made illegitimate.": Murray and Roscoe, eds., 236–237, PDF 186–187.

163: "For her [M'e Mpho] it was four years . . . for us both.": K. Limakatso Kendall, email to the author, September 14, 2016.

163: "stayed until May 2001, . . . returned to Lesotho.": Kendall.

163: Kendall's 2010 visit to M'e Mpho and their trip to the Indian Ocean, M'e Mpho's death in 2013: Kendall.

163: "This was her favorite of hundreds of pictures . . . mountain grasses.": K. Limakatso Kendall, "Mpho Nthunya in Her Basotho Hat," Flickr, August 4, 2008, https://www.flickr.com/photos /kkendall/2733686652/in/photolist-2fwiF2-8HNAwE -5auWNk-8HNAUu-5azd4G-5auWVg-2fANmA-5ayRNu -2fwhsn-2fwjxT.

164: "happy—very satisfied with the work . . . told her story.": Kendall, telephone conversation.

164: "In the old days friendship was very beautiful . . . long ago.": Nthunya, *Singing away the Hunger*, 72.

PART III: WHAT'S AHEAD: THE CHEVALIER D'ÉON AND MADEMOISELLE DE BEAUMONT WERE THE SAME PERSON

166: Born and lived the first half of his life: Robert Aldrich, *Gay Lives* (New York: Thames & Hudson, 2012), 68–73.

166: Background on the Chevalier d'Éon: d'Éon de Beaumont, *The Maiden of Tonnerre: The Vicissitudes of the Chevalier and the Chevalière d'Éon*, trans., ed. Roland A. Champagne, Nina C. Ekstein, and Gary Kates (Baltimore: John Hopkins University Press, 2001), xiii–xiv.

166: "intelligence intended for a possible French invasion of the British Isles.": Aldrich, *Gay Lives*, 71.

166–167: Bets were placed, "over £200,000": Aldrich, 71–72; d'Éon de Beaumont, *Maiden of Tonnerre*, xv.

167: Calculating how much today: "UK Pound Values," Measuring Worth.

167: Calculating how much in US dollars: "Pounds to Dollars," Foreign Exchange.

167: In 1785 moved to London and lived as a woman.: Aldrich, *Gay Lives*, 72; d'Éon de Beaumont, *Maiden of Tonnerre*, xiii–xiv.

167: One final twist: Aldrich, *Gay Lives* 72; d'Éon de Beaumont, *Maiden of Tonnerre*, xiii–xiv.

167: What a life outside gender boundaries: Aldrich, *Gay Lives*, 68–73.

CHAPTER 9: PHARAOH HATSHEPSUT

169: "My foes shall not exist . . . the king of the Two Lands.": David Warburton, *Architecture, Power, and Religion: Hatshepsut, Amun & Karnak in Context* (Münster, Germany: LIT Verlag Münster, 2012), 230. Professor Warburton has provided a new rendering of Hatshepsut's Oracle Text especially for this book.

170: Background on ancient Egyptian beliefs: Kara Cooney, *The Woman Who Would Be King: Hatshepsut's Rise to Power in Ancient Egypt* (New York: Crown, 2014), 12. All excerpts from *The Woman Who Would Be King* copyright © 2014 by Kara Cooney used by permission of Crown Books, an imprint of Random House, a division of Penguin Random House LLC. All rights reserved.

170: Who was Hatshepsut?: Kara Cooney, "Hatshepsut: How a Woman Ascended the Throne of Ancient Egypt," lecture at the Getty Villa in Los Angeles, January 28, 2015.

170–171: Thutmose II death and family dynasty: Cooney lecture.

171: Hatshepsut as regent: Cooney lecture.

171: "ticket to power was that nephew": Cooney lecture.

171: "the one to whom Ra has actually given the Kingship": Cooney lecture.

171: Crowned co-king: Cooney lecture.

171: Hatshepsut's death: Cooney lecture.

171: How Hatshepsut kept power: Cooney lecture.

172: "Her Majesty praised me and she loved me. . . . She made me great.": Cooney lecture.

172: Monument building: Cooney lecture.

172: Expeditions to other lands: Cooney lecture; Cooney, *The Woman Who Would Be King*, 11, 133–134.

172: Nubia, Punt, Yemen today: Cooney, 133.

172: Hatshepsut's second key to power: Cooney lecture.

172: Hatshepsut's Temple of Millions of Years, photo caption: Cooney lecture.

173: The Oracle Text, "His majesty [the god Amen] proceeded to the omens . . . all that you command.": Warburton, *Architecture, Power, and Religion*, 226–227.

174: "I place you upon my thrones . . . before the entire land.": Warburton, 227–228.

174–175: "I am beneficent king . . . king of the two lands.": Warburton, 230.

175–176: "Hatshepsut's young co-king was almost a man. . . . Something had to change.": Cooney, *The Woman Who Would Be King*, 153.

176: Hatshepsut's evolving presentation of gender, "wearing the long dress of a woman and the crown of a king.": Cooney, 153–158.

177: "depict an elite woman who stayed indoors . . . color scheme for Egyptian art.": Cooney, 154–155, second photo page after 144.

177: "Masculinity was a key component . . . referring to 'she' and 'her.'": Cooney, 156–157.

177–179: The Sed festival: "the biggest celebration . . . she claims Thutmose I did for her.": Cooney, 159–162.

178: Hatshepsut's Sed festival math: Cooney, 159–160.

179: "no temple image ever shows her as a woman . . . son of Thutmose I.": Cooney, 161.

179: "One image shows the sacred animal . . . predestined son of Re.": Cooney, 167.

179: "The Foremost of Nobel Women.": Cooney, 157.

179–180: "Just after her accession, she had added the phrase . . . 'The Female One Who Unites with Amen'": Cooney, 157–158.

180: After twenty-two years of rule, Hatshepsut died: Cooney, 189.

180–181: Tricky tricks, Thutmose III efforts to erase Hatshepsut from history: Cooney, 211–219; Cooney lecture.

181: Prized temple dismantled: Cooney, *The Woman Who Would Be King*, 215; Warburton, *Architecture, Power, and Religion*, 225.

181: "they changed the name of the king . . . 'Amen is satisfied by her monuments.'": Cooney, *The Woman Who Would Be King*, 214.

181: More of the story, Hatshepsut's legacy survived: Cooney lecture.

182: One more role, Hatshepsut was also a mother, "was a key player for both monarchs . . . pure royal blood.": Cooney, *The Woman Who Would Be King*, 169–171, 176.

182: "Nefrure was labeled on a Sinai inscription . . . in her own right.": Cooney, 171, 176–178.

CHAPTER 10: CATALINA DE ERAUSO, THE LIEUTENANT NUN

185: "I kissed the foot . . . my life dressed as a man.": Dan Harvey Pedrick, "The Sword & the Veil: An Annotated Translation of the Autobiography of doña Catalina de Erauso, Part II— The Autobiography of doña Catalina de Erauso, Chapter 1," Dan Harvey Pedrick, accessed June 13, 2020, http://carriagehousebandb.ca/catalina%20de%20erauso/Thesis-Section2.htm, part II, chap. 25.

186: Women in Spain in late 1500s and early 1600s: Theresa Ann Smith, *The Emerging Female Citizen: Gender and Enlightenment in Spain* (Oakland: University of California Press, 2006), 23–25.

186: The Spanish Inquisition: "This Day in History: March 31, 1492; Spain Announces It Will Expel All Jews," History, November 12, 2019, https://www.history.com/this-day-in-history/spain-announces-it-will-expel-all-jews; "Inquisition," History, August 21, 2018, https://www.history.com/topics/religion/inquisition.

186: "an imperfect and even monstrous creature . . . produces a female.": Smith, *Emerging Female Citizen*, 28–29.

186: "women's enclosure in either convents or marriage . . . male relatives.": Smith, 23.

186: "As men are made for public, . . . cover themselves.": Smith, 24.

187–188: The Autobiography of doña Catalina de Erauso, "Near the end of my novitiate year I had a quarrel . . . threw it away.": Erauso, translated by Pedrick, "The Sword & the Veil."

188: "Pieces of Eight," The British Museum, BBC, accessed June 14, 2020, http://www.bbc.co.uk/ahistoryoftheworld/objects/JO391t6cRtGxstjbE4EEmg.

188: Defining a scapular: Linda Alchin, "Medieval Nun's Clothing," Medieval Life and Times, accessed June 14, 2020, http://www.medieval-life-and-times.info/medieval-clothing/medieval-nuns-clothing.htm.

188: Living as Francisco Loyola: Erauso, translated by Pedrick, "The Sword & the Veil."

188: Spanish law banning people with female bodies dressing as men, "The ban, obviously, proved ineffective . . . to be renewed.": Catalina de Erauso, *Lieutenant Nun: Memoir of a Basque Transvestite in the New World*, trans. Michele Stepto and Gariel Stepto, forward by Marjorie Garber (Boston: Beacon, 1996), xi.

189–190: "I was standing at the doorway . . . like a feather in the wind.":
Erauso, translated by Pedrick, "The Sword & the Veil."

190: "my uncle, my mother's cousin": Erauso, translated by Pedrick, chap. 2.

190–191: "I went through some hard times. . . . They weighed anchor and
set sail.": Erauso, translated by Pedrick. chap. 2.

191–192: "One holiday I had just taken a seat . . . in stocks and shackles.":
Erauso, translated by Pedrick, chap. 3.

192: "a deputy to the sergeant-major . . . down through the place": Erauso,
translated by Pedrick, chap. 8, 9.

193: Does not reveal connection to brother: Erauso, translated by Pedrick,
chap. 6, 9.

193: "I remained with my brother. . . . I had to go.": Erauso, translated by
Pedrick, chap. 6.

194–195: "After having lived so pleasantly, I had to go. . . . I was very
pleased.": Erauso, translated by Pedrick, chap. 6.

195: "stunned . . . with God only knows what grief": Erauso, translated by
Pedrick, chap. 6.

195–196: "The daughter was very dark . . . property to me.": Erauso,
translated by Pedrick, chap. 7.

196: "on various pretexts . . . the canon's niece afterwards.": Erauso,
translated by Pedrick, chap. 7.

197–198: "The next morning at around ten . . . I missed him very much.":
Erauso, translated by Pedrick, chap. 20.

198: "We entered Lima . . . see the 'Nun Lieutenant.'": Erauso, translated
by Pedrick, chap. 21.

198–199: "in which I gave somebody . . . knife I had": Erauso, translated by
Pedrick, chap. 22.

199: "From Cadiz I went to Seville . . . dressed in male attire.": Erauso,
translated by Pedrick, chap. 23.

199–200: "I kissed the foot . . . good thing about me.": Erauso, translated
by Pedrick, part II, chap. 25.

199: "Thou shall not kill": "The Book of Exodus: Chapter 20: The Ten
Commandments," Latin Vulgate, accessed June 14, 2020,
http://www.latinvulgate.com/verse.aspx?t=0&b=2&c=20.

199: The Abrahamic faiths all teach the Ten Commandments: Seth Ward,
"Are the Ten Commandments Found in Islam? Notes on the
Decalogue," Moses, Jesus & Muhammad: RELI-4160-01,
University of Wisconsin, accessed June 14, 2020, https://
uwyo.instructure.com/courses/444647/pages/are-the-ten
-commandments-found-in-islam.

200–201: "The Nun Lieutenant arrived in Mexico . . . to prevent the
duel.": Vicente Riva Palacio, translated by Pedrick, "The Sword
& the Veil," part I, 7, translation of Vicente Riva Palacio, *Méjico
através de los siglos* (Mexico: Porrúa S.A. 1946) 166.

201: "Erauso's behavior could be forgiven . . . to become a man.": Smith, *Emerging Female Citizen*, 22.

202: "Tall and sturdy of stature . . . occasionally gesture effeminately.": Pietro Della Valle, translated by Dan Pedrick, "The Sword & the Veil: An Annotated Translation of the Autobiography of doña Catalina de Erauso," translation of José María de Heredia's introduction to Joaquín María de Ferrer, *Historia de la Monja Alférez* (Doña Catalina de Erauso) (Madrid: Tipp Renovación, 1918), vii–viii; Dan Pedrick, part 1, 7, June 14, 2020, http://carriagehousebandb.ca/catalina%20de%20erauso /Thesis-Section1.htm.

203: Tricky tricks, changing the history of the Lieutenant Nun, "neutralizes the lesbian episodes . . . duped by her disguise.": Sherry Velasco, *The Lieutenant Nun: Transgenderism, Lesbian Desire, and Catalina de Erauso* (Austin: University of Texas Press, 2000), 92–93.

203: Reaction to the Lieutenant Nun's story changing over time: Velasco, 94–95.

203: "A woman? . . . 'verdad histórica' (historical truth)": Velasco, 95, 98.

204: The 1996 English translation of the Lieutenant Nun's autobiography: Catalina de Erauso, translated from Michele Stepto and Gabriel Stepto, *Lieutenant Nun: Memoir of a Basque Transvestite in the New World* (Boston: Beacon, 1996), https://books.google .com/books?id=oCfAeDogtssC&printsec=frontcover&dq =Lieutenant+Nun:+Memoir+of+a+Basque+Transvestite+in+the +New+World&hl=en&sa=X&ved=0ahUKEwj92sGGg -DLAhWIKGMKHWcPDxYQ6AEIHTAA#v=onepage&q =Lieutenant%20Nun%3A%20Memoir%20of%20a%20 Basque%20Transvestite%20in%20the%20New%20World&f =false.

204: Corroboration of the Lieutenant Nun's story: Pedrick, "The Sword & the Veil," part I, introduction; Dan Harvey Pedrick, "The Sword & the Veil: An Annotated Translation of the Autobiography of doña Catalina de Erauso," part III—conclusion, Dan Pedrick, accessed June 14, 2020, http:// carriagehousebandb.ca/catalina%20de%20erauso/Thesis -Section3.htm, conclusion, appendix B.

204: "While strolling along the wharf in Naples . . . slipped away.": Erauso, translated by Pedrick, "The Sword & the Veil," part II, chap. 26.

CHAPTER 11: WE'WHA

207: "The Medicine Wheel represents . . . the creator's purpose for us.": Chadwick Moore, "'The Medicine Wheel Represents Men on One Side and Women on the Other, but There's a Space in Between That Is for the Two Spirits. We Join the Men and Women and Complete the Circle That Is Our Place in

Life. That Is the Creator's Purpose for Us.' Chadwick Moore Journeys to the Annual Gathering of the Two Spirit Society in Montana," *OUT*, October 2015, 68.

208: "in every region of the continent . . . neither men and women": Will Roscoe, *The Zuni Man-Woman* (Albuquerque: University of New Mexico Press, 1991), 5, 147.

208: Tribes listed in Roscoe's index: Will Roscoe, *Changing Ones: Third and Fourth Genders in Native North America* (New York: St. Martin's, 1998) 223–247; Will Roscoe, email message to the author, October 23, 2016.

208: Other names for Native third and fourth gender people: Roscoe, *The Zuni Man-Woman*, 4–5.

209: Counting genders: Will Roscoe, "Sexual and Gender Diversity in Native America and the Pacific Islands," in "LGBTQ America: A Theme Study of Lesbian, Gay, Bisexual, Transgender and Queer History," ed. Megan E. Springate, National Park Service Department of the Interior: Cultural Resources, Partnerships, and Science, National Park Foundation, accessed June 16, 2020, https://www.nps.gov/subjects/tellingallamericansstories /lgbtqthemestudy.htm; Donna M. Dean, "Dualism's Just a Construct," review of Will Roscoe, *Changing Ones: Third and Fourth Genders in Native America*, H-Net, October 2000, http:// www.h-net.org/reviews/showrev.php?id=4588.

209: "It is the sound between syllables of the expression 'oh-oh.'" Paul Kroskrity, UCLA professor of anthropology, email to the author, November 8, 2016.

209: "Winkte is gay with ceremonial powers.": Roscoe, *The Zuni Man-Woman*, 206.

209: Navajo third gender people and name, "from a word that refers to a constant state of change": Moore, "The Medicine Wheel," 66–71.

209: A:shiwi (Zuni people) third gender people and name: Roscoe, *The Zuni Man-Woman*, 22.

210: Kolhamana, "One side wound through a board . . . in the male style.": Roscoe, 24.

210: Mural with the same both male and female and neither male or female hairstyle: Roscoe, 24–25, 78.

210–211: Matilda Coxe Stevenson arrives to study the A:shiwi: Roscoe, 11.

210: Zuñi without a tilde and with: Pueblo of Zuni; Matilda Coxe Stevenson, "The Zuñi Indians: Their Mythology, Esoteric Societies and Ceremonies," in *Twenty-Third Annual Report of the Bureau of American Ethnology to the Secretary of the Smithsonian Institution 1901–1902, J.W. Powell, Director* (Washington: Government Printing Office, 1904), https://archive.org/details /b24862058, 3.

211: Centering and respecting native languages, including Shiwi'ma: Pueblo of Zuni, accessed June 18, 2020, http://www.ashiwi.org/.

211: Shiwi'ma "emerged around 7,000 years ago": Christopher Muscato, "Zuni Tribe: Facts, History & Culture," Study.com, accessed June 18, 2020, https://study.com/academy/lesson/zuni-tribe -facts-history-culture.html.

211–212: "We'wha, undoubtable the most remarkable member . . . a scolding from her.": Stevenson, "The Zuñi Indians," 310–311.

212: No gender pronouns in Shiwi'ma: Matthew S. Dryer and Martin Haspelmath, eds., "Language Zuni," World Atlas of Language Structures Online, accessed June 23, 2020, https://wals.info /languoid/lect/wals_code_zun; Stevenson, "The Zuñi Indians," 310–311.

212–213: We'wha was also an artist, "fine art . . . intellectual and social equals": Roscoe, *The Zuni Man-Woman*, 121–122.

213–214: "On one occasion . . . unconscious of the weight.": Stevenson, "The Zuñi Indians," 374.

213: "political correctness dishonors . . . or the white media.": Native Sun News Editorial Board, "Native American vs. American Indian: Political Correctness Dishonors Traditional Chiefs of Old," *Native American Times*, April 12, 2015, https://www.nativetimes .com/index.php/life/commentary/11389-native-american-vs -american-indian-political-correctness-dishonors-traditional -chiefs-of-old.

214: "She had a good memory . . . join in conversation.": Stevenson, "The Zuñi Indians," 310.

215: More on the Anthropologist: Roscoe, *The Zuni Man-Woman*, 8–9.

215: "Though you are a woman . . . such as men make.": Roscoe, 9–10; Stevenson, "The Zuñi Indians," 119.

216: "an Indian Princess of the Zuni tribe": Roscoe, *The Zuni Man-Woman*, 56.

216–217: *Washington Chronicle* article, "The princess is an eccentric child of nature. . . . She had completed it.": Roscoe, 55.

217: We'wha in Washington, DC, "especially anxious to obtain . . . from squatters and encroachment": Roscoe, 53–73.

217: We'wha seen as a joke: Roscoe, 72–73.

217–218: "I can't think of any thing . . . especially scientific Washington.": Roscoe, 72–73.

218: We'wha did not have her own children, but was "beloved by all the children, to whom he was ever kind": Roscoe, 84.

218: An 1893 confrontation with an officer: Roscoe, 104–111.

218–219: "An officer who with the sheriff went . . . a free man.": Roscoe, 106.

219: We'wha arrested and then four years later preparing for their religious festival: Roscoe, 2–3, 104–110.

219: "When a week or more had passed . . . to her beloved Ko'thluwala'wa [Sacred Lake]": Roscoe, 3.

219: We'wha's death: Roscoe, 111.

219: "caused universal regret and distress in Zuñi": Stevenson, "The Zuñi Indians," 310–312.

220: Tricky tricks, "This is one of the most unaccountable . . . fully recorded.": George Catlin, *Letters and Notes on the Manners, Customs, and Condition of the North American Indians: Written during Eight Years' Travel amongst the Wildest Tribes of Indians In North America, in 1932, 33, 34, 35, 36, 37, 38 and 39, in Two Volumes, with Four Hundred Illustrations, Carefully Engraved from His Original Paintings. Third Edition. Volume II* (New York: Wiley and Putnam, 1844), https://archive.org/details /lettersandnotes02catlgoog, 215.

220: "All the difficult labor . . . I wish to reverse their labors.": Roscoe, *The Zuni Man-Woman*, 43.

221: Boarding schools as part of the efforts to erase Native cultures: "Boarding Schools: Struggling with Cultural Repression," *Native Words, Native Warriors*, accessed June 22, 2020, https:// americanindian.si.edu/education/codetalkers/html/chapter3 .html; Roscoe, *The Zuni Man-Woman*, 199; Harlan Pruden and Se-ah-dom Edmo, "Two-Spirit People: Sex, Gender & Sexuality in Historic and Contemporary Native America," National Congress of American Indians, accessed June 23, 2020, http://www.ncai.org/policy-research-center/initiatives /Pruden-Edmo_TwoSpiritPeople.pdf.

221: "kill the Indian and save the man": "Kill the Indian and Save the Man," Digital History, accessed June 23, 2020, http://www .digitalhistory.uh.edu/disp_textbook.cfm?smtID=2&psid=3505.

221: "white GI attitudes": Roscoe, *The Zuni Man-Woman*, 201.

221–222: "It was agreed generally . . . vision of the moon.": Nancy Oestreich Lurie, "Winnebago Berdache," *American Anthropologist* 55 (1953), 708, http://onlinelibrary.wiley.com/doi/10.1525/aa.1953 .55.5.02a00090/epdf.

222: "between white intolerance . . . no mention of them at all.": Roscoe, *The Zuni Man-Woman*, 194.

223: Ruth Benedict, "We have only to turn to other cultures . . . they have even been especially acclaimed.": Roscoe, x–xi.

223: Linda Rapp, "Benedict, Ruth (1887–1948)," *GLBTQ Encyclopedia*, accessed June 23, 2020, http://www.glbtqarchive.com/ssh /benedict_r_S.pdf.

223: Two Spirit identity still exists: Moore, "The Medicine Wheel," 66–71.

223: "Tradition is reinvented in every generation.": Roscoe email.

223: Steven Barrios, "perhaps the most respected person . . . benevolent figure": Moore, "The Medicine Wheel," 70.

223: "a studly woman decked out in beads, with cascading gray hair": Moore, 68.

224: "The Medicine Wheel represents . . . the creator's purpose for us.": Moore, 68.

224: "Sometimes young people come. . . . They feel like they belong.": Moore, 70.

224: Geo Neptune, "While the label has only . . . anyone in between.": "What Does 'Two-Spirit' Mean? | InQueery | Them," YouTube video posted by them, December 11, 2018, 6:16, https://youtu.be/A4lBibGzUnE.

CHAPTER 12: CHRISTINE JORGENSEN

227: "I think we (the doctors and I) . . . rather than vice-versa.": Christine Jorgensen, *Christine Jorgensen: A Personal Autobiography* (New York: Paul S. Eriksson, 1967), 109.

228: "There had been perhaps thirty cases of sex conversion on record before mine.": Jorgensen, xiv.

228: "asking God for a pretty doll . . . bright red railway train.": Jorgensen, 11.

228–229: "It must have been about this stage . . . 'I don't like the kind of surprise God made me!'": Jorgensen, 12.

228: Brud was Christine's childhood nickname.: Jorgensen, 7.

229: "feminine ways . . . so much as a child": Jorgensen, 20.

229: "deep within myself . . . influenced by outside conditions": Jorgensen, 20.

229: Dr. Harry Benjamin on Christine, "This was a little girl . . . from my personal observation": Jorgensen, vii–viii.

229–230: "A few years ago, Christine . . . 'She is ours and we love her.'": Jorgensen, viii.

230: "To me, it was a matter of survival. . . . turn out to be.": Jorgensen, xi–xii.

230: "I remember being overwhelmed . . . to cope with life.": Jorgensen, 29–30.

230: Christine accepted into the army: Jorgensen, 35.

231: "When the examining psychiatrist asked me, . . . I answered simply, 'Yes.'": Jorgensen, 35.

231: "I looked into the vastness . . . 'but am I not a work of God, too?'": Jorgensen, 48.

231–232: "If, I wondered, hormones . . . 'through the magic of chemistry?'": Jorgensen, 80.

232: Christine buys bottle of estrogen pills, "unproductive attempts to find professional medical aid . . . more feminine": Jorgensen, 77, 85–88.

232: "How strange it seemed to me . . . a whole person.": Jorgensen, 86.

232: "transition to womanhood": Jorgensen, 95.

232: "All of my planning . . . point of no return as George Jorgensen.": Jorgensen, 95.

233: Christine finds Dr. Christian Hamburger.: Jorgensen, 102.

233: "No, I would not charge you . . . over long periods of time.": Jorgensen, 102.

233: "Just refer to me as guinea pig 0000!": Jorgensen, 103.

233: "Can you realize what success . . . that makes the real person.": Jorgensen, 109.

233: Christine names herself.: Jorgensen, 104–120.

234: Christine writes "the most important letter of my life": Jorgensen, 123.

234–235: Christine's coming out letter, "June 8, 1952 . . . Love, Chris ('Brud')": Jorgensen, 123–126.

236: "They were deeply upset. . . . WE LOVE YOU MORE THAN EVER. MOM AND DAD.": Jorgensen, 127.

236: The reporter showed up in Christine's hospital room, "tomorrow's newspapers will carry this story in banner headlines": Jorgensen, 138–139.

236: "BRONX GI BECOMES A WOMAN . . . YOUR DAUGHTER.": Jorgensen, 138.

236–237: "In the first shock-waves, . . . that hospital room.": Jorgensen, 138–139.

237: "I think this letter is probably . . . undesired by most trans folds.": Johanna Olson-Kennedy, email message to the author, December 6, 2016.

237: "avoid the development . . . matches their gender": Johanna Olson-Kennedy, email message to the author, December 6, 2016.

238–239: Christine's parents wrote her on December 3, 1952, "My Dear Chris, . . . Love, Dad": Jorgensen, *Christine Jorgensen*, 147–148.

239: "Like an avalanche, letters and cables . . . and extravagant offers.": Jorgensen, 144, 156–157.

239: Calculating how much today: "Seven Ways to Compute the Relative Value of a U.S. Dollar Amount—1790 to Present," Measuring Worth, accessed September 5, 2020, https://www.measuringworth.com/calculators/uscompare/relativevalue.php.

239: "What had been to me . . . atmosphere of love.": Jorgensen, *Christine Jorgensen*, 167.

239: Christine flies back to the U.S.: Jorgensen, 180–183.

239–240: "I stepped out of the doorway . . . 'Just one more!'": Jorgensen, 182–183.

240: Christine was a celebrity, "translated into fourteen languages and distributed throughout seventy countries": Jorgensen, 188.

240: Fame came with challenges: Jorgensen, 189–190.

240: "the largest world-wide coverage . . . person in the world": Jorgensen, 249–250.

241: Christine couldn't go back to photography, "Look, Chris, you're a world-famous personality . . . quiet life.": Jorgensen, 203.

241: "Off Limits!": Jorgensen, xii-xiii; Boston Institute for Nonprofit Journalism, research by Nyadenya Inyagwa, "Throwback: Boston Bans Trans Performer," *Medium*, June 12, 2016, https://medium.com/binj-reports/throwback-boston-bans-trans-performer-63c692207294.

241: "Many times, I've been accused . . . living the lie.": Jorgensen, *Christine Jorgensen*, 329.

241–242: "In Miami Beach at the Club Morocco . . . I combed my hair.": Jorgensen, 248.

242: "At one time or another . . . table or chair.": Jorgensen, xiv.

243: Christine worked hard to be a "true performer . . . boundaries of notoriety": Jorgensen, 272, 308.

243: Christine's engagement to John Traub, "storm of publicity . . . BAR WEDDING FOR CHRISTINE": Jorgensen, 287–293.

243: Christine interviewed about her romantic life, "I've been in love . . . pretty female syndrome": "Christine Jorgensen—HOUR magazine," YouTube video, 9:59, posted by Finding by William French, July 26, 2010, https://youtu.be/lDlGUeF1Bg0, 8:36.

243–244: Christine's 1982 TV interview with Tom Snyder "TOM. If George Jorgensen . . . CHRISTINE. . . . The *New York Daily News* made me.": "Christine Jorgensen, Tom Snyder—1982 Interview and Song," YouTube video, 14.55, posted by Alan Eichler in 2015, https://youtu.be/HWOsIBJVFes, 7:12.

244: Christine had a sense of humor too: John T. McQuiston, "Obituaries: Christine Jorgensen, 62, Is Dead; Was First to Have a Sex Change," *New York Times*, May 4, 1989, http://www.nytimes.com/1989/05/04/obituaries/christine-jorgensen-62-is-dead-was-first-to-have-a-sex-change.html.

244: Christine died in 1989: McQuiston.

244–245: "I suppose the final question . . . to be myself.": Jorgensen, *Christine Jorgensen*, 332.

245: "People always refer to the surgery. . . . The surgery is easy.": "Christine Jorgensen, Tom Snyder," YouTube video, 6:14.

CONCLUSION: IT'S NOT ABOUT THE NUMBERS, IT'S ABOUT A SAFE SPACE

246: Queer people as percentage of population: Gary J. Gates, "How Many People Are Lesbian, Gay, Bisexual, and Transgender?," Williams Institute, accessed June 27, 2020, https://williamsinstitute.law.ucla.edu/publications/how-many-people-lgbt/; "Kinsey Institute: Research: FAQ," Kinsey Institute, accessed June 27, 2020, https://kinseyinstitute.org/research/faq.php.

246: Sufism: Megan Specia, "Who Are Sufi Muslims and Why Do Some Extremists Hate Them?," *New York Times*, November 24, 2017, https://www.nytimes.com/2017/11/24/world/middleeast/sufi-muslim-explainer.html.

247: Lines from Rumi's poem,"I saw you last night in the gathering, / . . . / pretending to talk privately": Rumi, *The Essential Rumi*, translations by Coleman Barks with John Moyne (New York: HarperCollins, 1995), 98.

CONCLUSION: THE HISTORY OF THE RAINBOW FLAG THAT BROUGHT IT ALL TOGETHER

248: The Rainbow Pride flag history: "A Brief History of the Rainbow Flag," San Francisco Travel Association, accessed June 27, 2020, http://www.sanfrancisco.travel/article/brief-history-rainbow-flag.

248–249: "It all goes back to the first moment . . . of my life.": San Francisco Travel Association.

249: Gay Pride flag colors: Hilary Greenbaum, "Who Made That Rainbow Flag?," *The 6th Floor*: Eavesdropping on *the Times* Magazine, *New York Times*, June 29, 2011, https://6thfloor.blogs.nytimes.com/2011/06/29/who-made-that-rainbow-flag/.

249: Diversity Pride flag: "More Colors. More Pride," Tierney, accessed June 27, 2020, https://hellotierney.com/work/more-color-more-pride-2/; Ernest Owens, "Philly's Pride Flag to Get Two New Stripes: Black and Brown," *Philadelphia Magazine*, June 8, 2017, https://www.phillymag.com/news/2017/06/08/philly-pride-flag-black-brown/.

RECOMMENDED RESOURCES

Alsenas, Linas. *Gay America: Struggle for Equality.* New York: Amulet Books, 2008.

Brother Outsider: The Life of Bayard Rustin. DVD. Produced by Sam Pollard and Mridu Chandra. Directed by Nancy Kates and Bennett Singer. New York: Question Why Films, 2003.

"Christine Jorgensen, Tom Snyder—1982 Interview and Song." YouTube video, 14.55. Posted by Alan Eichler in 2015. https://youtu.be/HWOsIBJVFes.

Churchill, Sarah, Duchess of Marlborough, and Nathaniel Hooke. *An Account of the Conduct of the Dowager Duchess of Marlborough, from her First Coming to Court, to the Year 1710—In a Letter from Herself to My Lord—.* London: James Bettenham, for George Hawkins, 1742.

Cooney, Kara. *The Woman Who Would Be King: Hatshepsut's Rise to Power in Ancient Egypt.* New York: Crown, 2014.

Ferrer, Joaquin Maria de. *The Autobiography of doña Catalina de Erauso and Historia de la Monja Alférez (Doña Catalina de Erauso).* Translation by Dan Harvey Pedrick. Madrid: Tipo Renovación, 1918. Available online at Early Americas Digital Archive. http://mith.umd.edu/eada/html/display.php?docs=erauso_autobiography.xml.

Field, Ophelia. *Sarah Churchill, Duchess of Marlborough: The Queen's Favourite.* New York: St. Martin's, 2003.

Gandhi, Mohandas. *The Collected Works of Mahatma Gandhi.* New Delhi: Publications Division Government of India, 1999.

Houtman, Jacqueline, Walter Naegle, and Michael G. Long. *Bayard Rustin: The Invisible Activist.* Philadelphia: Quaker, 2014.

Jorgensen, Christine. *Christine Jorgensen: A Personal Autobiography.* New York: Paul S. Eriksson, 1967.

Kincaid, Robert L. "Joshua Fry Speed, 1814–1882, Abraham Lincoln's Most Intimate Friend." *Filson Club History Quarterly* 17 (April 1943): 123.

Lelyveld, Joseph. *Great Soul: Mahatma Gandhi and His Struggle with India.* New York: Alfred A. Knopf, 2011.

LGBT History Month Icons: Icons from All Years http://www.lgbthistorymonth.com/icon_search/all

Lincoln, Abraham. *Abraham Lincoln, Complete Works: Comprising His Speeches, Letters, State Papers, and Miscellaneous Writings, Volume One.* Edited by John G. Nicolay and John Hay. New York: Century, 1894.

Miller, Calvin Craig. *No Easy Answers: Bayard Rustin and the Civil Rights Movement.* Greensboro, NC: Morgan Reynolds, 2005.

Murray, Stephen O., and Will Roscoe, eds. *Boy-Wives and Female Husbands: Studies in African Homosexualities*. New York: St. Martin's, 1998.

Nthunya, Mpho 'M'Atsepo. *Singing away the Hunger: The Autobiography of an African Woman*. Edited by K. Limakatso Kendall. Bloomington: Indiana University Press, 1997.

Pohlen, Jerome. *Gay & Lesbian History for Kids: The Century-Long Struggle for LGBT Rights, with 21 Activities*. Chicago: Chicago Review, 2016.

Roscoe, Will. "Sexual and Gender Diversity in Native America and the Pacific Islands." In *LGBTQ America: A Theme Study of Lesbian, Gay, Bisexual, Transgender and Queer History*. Edited by Megan E. Springate. Washington, DC: National Park Foundation, 2016. https://www.nps.gov /subjects/tellingallamericansstories/lgbtqthemestudy.htm.

———. *The Zuni Man-Woman*. Albuquerque: University of New Mexico Press, 1991.

Rustin, Bayard, Devon W. Carbado, and Donald Weise. *Time on Two Crosses: The Collected Writings of Bayard Rustin*. New York: Cleis, 2015.

Sappho. *Sappho*. Translated by Mary Barnard. Berkeley: University of California Press, 1958.

Shakespeare, William. *The Riverside Shakespeare*. Edited by G. Blakemore Evans. Boston: Houghton Mifflin, 1974.

Snyder, Jane McIntosh, and Camille-Yvette Welsch. *Sappho*. Philadelphia: Chelsea House, 2005.

Stevenson, Matilda Coxe. "The Zuni Indians: Their Mythology, Esoteric Societies and Ceremonies." In *Twenty-Third Annual Report of the Bureau of American Ethnology to the Secretary of the Smithsonian Institution 1901–1902, J. W. Powell, Director*. Washington, DC: Government Printing Office, 1904. Available online at Internet Archive. https://archive.org/details /thezueniindians00stevrich.

Streitmatter, Rodger. *Outlaw Marriages: The Hidden Histories of Fifteen Extraordinary Same-Sex Couples*. Boston: Beacon, 2012.

Streitmatter, Rodger, ed. *Empty without You: The Intimate Letters of Eleanor Roosevelt and Lorena Hickok*. New York: Free Press, 1998.

For additional recommendations and acknowledgments, please visit www.leewind.org.

INDEX

PHOTO ACKNOWLEDGMENTS

Image credits: Ktrinko/Wikimedia Commons (CC0 1.0), p. 5; Pahl, Georg/Wikimedia Commons (CC-BY-SA 3.0), p. 9; © Paramount Pictures/Photofest, p. 11; Jörg Bittner Unna/Wikimedia Commons (CC BY 3.0), p. 12; Ken Goldstein/flickr, p. 14; West Yorkshire Archive Service, Calderdale. Document reference: SH:7/ML/E/4., p. 15; Design by Landyn Pan, Illustration by Anna Moore, p. 23; Library of Congress/Wikimedia Commons (public domain), p. 30; © Photofest, p. 31; University of Florida, George A. Smathers Libraries/Wikimedia Commons (public domain), p. 33; Studio Sarah Lou/flickr (CC BY 2.0), p. 35; It's No Game/flickr (CC BY 2.0), p. 41; Wellcome Library, London/Wikimedia Commons (CC BY 4.0), p. 44; Library of Congress (LC-USZ62-16377), p. 47; Filson Historical Society/Wikimedia Commons (public domain), p. 48; Library of Congress/Wikimedia Commons (public domain), pp. 49, 139, 166; Todd Strand/Independent Picture Service, p. 55; National Portrait Gallery/Wikimedia Commons (public domain), p. 56; Gregory F. Maxwell/Wikimedia Commons (public domain), p. 58; Wikimedia Commons (public domain), pp. 61, 64, 67, 79, 96, 99, 105, 117, 119, 120, 167, 216; William J Scott, Jr, p. 82; Estate of Bayard Rustin, pp. 84, 92; Bibi Saint-Pol/Wikimedia Commons (pubic domain), p. 102; Masur/Wikimedia Commons (CC BY-SA 2.5), p. 111; Sir Godfrey Kneller, Bt /Wikimedia Commons (public domain), p. 124; National Library of Scotland/Wikimedia Commons (public domain), p. 127; Elias Gayles/flickr (CC BY 2.0), p. 128; Library of Congress (LC-USZ62-25812), p. 135; U.S. Air Force photo/Wikimedia Commons (public domain), p. 137; By Unknown or not provided (U.S. National Archives and Records Administration)/Wikimedia Commons (public domain), p. 147; K. Kendall/Wikimedia Commons (CC BY 2.0), p. 153; Courtesy of Kendall, pp. 159, 160; K. Kendall/flickr (CC BY 2.0), p. 163; wrangel/iStock/Getty Images, p. 169; MarcPo/iStock Editorial/Getty Images, p. 172; Rogers Fund, 1929, Torso lent by Rijksmuseum van Oudheden, Leiden (L.1998.80)/The Metropolitan Museum of Art (public domain), p. 176 (left); Rogers Fund, 1929/The Metropolitan Museum of Art (public domain), pp. 176 (right), 177; pantonov/iStock/Getty Images, p. 180; Wellcome Collection gallery/Wikimedia Commons (CC-BY-4.0), p. 185; Isaac Vásquez Prado/Wikimedia Commons (CC BY-SA 4.0), p. 201; The National Archives/Wikimedia Commons (public domain), p. 207; Internet Book Archive/flickr (public domain), p. 210; National Antropological Archives, Smithsonian Institution NAA INV 01146100, p. 215; Fred Morgan/NY Daily News Archive via/Getty Images, p. 228; NY Daily News Archive/Getty Images, p. 238; Photo by Maurice Seymour, New York/Wikimedia Commons (public domain), p. 243; Ktrinko/Wikimedia Commons (CC0 1.0), p. 295.

Cover: Library of Congress/Wikimedia Commons (public domain), (Abraham Lincoln); Wikimedia Commons (public domain) (Mohandas Gandhi & We'wha); Library of Congress (LC-USZ62-25812) (Anna Eleanor Roosevelt).

ACKNOWLEDGMENTS

I suppose some books have direct paths to publication, where all the gates open up, everyone says "yes" in a tidy row, and the manuscript *flows* into a published book.

This book did not have that journey.

But *No Way, They Were Gay?* did, does, and continues to have its champions, to whom I am so grateful.

A rainbow of gratitude to:

The late Randy Harrison, whose talk about Abraham Lincoln's letters to Joshua Fry Speed cracked the false façade of history for me.

Melissa Stewart and Claire Bidwell Smith, for their advice shaping the initial book proposal back in 2013.

All the many intrepid and kind librarians who helped me track down sources and facts.

Judy Grahn, Martin Greif, Paul Russell, Rodger Streitmatter, Christine Downing, Robert Aldrich, Kara Cooney, Will Roscoe, Eric Marcus, and the many other historians of our LGBTQ legacy for their scholarship and inspiration.

My agent Marietta Zacker, whose belief in this project—and in me—makes such a difference.

Victoria Sutherland and Hallie Warshaw, for seeing Zest Books and Lerner as the perfect publishing home for this book—and Ashley Kuehl, Shaina Olmanson, and the entire Lerner team for making that promise a reality.

My community of Kickstarter supporters for *Queer as a Five-Dollar Bill*. Those 180 people I'm not related to stood up and put down real money to support my creative voice and a shared vision that knowing our queer history can empower young LGBTQ people today. That support kept me going.

Betsy Bird, Linda Sue Park, Ellen Hopkins, Michael D. Cohen, Lesléa Newman, Kathleen Krull, Susan Yaegley, Yapha Mason, Ellen Wittlinger, Jessica Weissbuch, Bruce Coville, Elisabeth Abarbanel, Alex Sanchez, Steve Krantz, and Matthew C. Winner, for their full-on sprint to give this book early support.

My SCBWI, IBPA, and Kid Lit communities, for being my colleagues and friends.

My family, for loving me back when it looked like this book would never be published, and now, and every moment in between.

And you. I hope if you've read this far, I can now count you among this book's champions too.

Thank you, all.

Do you see our familiar world differently now?
There is so much more queer history to discover . . .

ABOUT THE AUTHOR

Lee Wind is a lighthouse of stories—true and fictional—that center on marginalized kids and teens and celebrate their power to change the world. Closeted until his twenties, Lee writes the books that would have changed his life as a young gay kid. His master's degree from Harvard in education didn't include blueprints for a time machine to go back and tell these stories to himself, so Lee pays it forward with a popular blog with over three million page views (*I'm Here. I'm Queer. What the Hell Do I Read?*) and books for kids and teens. In addition to *No Way, They Were Gay?* he is the author of the award-winning young adult novel *Queer as a Five-Dollar Bill* and the upcoming picture book *Red and Green and Blue and White*. With day jobs for the Independent Book Publishers Association (as their director of marketing and programing) and the Society of Children's Book Writers and Illustrators (as their official blogger), Lee's hero job is storytelling to empower readers to shine with their own light. Visit www.leewind.org to subscribe to Lee's newsletter and continue your journey to discover our past and live your future.

Photo credit: Michele Baron